AF478132

Sandra J. MacLean, Sherri A. Brown and Pieter Fourie (*editors*)
HEALTH FOR SOME
The Political Economy of Global Health Governance

Craig N. Murphy (*editor*)
EGALITARIAN POLITICS IN THE AGE OF GLOBALIZATION

George Myconos
THE GLOBALIZATION OF ORGANIZED LABOUR
1945–2004

John Nauright and Kimberly S. Schimmel (*editors*)
THE POLITICAL ECONOMY OF SPORT

Morten Ougaard
THE GLOBALIZATION OF POLITICS
Power, Social Forces and Governance

Jørgen Dige Pedersen
GLOBALIZATION, DEVELOPMENT AND THE STATE
The Performance of India and Brazil Since 1990

Markus Perkmann and Ngai-Ling Sum
GLOBALIZATION, REGIONALIZATION AND CROSS-BORDER REGIONS

Marc Schelhase
GLOBALIZATION, REGIONALIZATION AND BUSINESS
Conflict, Convergence and Influence

Herman M. Schwartz and Leonard Seabrooke (*editors*)
THE POLITICS OF HOUSING BOOMS AND BUSTS

Leonard Seabrooke
US POWER IN INTERNATIONAL FINANCE
The Victory of Dividends

Timothy J. Sinclair and Kenneth P. Thomas (*editors*)
STRUCTURE AND AGENCY IN INTERNATIONAL CAPITAL MOBILITY

Fredrik Söderbaum and Timothy M. Shaw (*editors*)
THEORIES OF NEW REGIONALISM

Susanne Soederberg, Georg Menz and Philip G. Cerny (*editors*)
INTERNALIZING GLOBALIZATION
The Rise of Neoliberalism and the Decline of National Varieties of Capitalism

Ritu Vij (*editor*)
GLOBALIZATION AND WELFARE
A Critical Reader

Matthew Watson
THE POLITICAL ECONOMY OF INTERNATIONAL CAPITAL MOBILITY

Owen Worth and Phoebe Moore
GLOBALIZATION AND THE 'NEW' SEMI-PERIPHERIES

International Political Economy Series
Series Standing Order ISBN 978–0–333–71708–0 hardcover
Series Standing Order ISBN 978–0–333–71110–1 paperback
(*outside North America only*)

You can receive future titles in this series as they are published by placing a standing order.
Please contact your bookseller or, in case of difficulty, write to us at the address below with
your name and address, the title of the series and one of the ISBNs quoted above.

Customer Services Department, Macmillan Distribution Ltd, Houndmills, Basingstoke,
Hampshire RG21 6XS, England

Globalization and the 'New' Semi-Peripheries

Edited by

Owen Worth
Lecturer in International Relations, University of Limerick, Ireland

Phoebe Moore
Lecturer in International Relations, University of Salford, UK

First published 2009 by
PALGRAVE MACMILLAN

Palgrave Macmillan in the UK is an imprint of Macmillan Publishers Limited, registered in England, company number 785998, of Houndmills, Basingstoke, Hampshire RG21 6XS.

Palgrave Macmillan in the US is a division of St Martin's Press LLC, 175 Fifth Avenue, New York, NY 10010.

Palgrave Macmillan is the global academic imprint of the above companies and has companies and representatives throughout the world.

Palgrave® and Macmillan® are registered trademarks in the United States, the United Kingdom, Europe and other countries.

ISBN-13: 978–0–230–22075–1 hardback

This book is printed on paper suitable for recycling and made from fully managed and sustained forest sources. Logging, pulping and manufacturing processes are expected to conform to the environmental regulations of the country of origin.

A catalogue record for this book is available from the British Library.

A catalog record for this book is available from the Library of Congress.

10   9   8   7   6   5   4   3   2   1
18 17 16 15 14 13 12 11 10 09

Printed in the United States of America

Contents

Acknowledgements

As we mention in the introduction this book began life as a workshop held at the Kilmurry Lodge Hotel in Limerick, Ireland in March 2006. We would like to thank the department of Politics and Public Administration at Limerick and particularly Neil Robinson for sponsoring the event. We have also developed the ideas here with the contributors at subsequent panels at the International Studies Association (New York 2009). There were a number of paper givers at both events who have not featured in this book, but have made significant contributions to its development as a collection. In particular, we would like to thank Neil Robinson (again), Kevin Gray, Marina Blagojevic, Chris Farrands, Athina Karatzogianni, Andrew Robinson and Or Raviv. We would also like to thank Kyle Murray for his contribution to the debates. At Palgrave we would like to thank Alexandra Webster and Renée Takken for their help and commitment to the project. Finally, we would like to thank the International Political Economy series editor, Tim Shaw for his support and interest towards the book.

Owen Worth
Phoebe Moore

Notes on Contributors

Dr Jason P. Abbott is currently lecturing in International Politics and Political Economy at the University of Surrey. His publications include *The Political Economy of the Internet in Asia and the Pacific* (Greenwood, 2004), *Developmentalism and Dependency in South East Asia* (Routledge, 2003), and *State Strategies in the Global Political Economy* (Palgrave, 1999 with Dr Ronen Palan). He is also the co-editor with Owen Worth of *Critical Perspectives on International Political Economy* (Palgrave, 2002), and *Offshore Finance Centres and Tax Havens: The Rise of Global Capital* (Palgrave, 1999 with Mark Hampton). Jason has also published in *Asian Affairs, Asian Studies Review, Development Policy Review, Pacifica Review, Roundtable: The Commonwealth Journal of International Affairs, Security Dialogue and Third World Quarterly*.

Terry Boswell (1955–2006) was a Professor in Sociology at the University of Emory, who wrote extensively on labour organisation and world-systems analysis. He was author of a number of books and over 40 articles, including *The Spiral of Capitalism and Socialism: Towards Global Democracy* (with Christopher Chase-Dunn, Lynne Rienner, 2000).

Christopher Chase-Dunn is a distinguished Professor of Sociology and Director of the Institute for Research on World-Systems at the University of Riverside in California. He is the founding editor of the *Journal of World-Systems Research* and author, co-author, editor or co-editor of over a dozen books, including *Global Formations: Structures of the World Economy* (Blackwell, 1998), *Rise and Demise: Comparing World Systems* (Westview) and *The Spiral of Capitalism and Socialism: Towards Global Democracy* (Lynne Rienner, 2000).

Charles Dannreuther is Lecturer in European Political Economy at the University of Leeds, working in the area of EU studies and EU enlargement. His work has been published in *Comparative European Politics* and *Competition and Change*.

Gerard Downes teaches political science at the University of Limerick, Ireland. He recently completed a PhD on the World Trade Organization's

(WTO) Trade-Related Aspects of Intellectual Property Rights Agreement (TRIPs) which assessed the impact of the agreement on product and process patents on pharmaceuticals in India.

Kirk Lawrence is a graduate student in sociology at the University of California, Riverside. His emphases are in political economy and theory, with particular interest in the interaction of humans and the biosphere during the evolution of world-systems.

Phoebe Moore is Lecturer in International Relations for University of Salford, and has served on the Editorial Board for Capital and Class since 2006. Her recent publications include the hosting of the special issue titled 'Visions of Peer to Peer Production' (January 2009) and the monograph *International Political Economy of Employability: Skills Revolutions, East and West* (Palgrave Macmillan IPE series, forthcoming).

Hugo Radice is Research Fellow at the School of Politics and International Studies, University of Leeds, working in the fields of international political economy and Marxist theory. Recent papers include 'The developmental state under global neoliberalism', *Third World Quarterly* 29/6, 2008; and 'Life after death: The Soviet system in British higher education', *International Journal of Management Concepts and Philosophy* 3/2, 2008.

Stuart Shields is Lecturer in International Political Economy at the University of Manchester, specialising in the area of Eastern Europe and IPE. His most recent work has been published in *Global Society* and *Competition and Change* and his book 'The Political Economy of Transition' was published by Routledge in 2009. He is also the convenor for the International Political Economy Group (IPEG) for the British International Studies Association (BISA).

Rick Simon teaches Politics at Nottingham Trent University, UK. He is the author of *Labour and Political Transformation in Russia and Ukraine* (Ashgate 2000). He is particularly interested in state formation and in the political economy of Russia.

Gerard Strange is Reader in Political Economy at the University of Lincoln, UK. He has written extensively on critical analyses of globalization, regionalism, political ecology and British trade union engagement with the political economy of European Union.

Ernesto Vivares is a Teaching Associate in Development Studies at the University of Bath. He completed PhD at the University of Sheffield on South America and neoliberal World Order.

William Vlcek was Lecturer in International Politics at the Institute of Commonwealth Studies, University of London, when his contribution was completed. He is the author of *Offshore Finance and Small States: Sovereignty, Size and Money* (Palgrave Macmillan, 2008).

Owen Worth is Lecturer in International Relations at the University of Limerick. He is the author of *Hegemony, International Political Economy and Post-Communist* Russia (Ashgate, 2005) and has authored a number of articles. His most recent work has appeared in *International Politics, Third World Quarterly* and *Review of International Studies*.

Introduction

Owen Worth and Phoebe Moore

Global Politics in the twenty-first century has brought with it fresh challenges and fresh enquires into the nature and stability of the workings of the contemporary world. In terms of theory, the recent 'critical' literature on globalisation and Global Political Economy has led to an extension of the central concepts of core–semi-periphery–periphery that were developed by world-system theorists and by dependency theorists during the Cold-War era of western Marxism. Within these models, great emphasis was placed upon the role of the semi-peripheral state as an agent for change and transformation (Frank, 1966; Wallerstein, 1979; Chase-Dunn, 1989). With the end of the Cold War, the rise of the 'globalisation' phenomenon and the emergence of the discipline of International (or Global) Political Economy (IPE) as a distinct field within International Politics, previous 'statist' observations became both unfashionable and criticised. Factors such as the rise of neoliberalism and the 'globalising' of the economy have led to a new set of critical enquiries (Abbott and Worth, 2002) as well as radical questions about how the international division of labour has emerged in ways that distinctly affect people (see, for example, Moore and Taylor, 2009) not seen in the industrial context of the authoring of World Systems analysis (WSA). Without the concept of the semi-periphery the 'world system' as understood by the WSA theorists has no significance, and with the rise of the 'global' system (Robinson, 2004), a reconsideration of the characteristics of any kind of 'system' must be conducted. The semi-periphery as a unique avenue of study within global politics outside the more specialised area of world-systems research (or more specifically, within IPE) has waned and as a result, we aim to bring the concept back to the drawing board, but to first, decide how it must be altered to represent our contemporary post-globalised world.

What the chapters of this volume maintain is that whilst the term as an explanatory tool at first glance might have altered or declined, globalisation has brought with it a number of characteristics which add to a wider understanding of what we might interpret as 'semi-peripheral'. Factors such as capital mobility, labour drains caused by increased emigration, the co-ordination of macro-policy and increased inequality both above and below the state have produced a whole set of what we might define as 'new semi-peripheries in the Twenty-First century'. One of the main enquiries that we engage within this collection is whether these new semi-peripheral developments that have occurred since the onset of neoliberal globalisation still retain the same character that some earlier accounts had insisted. By illustrating how traditional semi-peripheral states and new semi-peripheral developments have been reshaped by globalising processes, the examples in this book have generally followed the trends made within IPE as a whole. Rather than following the 'statist' cyclical systemic interpretations that previous understandings might have favoured, these have generally moved to a position that understands the semi-periphery within a more complex international society and one that – to use a term that is borrowed in both Chapters 2 and 3 – 'takes globalisation seriously'. Thus one of the main enquires here asks how 'second-world' or the semi-periphery have responded to the forces of globalisation – especially in light of the fall of state-socialism.

Recent events and instabilities have brought global capitalism to new forms of crisis and have placed greater significance on studies of semi-peripherality. Previous accounts have often suggested that the semi-periphery can play a unique role during economic crisis – this might have been previously indicated through events such as the Russian Revolution and more towards neo-mercantilism in the post-war era, allowing us to tentatively suggest that in the current climate of economic unrest the semi-periphery (however it might be defined) might attract greater significance. However, the genesis of this book was in a workshop that took place at the University of Limerick in early 2006 at a time when the global economy was still – albeit slightly retracted – in a state of general stability. Thus, the main crux of the workshop remained to evaluate both the concept of and the effects that globalisation has had upon what he considered to be semi-peripheral. Not all chapters' authors within the present book participated at the workshop, but the collection can be seen as the sum of what was discussed during the day.

The book is divided into three separate parts, each of which examines a distinct part of the book's overriding theme. The first section, 'theoretical reflections: globalisation and the semi-periphery' is an attempt to re-examine the concept of the semi-periphery, in light of the development of International Political Economy (IPE). Chapter 1 outlines the origins of the concept of the semi-periphery and questions, why, despite its historical richness, its usefulness has diminished. It argues instead that the semi-periphery has seemed to alter its strategy since the onset of neoliberal globalisation from being one that has contended to contest the character of the world order to one that contests it. Hugo Radice in Chapter 2, however, offers a different overview of the semi-periphery. For him the term grew into one that became intertwined with world-systems theory to the extent that when political and economic relations became more globalised, the term became redundant. Instead of reverting back to structural definitions (no matter how loose), the chapter argues that we instead should look more at the reconfiguration of class relations to explain changes to global capitalism. The last chapter in this section takes in much of what the previous chapter argued in terms of the reconstruction of class relations, but argues that the current era has to be seen as one of a post-Fordist character in which manufacturing is deployed to the semi-periphery. For Strange, the significance of the 'new' semi-peripheries should not be underestimated, for as post-Fordism enters an era of crisis, then such states (in particular China) will take up greater prominence.

If the first section looked provided a theoretical overview of the relevance of the semi-periphery, then the second section 'Globalisation and change in the semi-periphery' looks at the effects globalisation and global change have had on what we might define as 'traditional semi-peripheral' states. In Chapter 4 Ernesto Vivares looks at recent development in Argentina and Brazil. He illustrates how, in the last 30 or so years, South America has been transformed and re-situated from one world order to another. As a result, its social forces and political ideology have been transformed and restructured in tandem with broader changes from above. The other region where semi-peripheral development has historically been prominent has been in Southeast Asia. In Chapter 5 Jason Abbott argues that we can look at this region as one that can still be seen in terms of dependency. Whilst much of the early work on dependency theory might have been criticised due to the emergence of East and Southeast Asia as autonomous regions, a closer examination of industrial production and recent transformations in these areas reveal a more complex relationship with the global economic order which should be seen as a form of dependency. To illustrate his argument, Abbott focuses upon the nature and workings of the motor industry in Malaysia and Thailand.

One of the themes throughout this book is the prominence and character of China as a new major player in the global economy. In Chapter 6, Gerard Downes takes up both the cases of China and India and argues that both can be regarded as semi-peripheral powerhouses, as whilst their emergence has attracted great investment, it has done so through its promotion of cheaper skilled labour, without developing its social or political infrastructure. To a certain extent, Russia is seen alongside China and India as a key semi-peripheral player in the global economy. Chapter 7 examines the transformation of Russia since its prominence as a 'Communist power' and demonstrates that Russia has entered the global capitalist economy as a semi-peripheral power that has become heavily dependent upon energy. In addition to the new regional leadership roles that China and India have assumed, Russia has maintained and indeed strengthened its position as a geopolitical power. Then, Chapter 8 focuses upon another power on the fringes of Europe that has often been described as semi-peripheral – Turkey. In assessing its development and recent transformation and by favouring a more traditional WSA approach, Moore and Dannreuther argue that Turkey's historical development and its contemporary relationship with the EU reveal a unique semi-peripheral character that itself brings to light the importance of a re-visitation of this concept.

The final section of this book 'New semi-peripheral developments and possible futures' looks at both new forms of the semi-periphery that have emerged since the end of the Cold War and the onset of globalisation, and looks at what might emerge from the semi-periphery in the future. In looking at Eastern European transition, Stuart Shields illustrates how the ideological project of neoliberalism has been centralised into Eastern European through the mobilisation of social forces that have been shaped by transnational elites. By focussing in particular on Poland, Shields argues that the best way we can interpret new semi-periphery formations in Eastern Europe is through understanding the transnational development of neoliberal hegemony. Another result of neoliberal globalisation has been the movement of capital to tax havens and off-shore finance havens. Chapter 10 argues that such havens represent a new form of semi-peripherality, as they are both dependent upon flights of capital from key players in the global economy on the one hand and maintain its overriding principles on the other. As a result they represent a new form of semi-peripheral development that has been the direct result of globalisation.

The last two chapters focus upon the belief that resistance and transformation are more likely to emerge from the semi-periphery. Both also question the sustainability of the contemporary capitalist system and look at potential developments from the semi-periphery in order to imagine potential futures. Chapter 11 focuses on the question of energy and on the contemporary system's reliance on the commodification of energy. Kirk Lawrence argues that this dependency is far more than many accounts have previously suggested and is unsustainable in its present form. As a result, developments from the semi-periphery might move to transform the system. The final chapter by Chase-Dunn and Boswell follows on from this by assessing the emergence of social movements geared towards contesting the legitimacy of the current world system, and argues that due to its nature, there is a higher likelihood that socially progressive and democratic movements are more likely to emerge from semi-peripheral states or regions. In this way, it is imperative that greater attention is placed onto examining this potential dynamic.

As the international system enters a new era of uncertainty, the timing of this collection, we believe, is significant. The new relationships and power structures that global capitalism has produced are being re-assessed at the practice level of politics. As a result it seems a poignant opportunity to asses how the semi-periphery has been transformed and what these transformations might lead to in the foreseeable future. This book brings a wide range of authors from different positions to debate such developments.

Part I

Theoretical Reflections: Globalisation and the Semi-Periphery

1
Whatever Happened to the Semi-Periphery?

Owen Worth

International Political Economy (IPE) has in recent years seen an influx of critical writing on the theme of globalisation and world order which has radicalised the way that power has been conceived within the global political economy. The much heralded work of Susan Strange, followed by interventions from Robert Cox and the birth of 'new international political economy' opened up new ways of understanding the emergence of the globalised economy and non-state and institutional actors (Strange, 1987; Murphy and Tooze, 1991; Cox, 1996). This body of work, some of which – but by no means all – have been influenced by Marxist literature, has often been presented as one that transcended former Marxist-inspired interpretations of power that had generally been expressed through the relationship of core-periphery. The central concepts of core-periphery favoured by world-system and dependency theorists were criticised for undermining the complexities of structural power in their reproduction of international capitalism and equally for being unable to account for transformation and change (Strange, 1987: 24–29; Linklater, 1990: 97–139; Cox, 1996: 510–513). These criticisms (which themselves often appraised as much as criticised the work[1]) have led to a body of 'critique' that seems to be quick to dismiss much of the language inherent within world-systems.

One of the more underplayed concepts inherent within world-system theory is the role played by the semi-periphery. Here, great emphasis is placed upon the role of the semi-peripheral state as an agent for change and transformation (Wallerstein, 1974, 1979; Gereffi and Evans, 1981; Arrighi, 1985; Chase-Dunn, 1990). Yet, despite the appeal of Coxian-inspired accounts of world order, empirical work has tended to favour the study of influential states and regions (Gill, 1990; Cox, 2002), and whilst semi-peripheral areas have been studied (Gill, 1993a; Robinson,

2003; Moore, 2007b; Morton, 2007), the focus has tended to be on how semi-peripheral states have integrated into the world economy, rather than how they might transform it. This chapter seeks to re-engage with how we should look at the concept of the semi-periphery and then ask whether semi-periphery states still maintain their uniqueness in the era of globalisation.

The semi-periphery: Problems with definition

As stated above, the criticisms placed to world-systems and dependency theorists have tended – rightly or wrongly – to focus upon problems of reductionism and on the failure to account for factors such as the rise of neoliberalism and the 'globalising' of the economy. These might be reasonable accusations. The charge of reductionism stems partly from Cox's criticism that world-systems theories have been too preoccupied with structure and that there is a lack of engagement with the functional processes involve within a system or order (Cox, 1996: 513). In addition, there is a charge of 'state-centric reductionism' that stems from the observation that world-systems theorists tend to suffer from the same problem as Waltzian realists in that they tend to reduce state and the state-system to units within a system, the only significant difference being that they appear as economic, as opposed to military units (Skocpol, 1977; Cox, 1987: 357).

Perhaps even more relevant is the method employed by world-systems theorists, especially when analysing the nature of various components that bind systems together. Again criticisms here are centred upon the claim that world-systems theories fall into a positivist trap, which overly relies on economic data and indices in order to make specific conclusions (Linklater, 1990). It is perhaps the method of analysis that allows us at first to re-think the very nature of the semi-periphery. Rather than revisit the debates inherent within International Relations (IR) on which brand of Marxism is less susceptible to charges of 'vulgar economism', we should critically reflect on the manner in which the semi-periphery is defined. Generally speaking, semi-peripheral states are those states which contain an equal level of basic and advanced forms of production (Wallerstein, 1985; Peschard, 2005), and have a GDP per capita somewhere between the advanced powerhouses of North America and Europe and underdeveloped states currently associated with structural adjustment and the heavily indebted poor counties (HIPC). In addition, semi-peripheral states are often characterised as those which are heavily reliant upon manufacturing (as typified by the East Asian states that succeeded in maximising manufacturing exports in the post-war era), and are marked by certain instabilities. Politically, these might include weak or venerable state structures, whilst socially these might include factors such as increasing inequality, changes in population (either due to emigration or an increase in the rate of population) and a steady increase in urbanisation. Yet, these broad terms are in no way uniform and any measurement of semi-peripherality is not just subjective in terms of its appliance, but also dependent upon its definition.

The semi-periphery remains a contested term that largely has its origins in sociological thought and that has been applied within separate disciplines of the social sciences. Whilst the semi-peripheral state might have become associated with world-system analysis, its elementary roots lie within classical sociological studies. In different ways the social enquiries of Marx, Weber and Durkheim all mention the semi-periphery in their contrasted visions of the project of modernity. Whilst we are now familiar with the concept as part of a backlash against the principals of modernisation and in particular of the Rostowian developmental model, it should equally be acknowledged that such theorists used similar criteria for defining the semi-periphery as their critics. In addition, Rostow placed a similar degree of importance to the semi-peripheral state's mobilisation as being central to social change. For, let us not forget that the crux of his model centred on the 'take-off' stage, which focussed upon states that could all be defined as 'semi-periphery' (Rostow, 1960). At the same time Marx's classic recipe of 'primitive accumulation' was employed to understand the development of capital in the same stage that Rostow set out to examine (Marx, 1990). It seems that there is often a reluctance to disable the term from its neo-Imperialist origins, which tends to determine semi-peripheral states within a system that is ultimately ordered by a rigid relationship of dependency. This is equally perhaps why those that borrow from the Coxian-inspired form of IPE have tended to keep such a distance between structural concepts which they stress that they are moving beyond. Nevertheless, if we are merely to define the semi-periphery as a state that rests between advanced industrial states and underdeveloped state, then we equally should expand beyond its association with world-systems research.

Another problem that faces those that study the semi-periphery is precisely what states should be included in the category as it remains difficult to define exactly what is meant/required to be semi-peripheral and indeed how the term should be defined. Classical semi-peripheral states have generally included states within Latin America, East Asia and post-Communist or 'post-authoritarian' states such as Russia, Central Asia and South America (Arrighi and Drangel, 1986). Yet certain common definitions often mark the fluid movement that occurs in short spaces of time have suggested a re-examination. Whilst Arrighi (1985) might have insisted that the semi-periphery is a permanent feature of the world economy, the states included within the concept – and I would further argue, more significantly its function – alter and change over time. In terms of states for example, Eastern Europe, Southern Europe and Ireland were seen as amongst those cited as additions, when many were empirically debating examples in the 1980s (Martin, 1990). If we were to use convention indicators such as GDP and the diversity of production activity in contemporary terms then it would be hard to argue that any state in either South or Eastern Europe would fit this category, and would be plain absurd to argue that Ireland – which currently holds one of the highest GDP per capita figures in Europe – could be considered semi-peripheral. On the other hand, states such as India and China have emerged as states that adequately fit these definitions, with an increasing global economy viewing them as ideal locations for cheap skilled and semi-skilled manufacturing labour (see Downes', Chapter 6, in this volume).

Other accounts have focussed upon states that are subordinate/peripheral to a strong power, but find themselves located within regional organisations and inter-state partnerships that exploit, or at least contribute to mechanisms that disadvantage underdeveloped states. Such definitions have provided studies on countries such as Canada, Norway, Australia (Glenday, 1989; Cohen and Clarkson, 2004[2]) and Ireland (Kirby, 2002) arguing that whilst these respective countries may appear at the top-end of respective crude economic indices, they remain semi-periphery in terms of 'middle powers' and act as an important clog by legitimating a specific power system. These however, could equally be described as states that appear at the 'periphery of the core', as opposed to genuinely semi-peripheral, as they have all the characteristics of advanced countries, without necessarily possessing the structural power or influence (Strange, 1988).

This leads us to the wider question of how the phenomenon of globalisation has further problematised how we define the semi-periphery. The increase in capital flows, reliance of Foreign Direct Investment (FDI) and the rise in the prominence of multinational enterprises as an actor for economic generation has had a significant effect upon the semi-periphery, with states such as Brazil, Mexico, Malaysia and Indonesia moving away from the Import Substitution method of self-autonomy, as classically subscribed by Frank (1966), towards strategies of 'internationalisation', that create favourable conditions for global souring by MNCs (initially noted by Gereffi and Evans in the early 1980s). As a result, one could argue that the semi-periphery has changed its character from one that sought to resist the character of the overall system/order to one that has largely complied. For example, the Soviet-inspired projects of state socialism as well as the various forms of Import Substitution strategies were all intended to challenge existent dominant trends. The end of the Cold War has altered this dynamics as key states that resisted capitalist development in the twentieth century have re-entered the global economy as key contributory players.

Finally and perhaps more importantly, globalisation has also prompted some to point to the problems with state-centric classifications of core-periphery (something which I will deal with more below), which brings us back to one of the major flaws with dependency theory. In fairness, it was Frank himself who informed us that dependency operated at two-levels, with a core-periphery (or metropolis/satellite) relationship between essential both within the state and as its representative position outside (Frank, 1966). Globalisation however has blurred this even further and has brought with it renewed questions of spatial fluidity, which has made tradition models of state-centric neo-Imperialism problematic. This can be seen with Jan Nederveen Pieterse's observations that the corporation has emerged as a separate actor in dependency-based relationships. Equally or perhaps more important is his observation that some of these corporations originate from semi-peripheral countries themselves and often operate in (often deprived areas) of advanced (or 'core') industrial states, creating a situation of 'reverse-dependency' (Nederveen Pieterse, 2000). Indeed, one might be inclined to agree with Nederveen Pieterse here that such globalising trends have made it necessary to re-think statist categorisations.

Problems with '20th century' model

The traditional statist model of the semi-periphery should be seen as one that is a product of the twentieth century that was entrancingly linked to the dependency models, inspired by Frank, that and to world-systems theory, associated primarily by Wallerstein. Despite the close proximity between these approaches there remain distinct differences within and between them in how the semi-periphery is perceived and understood. Before looking at how we need to move beyond these models, it is necessary to briefly outline how these traditions developed their respective positions.

Dependency theories obviously owed a lot to the original contributions of the late Andre Gunder Frank and his work, and from his seminal observation that an increase in international trade results in the renewed neo-colonial relationship between advanced states and underdeveloped states (Frank, 1966). The semi-periphery facilitates an important role in this relationship as they consist of states in which urbanisation have been mobilised to allow for a smooth running of the international capitalist trading system (Frank, 1967; Emmanuel, 1972). This was further modified to take into account differences in the historical development of such semi-peripheral states, and also for the contrasting modes of production that specific states have pursued through complex state sociological strategies (Emmanuel, 1972; Amin, 1976; Cardoso and Faletto, 1979). Here then, attempts were made to broaden the scope and type of dependency relationship, so that charges of linear generalisation can be dismissed. In addition, comparative historical studies of semi-peripheral states show how they have responded to the wider relationship of dependency, by perusing a contrasting number of economic directions that have included the Asian Tigers, state socialism and Latin American militarism. Whilst Frank et al. did not approve of the authoritarian regimes that had emerged throughout the twentieth century he (they) nevertheless insisted that semi-peripheral states, unlike their colonialised counterparts did have the option to opt out of the world economic system through pursuing nationalist and mercantilist policies in order to assert economic self-autonomy which would weaken the systemic reliance upon dependency (Frank, 1966).

World-systems theory, on the other hand, saw the semi-periphery as a necessary structure that facilitates the mechanical workings of the international system and as such is a focal area of study in its own right as it makes up a key part of the three-way relationship that makes up the overall world-system. In terms of a systems share of wealth semi-peripheral states are those that are distinctive as they 'appropriate benefits in excess of the long-run costs of participation in the world division of labour but less than what it is necessary to keep up with the standard of wealth set by core states' (Arrighi, 1990: 17). As indicated above and insisted by Wallerstein, the semi-periphery appears as a permanent feature of the modern world-system, despite the fact that 'the ever-changing patterns of productive activities which constantly threaten to redefine the internal mix of semi-peripheral countries in the direction of peripheralisation' (Wallerstein, 1995). Arrighi clarifies the contradictory position taken by the semi-periphery by illustrating how states both engage with and struggle against the processes of exploitation and exclusion. Exploitation can occur towards peripheral states through unequal exchange[3] whilst the specialisation of one specific commodity or resource can lead to the exclusion of peripheral states from competing in that area of trade. Likewise, semi-peripheral states consistently struggle against similar processes coming from core states, whereby the semi-peripheral state might wish to further specialise in a specific resource that might lead towards a favourable form of comparative advantage. Alternatively, the positioning of the semi-periphery within the world-system can lead a state to take certain measures to resist and challenge the overall system by trying to contest measures placed on it by the core (Arrighi and Drangel, 1986; Arrighi, 1990: 16–18).

The one unique feature of the semi-peripheral state, however, is found in its potential ability to transform a system. As Chase-Dunn argues, the semi-periphery is defined by political and economic instability and as such appears as the potential 'seabed of change' (Chase-Dunn, 1989; Chase-Dunn and Hall, 1997). This ability was noted by Frank, when he observed in his classic study on Brazil and Chile that as semi-peripheral generate greater wealth when the core-dependency relationship is in crisis, then the semi-periphery can act in a self-interested manner which can facilitate this strain, leading to the potential break-up of the dependency chain (Frank, 1966). Yet such interpretations seem to draw (although this is often not identified) from the earlier analysis of Imperialism undertaken by Lenin. Lenin classically argued that as early twentieth-century Russia was in a unique position at the 'fringes' of capitalist development – as it was not fully industrialised, yet still considered amongst the European elite – then revolution in Russia could break the Imperialist system through breaking its weakest link.[4]

Both Lenin and subsequent accounts of Leninism make certain false assumptions that dependency theorists were to repeat in another part of the semi-periphery. Indeed, it can be argued that *Imperialism: The Highest Stage of Capitalism* was the genesis for all Marxist-inspired state-centric systemic understandings of twentieth-century capitalism. Lenin's statistic observations of the rise of financial monopolisation and its outward expansion with advanced capitalist states led him to argue that the 'moment' of the old capitalism where 'free competition predominated' had passed to be replaced by the 'new capitalism' of state expansion and monopolies (Lenin, 1933: 37). Capitalism had thus reached a stage where it was not only at its most destructive, but also at a crucial stage as this advanced form of capitalism had mobilised opportunism that had created divisions within the labour movements of advanced capitalist states. Lenin's concern was that the bourgeoisification of the proletariat that had already resulted from such opportunism in Britain was becoming entrenched in Germany and France, leading to a strong correlation between this process and the larger economic pursuit of Imperialism (Lenin, 1933: 96–97). It was from this point of departure that Lenin turned his attention to the revolutionary objectives of the Russian proletariat and its role as the instigator of the wider upheaval of the capitalist system. Fifty years later, a more implicit tonic was being subscribed through the promotion of Import Substitution.

Lenin had ignored the complex semi-Asiatic nature of the Russian State in his own work on the Russian position (Wittfogel, 1957; Worth, 2005), but more importantly, in *Imperialism*, he simply misinterpreted the dynamics of capitalism and its tendency to reinvent itself in different forms. The assumptions made were largely driven through a rather crude positivism of determinism that was driven from empirical economic data. Frank's seminal piece, or at least the material on South America that became influential, made assumptions from a similar methodological base. Frank's overriding logic drove from the observation that the semi-periphery performed at a better level during the financial crisis at the core post-1929, due to the fact that the system that centred upon the core had floundered (Frank, 1966). Thus his hypothesis rested upon the notion that if a semi-peripheral state contested the system, it would break out of the overall mechanism of exploitation. Yet in both instances, activity at the semi-periphery ultimately failed to alter or significantly transform the capitalist world-system. In the case of the Soviet Union, rather than offering an alternative, world systems theorists generally viewed it as merely taking its place within the core (Wallerstein, 1979), yet the nature of capitalist production produced during what Hobsbawn terms as the Short Twentieth Century had certainly been shaped by the results of the Russian Revolution and the consolidation of the Soviet Union (Hobsbawn, 1994).

Thus, whilst, as Chase-Dunn recognises, semi-peripheral states have often adopted a disposition explicitly geared to revolutionising the internal and external positioning of a specific system, such developments have failed to significantly alter its working order. The failure of such alternative 'social' strategies has been recognised by certain pioneers of dependency theory themselves. In response to the charges of reductionism that had been levied against them, subsequent accounts have placed a greater focus on dialects (originally developed by Cardose) and on Amin's notion of unequal exchange (that itself was developed from the work of Emmanuel) that may have retained the importance of structure, but did give certain emphasis to the role of cultural agency. Part of this stemmed as a reply to Laclau and subsequently others, who critiqued dependency theory for favouring a simplistic systemic reduction of capitalism as opposed to a more complex articulation of contrasting modes of production (Brenner, 1977; Laclau, 1977). Therefore, as the components of the capitalist system are far more complex and far less determined in their respective roles, 'anti-systemic' strategies would not necessarily transform a system, but rather re-shape its legitimacy through the process of articulation (Ruccio and Simon, 1992).

Perhaps the most obvious practical occurrence that questioned the validity of the notion of the semi-periphery was the rise of the newly industrialised countries (NICs) in East Asia (see Abbott's, Chapter 5, in this collection). Here states from the margins were able to use their industrial strategies to compete on their own terms and challenge the productive hegemony of Western Europe and North America. Similarly, the oil crisis and the rise of the OPEC countries have also shown us that states are not necessarily confined to a system that is determined by the distribution of structures. Such developments were championed by neo-pluralists at the time as they believed that this was an indication that weaker states could transform themselves to co-operate and compete with mature democracies (Keohane, 1984; Fukuyama, 1992). Yet, Wallerstein's take on this would not necessarily demonstrate the contradictory consciousness of the semi-periphery, but re-enforce his own doubts on Chase-Dunn's claim that it provides the sea-bed of change. As noted by Arrighi, Wallerstein argued that the semi-periphery was essentially a safety valve for capitalist development in the world-system and provided 'capitalists the ability to shift capital from a declining sector to a rising sector' in order to 'profit from the wage-productivity squeeze of the leading sector' (Wallerstein, 1979; quoted in Arrighi, 1990). Arrighi feels that both Wallerstein and Chase-Dunn do not necessarily differ from their conceptions of the function of the semi-periphery, but demonstrate the apparent 'openness' of their potential roles. However, in contrast, Laclau's was quite adamant in his critique that Wallerstein has no room for such openness and that such a reading merely transfers all capitalist activity back to its systemic level (Laclau, 1977: 48).

Laclau's classic criticisms of systems theory brings us back to the major problem with traditional definitions of the semi-periphery – the separate, yet interlinking claims of reductionism, determinism and state-centricity, all of which have been enhanced by the advance of globalisation theory. To reiterate these within the study of Global Politics in recent years has led to the almost accepted narrative that world systems theory suffers from similar faults that were previously directed to 'vulgar Marxism'. Postgraduate text books in IR theory have long argued that this type of structural reductionism has more in common with the positivist method associated with Waltz's neo-realism than it does with any form of capitalist critique (Smith, Booth and Zalewski, 1996). Defined broadly as 'structuralism', such theories have been associated with the 'inter-paradigm' debate in the 1980s and along with the dual orthodoxies of realism/pluralism become open to epistemological criticisms, largely from the Marxist tradition. For example, Mark Rupert argues that world-systems theory can be seen in the same breath as realism as both are 'produced by abstracting one or the other aspect of (the) alienated relation of politics/economics, and then constructing abstract causal explanation in terms of this favoured primitive unit' (Rupert, 1993).

Charges of reductionism are complimented by the second charge of determinism and the third of state-centrism. The logic behind a structural interpretation of world politics is that its agents or units are ordered or shaped towards acting in a specific manner, reviving the spirit of Marx's overview of the rise of Louis Bonaparte and his immortal observation that whilst men may make history, they do not do so in the conditions of their choosing (Marx, 1967). However, the criticisms placed here suggest that in a world-systems analysis, the semi-periphery is merely a mechanical part of the global network of exchange, in which its functional body is dependent on the character of the system at a given historical time (Holman, 1993). Yet, whilst the Coxian-inspired literature has been presented in the recent history of IR theory as being one that has produced a vibrant form of critical Marxism, against the determinism of world-systems research, Wallerstein himself has denied such charges, arguing instead that his work has always been opposed to the irreversible laws of nature and maintains that once a system is on the point of disintegration, it is the social world that constructs a replacement (Wallerstein, 1992; Little, 1995). This leaves the criticism of state-centrism. This has become more evident with notions such as the 'internationalisation of the state' (Cox, 1987), the 'transnationalisation of classes' (van der Pijl, 1998; see Chapter 9 by Shields) and the 'erosion of the traditional paternalism' that socialised the composition of the state-system (Castells, 1996; Peschard, 2005). As the twentieth-century model of the semi-periphery was characterised by its centrality of the state and its economic output, then it was always unlikely to survive, or at least remain fashionable during an era of global change and transformation.

Globalisation, world order and the 'Cardoso effect'

If the concept of the semi-periphery was to become associated with variants of world-systems theory, then has the globalisation debate affectively consigned it to the dustbin? Whilst certain arguments would urge us to conclude that this to be the case (see Radice's, Chapter 2, in this volume), the recent studies and compilations mentioned above would suggest a resounding 'no'. However, whilst more refined studies have moved to successfully analyse globalisation through specific modifications of structural engagement, the more traditional accounts of world-systems have become increasingly specialised. In general, world-system's theory has been slow to examine the effects that neoliberal policy has had within semi-peripheral areas, coupled with the changing nature of global and institutional governance.[5] Equally, due to the societal effects that have resulted from technological change, it has become increasingly difficult to consistently identify states in terms of their structural might.

This should therefore present us with an opportunity to re-define and move beyond the ontology of dependency and world-systems to construct a theory of the semi-periphery that returns to the social enquiries that were instigated by Marx and which take into account contemporary developments that have emerged since the end of the Cold War and the rise of neoliberalism. One way in which this could be achieved is through the world order theory that might have been initiated by the hugely influential Cox, but was reproduced by a number of prominent academics to represent a fundamental change in thinking in the manner that the global political economy was ordered (Murphy and Tooze, 1991; Gamble and Payne, 1996). Following Cox 'new international political economists' suggest that International society is determined through the interaction between production and institutions. Borrowing from different interpretations of Gramsci's model of hegemony, they suggest that world orders emerge through a historical process where competing social forces struggle for hegemonic supremacy, which can only be obtained through passivity and consent (Cox, 1996). Unlike the world-system's interpretation of hegemony – that interprets the term as a structural progression which occurs when there is an unusually large concentration of power centred on one core state, the Coxian account relies more upon how economic and political ideas are constructed and contained, taking into account hegemonic agents that exist at various levels (Worth, 2005). The post-Cold War 'globalised' world is thus defined as one which has been defined by the consolidation of neoliberalism, maintained through policy initiatives that took shape from the World Bank's structural adjustment policy and by the creation of super-structural institutional agents such as the World Trade Organisation (WTO) and the World Economic Forum. In explanatory terms, world order theory has provided us with new Marxist approaches to the concept of agency within international politics, which had previously been primarily associated with plural orthodoxy and with constructivist accounts of the 'real world'. By placing greater emphasis on the functional articulation of agents in the international sphere, there has been a far greater development of the complex consciousness processes of base/super-structure than the structuralism inherent in much of the world-systems research (Bieler and Morton, 2001).

World order and globalisation theory might be better placed to account for the transformation of global politics in the past 30 or so years, but they have largely not adequately explained how the semi-periphery has responded to this transformation. Indeed one of the major concerns with world order theory is that it appears too Euro-centric in its nature (Linklater, 1990). Likewise, many empirical accounts seem to be based upon the formation and the influence of transnational social classes located in the industrial north. There have been far fewer accounts on how states associated with semi-peripherality have emerged and interacted with the dominant norms of the world order. The emergence of India, the re-emergence of Russia and China as semi-peripheral states, the restructuring of social relations in places such as post-Apartheid South Africa and Eastern Europe, and the continued and contrasting economic development and performance East Asia and Latin America all offer us areas to explore. Indeed their respective struggles in dealing with global transformation should tell us far more than more established regions about the workings and (in)stability of world order if we take Chase-Dunn's claim that, due to its unique character, the semi-periphery remains a potential sea-bed for change seriously (Worth, 2005).

Debates on the social dimensions of globalisation have further problematised structural studies on the semi-periphery. For example, whilst semi-peripheral states during the Cold War were prone to revolutionary and authoritarian turns, discontent with contemporary developments have often emerged from civil societal movements below the state (Gills, 2000). One such example here can be seen with the *Zapatistas* movement, an indigenous civil movement in Mexico that instigated an insurrection, after the NAFTA agreement eroded a constitutional pledge on land rights. In other semi-peripheral states, the resurgence of ethnic nationalism and competing ideological contestation has been a common feature of neoliberal transition. Yet, whilst these might represent civil forms of resistance within the semi-periphery they are not indicative of the ways that semi-peripheral states have responded to the onset of globalisation. In truth, the significance of such civil resistance, especially so-called progressive movements such as the *Zapatistas*, has been overplayed and has certainly made no significant impact on the overall direction that the state has taken. In contrast to the Import Substitution or era of state socialism, one of the features of the globalised world is that governments have felt inclined to 'toe the line' and compelled to integrate fully into the global economic. Even Castro insisted upon the need for Latin American states to 'join the fight against US Imperialism' from within the institutional confines of the WTO (Castro, 2000).

The effects of globalisation have thus altered the character of semi-peripheral states in two ways. Firstly – and arguably due to the collapse of the state socialist alternative – such states are no longer geared towards resistance in the same manner as they were during the second part of the twentieth century. Whilst certain states – Castro's Cuba and Chavez's Venezuela – have been outspoken in their criticisms of the unequal nature of global development, they have not sought to substantially provide a challenge. Secondly, due to the fluidity of investment and information, the distinction between resource-based and the industrial-based states have been made less clear, leaving the semi-periphery, which traditionally maintains a balance between the two in greater flux. Indeed, energy and manufacturing companies within these states have been able to create forms of 'reverse dependency' in areas within advanced industrial states (Nederveen Pieterse, 2000), whilst social indicators have revealed a greater increase in inequality and relative poverty (UNDP, 2005).

One popular argument put forward concerning recent trends is that globalisation has effectively made claims to dependency redundant and as such middle-ranking powers can no longer use the claim of semi-peripherality as an excuse for underdevelopment. This view is epitomised by former Latin American dependency theorist-turned Brazilian President Fernando Henrique Cardoso, who has argued that it is no longer acceptable to challenge movements from above as such a move risks the more dangerous threat of isolationism. To quote Cardoso in full:

> We are no longer talking about the south that was on the periphery
> of the capitalist core and tied to it in a classical relationship

of dependency…We are dealing in truth with a crueler (*sic*) phenomenon: either the south enters the democratic-technological-scientific race, invests heavily in R&D, and endures the 'information economy' metamorphosis, or it becomes unimportant, unexploited, and unexploitable.

(Cardoso, 2001)

Using the social-democratic 'third way thesis' associated with Giddens, Cardoso argued throughout his presidency that market reforms were required to allow investment to stimulate growth required to tackle social issues. Globalisation has thus become a mechanism that cannot be consigned merely as a specific form of capitalism, but as a process in which inclusion democratic interaction is required as a means of creating an equitable end (Cardoso, 2001).

The Cardoso 'effect' has been played out in the majority of states that maintain semi-peripheral characteristics. Strategies have been developed in East Asia, Eastern Europe, the post-Communist world – including Russia and China as well as in other states in Latin America that have found a way to adapt to the forces of globalisation (for example, see Shields, 2003; Worth, 2005; Moore, 2007b; Morton, 2007). The general premise here is that states on the semi-periphery should no longer aim to cut off from internationalism, but rather embrace it as an integral part of global development and as a result significantly alter western perceptions of development and progression.

Conclusion: The semi-peripheries of the twenty-first century

This chapter has argued that the unique character of the semi-periphery has often been sidelined within globalisation studies and that the development of perspectives from 'critical' or 'new' IPE that has accompanied globalisation analysis has either not explored or not neglected this development of study. As I have suggested here, this is partly due to its association with world-systems research, which many have argued has not adequately come to terms with the processes of globalisation and its effects on the state. As Radice argues in Chapter 2, the categorisation of core, periphery and semi-periphery relies upon territorially defined entities and specific strategic objectives, which could not account for the global onset of neoliberalism. Yet, the semi-periphery remains an important area of understanding of how neoliberal globalisation has spread and has been legitimised and equally how it might be contested. As some of the contributors to this collection illustrate, it seems crucial to enquire about the nature of and reliance on manufacturing powerhouses such as India and China and on avenues such as offshore centres, which represent contemporary forms of semi-peripherality. At the same here, this chapter has also endorsed and reaffirmed Chase-Dunn's claim that it is the semi-periphery – in whatever form or reproduction – that remains the focal point for instability and as a result provides us with a unique angle to understand the contemporary global world order.

In summary, we can make a number of claims that allow us to re-examine the role of the semi-periphery in world politics and make tentative suggestions for future research developments and agendas. Some of which are taken up in the later empirical chapters in this book.

- The term 'semi-periphery' is not 'dead in the water' as certain analysts would like to prescribe, but has been transformed by the rapid fluidity of globalisation.
- The definition of the semi-periphery should be re-evaluated so that it accounts for both the changing nature of production and the different strategies employed by successive governments to facilitate such changes.
- The role of the semi-periphery has moved from one that was neo-mercantilist in character to one that actively seeks engagement with the global political economy. In this sense it can fully engage with what Cerny calls the 'Competition State', whereby states seek to assume a positive that is competitively viable within the global political economy (Cerny, 1997).
- Such competitive strategies might mean a drive towards a more explicitly neoliberal polity, but could equally refer to states that are reliant upon certain commodities, that are used as a significant bargaining tool within the global economy. The most obvious examples here being energy-rich entities.
- Semi-peripheral activities remain fraught with instabilities, prompting great avenues of contestation. As a result they often provide us with richer explanations regarding the wider character and stability of the current era of globalisation.

Notes

1. Cox was quick to acknowledge the developments of world-systems analysis, arguing that whilst they were limited in terms of their structural and economic form of determinism, they did nevertheless bring the scope of human activity into the neo-realist-dominated field of International Relations at the time and forms the basis for a systemic approach of world politics that is at odds with

the Newtonian positivism associated with Kenneth Waltz at the time (Cox, 1996: 359–361).

2. The Cohen and Clarkson collection also includes the more traditional example of Mexico, which, whilst logical in one sense that Mexico, alongside Canada, is a NAFTA partner, is nevertheless seems out of place with the other, more developed, 'middle powers'.

3. The process of unequal exchange became a crucial feature of dependency theory in that it accounts for legitimating the diversity of wage and labour value through the practise of free trade. The invention of the trading system by advanced 'core' states allowed for an institution mechanism to structural manage the relationship of dependency. See Emmanuel (1972) and Amin (1980).

4. The term 'weakest link' is one that is often attributed to Lenin, despite the fact that there was no direct mention to the term throughout the theory of Imperialism. It was used by Stalin in the 1920s to illustrate Leninist revolutionary thought (Robinson, 2004) and became popularised in the west by Dinko Tomasic in the early 1950s, when examining the impact of the Russian cultural mindset on the development of Communism (Tomasic, 1953).

5. The difference approaches to globalisation can be seen in the Paradigm collections, run by Wallerstein through the Fernand Braudel centre in New York. Here certain contributors, such as Boswell, Reifer and Chase-Dunn placed renewed emphasis on system's theory through greater historical analysis, an expansion on the role of social agency and greater emphasis on the role of the semi-periphery, whilst others, such as Amin and Schwartzman have generally favoured an updated version of dependency (Reifer, 2004; Wallerstein, 2004b; Friedman and Chase-Dunn, 2005).

2

Halfway to Paradise? Making Sense of the Semi-Periphery

Hugo Radice

The purpose of this chapter is to examine critically the concept of the semi-periphery, in the context of the evolution of global capitalism over the last 30 years or so. Since the semi-periphery became a particular focus of world-systems theory (WST hereafter) in the 1980s, the first part of the chapter looks at how this concept fits into the development of development theory, starting from the well-known conflicting paradigms of modernisation and dependency, moving on to the more specific relationship between the latter and the world-systems approach, and from there to the concept of semi-periphery itself. The second part examines the concept in detail, focusing on the work of Arrighi (1990), Chase-Dunn (1989, 1990) and the contributors to Martin (1990); here it is argued that the world-systems approach had considerable difficulty in adapting to the rise of neoliberalism and the political economy of globalisation, and that the origins of this difficulty lies in a flawed understanding of the dynamics of global capitalism. The final part outlines an alternative approach which deploys a different understanding of capital, class and the state in making sense of recent changes in the regions and countries chiefly seen as being semi-peripheral.

Developmentalism, dependency and world-systems theory: Genesis of the concept of semi-periphery[1]

For 30 years after the end of the Second World War, global capitalism is widely seen as having enjoyed uninterrupted economic growth and prosperity, notwithstanding the perils of Cold War confrontation with the Soviet bloc and the troubled process of decolonisation in the global South. That period generated two conflicting views of the dynamics of global capitalism in relation to the post-colonial

South: while modernisation theory presented a story of transformation from backwardness to modernity, dependency theory depicted a story of polarisation in which the development of the centre was built upon, and perpetuated, the underdevelopment of the periphery. Despite the apparent gulf between these two theories, they shared a common understanding of the central concept of development, namely a process of economic growth, industrialisation and urbanisation culminating in the form of society represented by the most advanced industrial states. A significant further point of agreement was that the state – that is, the formal institutions of government in a given country – would play a central role in such development.

The differences lay in the two schools' understanding of the dynamics of capitalism, and in the policy prescriptions flowing from their analyses. Modernisation theory, represented most notably by Rostow (1960, 1984), was situated in the tradition of Adam Smith and classical political economy, and focused on the economic condition of a given 'traditional' economy. It argued that economic dynamism could be unleashed by the construction of appropriate institutions and policies for harnessing the positive benefits of nationalism, leading to sustained growth based on higher levels of investment. For the most part, writers belonging to this school recognised a positive role for the state as well as the private sector, including initial measures of protection from international competition; they also advocated public development aid as a valuable additional stimulus. Dependency theory, exemplified by the work of Frank (1967), by contrast saw capitalism as pre-eminently a global system which intrinsically generated polarisation between rich and poor countries. Underdeveloped countries faced cumulative disadvantages in attempting to transform their conditions, because dependent integration into global capitalism had over time created politically powerful domestic interests linked to the advanced capitalist powers and therefore uninterested in autochthonous industrialisation.

Following the end of the post-war boom in the early 1970s, both paradigms struggled to adapt to new trends and problems. In explaining the 'lost decade' in Africa and Latin America in the 1980s, modernisation theorists could attribute the failure to achieve take-off to factors such as government corruption, restrictive property regimes and poor education; in explaining the relative success of the newly industrialising countries (NICs), especially in East Asia, dependency theorists could cite advantageous resource endowments, fortuitous policy innovations such as land reform and selective protection, or generous financial aid motivated by Western security concerns. At the same time, the traditional developmentalist focus on industrialisation and urbanisation was undermined by the shift in global economic dynamism towards the service sector, as well as the recognition of the continuing importance of agriculture in providing food security and a source of export revenues.

In this context, WST came into prominence in the 1970s by offering a more sophisticated 'historical sociology' of global capitalism, which aimed to take account of the complex relationship between the system as a whole (world-system) and the experience of individual countries.[2] WST drew on the French *Annales* school in placing great emphasis on the interpretation of long-run economic, social and political history. It also established a clear if critical link to long-standing Marxist concerns with both the theory and the history of capitalism, including debates on the nature and origins of the capitalist mode of production and its relation to other modes, its historical periodisation, economic dynamics and international relations (IR). The focus in WST on hegemonic powers and their role in shaping global dynamics offered a riposte to the common criticism that dependency theory tended towards 'structuralist' economic determinism, while the willingness of WST scholars to make extensive use of standard economic data sets seemed an improvement on the reliance of much Marxist writing on rhetorical polemics. Bringing together history and cultural studies with the entire gamut of the social sciences helped to generate real innovations in scholarship, although their diffusion has always been severely hampered by the growing mutual isolation of disciplines in academia.

The relational concepts of *core* and *periphery* are fundamental to WST's take on global capitalism, and are deployed much as in dependency theory, the main difference being that WST's focus is on the world-system as a whole rather than the underdeveloped periphery. The term *semi-periphery* originates simply as an empirical observation, that there are countries which by standard measures such as GDP per capita fall between the advanced core and the underdeveloped periphery.[3] However, the term was then invested with considerable analytical significance in the dynamics of core-periphery relations. To begin with, the continued existence of an intermediate range of countries that belonged neither to the core nor to the periphery in itself undermined the central proposition that the world-system contained strongly polarising forces: why did intermediate countries not get either drawn into the core, or pushed out to the periphery?

More broadly, by the late 1980s, the analytical defences employed by dependency writers to explain the existence of relatively successful NICs were starting to wear thin. US military aid as a source of growth became less important in the context of détente between China and the USA and the increasingly clear signs of decline in the Soviet bloc, while favourable land reforms in Taiwan and South Korea were now well in the past. Above all, the concept of the developmental state (Amsden 1989, Wade 1990) offered a direct challenge to the idea that peripheral countries were permanently trapped in underdevelopment by outlining indigenous sources of real development in the economic, social and political arrangements of these countries. At the same time, in Latin America both authoritarian and democratic régimes were turning away from the development policies of 'vertical' Import-Substitution and public-sector investment, towards export-led growth, privatisation and regional integration. Although to a significant extent such policy changes were mandated by core-country creditors and the Bretton Woods institutions, it became clear that they were supported by substantial domestic interests, including local capitalists and unions; the changes were also linked to processes of democratisation in many cases. Lastly, the emergence of substantial *outward* investments by firms headquartered in NICs called into question the assumption of the innate competitive superiority of core enterprises. In short, it became urgently necessary to re-formulate or extend WST to develop a viable understanding of the new diversity of development experience. The concept of the semi-periphery appeared to offer a good starting point.

The semi-periphery as an explanatory concept

In their important *Review* article, Arrighi and Drangel (1986) begin by observing

> …the existence of a significant number of states that seem to be permanently stationed in an intermediate position between 'maturity' and 'backwardness', as modernization theorists would say, or between 'center' and 'periphery', as dependency theorists would say.
>
> (Arrighi and Drangel 1986, p. 9)[4]

They cite Cardoso and Faletto's concept of 'dependent development' (1979), among others, as attempting to address this issue, but argue that while this may be helpful for understanding certain Latin American cases, it is insufficiently general. Instead, they start from Wallerstein's suggestion (1979) that semi-peripheral states form a distinct intermediate group by virtue of containing a mixture of the sort of economic activities normally associated with either the core or the periphery, the distinction being defined by the relative appropriation of the total surplus generated in the commodity chains that constitute the material basis of the capitalist world-economy. They propose to investigate whether such an intermediate group exists, whether it can be structurally identified and whether it has 'remained more or less constant… over the last 45 years' (Arrighi and Drangel 1986, p. 13).

Noting that the empirical identification of the semi-periphery has proved problematic, they then seek to specify it theoretically. First, they argue that the term should only be used 'to refer to a position in relation to the world division of labour and never to refer to a position in the interstate system' (ibid., p. 15). Second, they specify that the idea of 'commodity chain' should focus not on the distribution of the total product between different factors of production, but on its distribution between locational 'nodes' in the chain. Activities are defined as core activities if the nodes at which they occur are able to 'incorporate most if not all of the overall benefits of the world division of labour' (ibid., p. 17), while peripheral activities are remunerated at levels only marginally above those available outside that division of labour. The mechanism through which this unequal distribution of rewards is sustained is, in essence, that of market structure: businesses and zones engaging in core activities have market power based on superior technology, management and access to finance, while those engaging in peripheral activities have only generic resources of cheap land and unskilled labour, the markets for which are highly competitive. Core activities vary through time as Schumpeterian processes of creative destruction throw up new dynamic sectors; such processes, they suggest, tend to cluster not only in time, but also in space, forming a locus of 'core capital', and where such activities generate mutually beneficial externalities, a 'core zone' (ibid., p. 21).

Overlaying the global map of core and periphery activities and zones is a political system of multiple states, which have the legal right to control activities within and movement across their boundaries. Subject to the constraints of interstate competition, a given state may have the capacity to promote sufficient core activities within its territory to link together a critical mass of core capital, and thereby become a core state, able to maintain the necessary infrastructure to reproduce its core zones through time.

Having thus specified the joint concept of core and periphery, they then offer their central proposition concerning the structural role of the semi-periphery in the world-economy: semi-peripheral states contain enough core activities to generate revenues which can block the forces making for peripheralisation, but also enough low-revenue peripheral activities to prevent them from achieving core status (ibid., p. 27). The crux of the matter is that semi-peripheral states seeking to enlarge their share of global core activities can do so in one of two ways: either they can use revenues to protect indigenous core activities from global competition, in which case they isolate their core-activity businesses from the wider global flow of innovations that is central to an activity retaining its core character; or they improve the international competitiveness of their core activities through cost-reduction, but then find that other states follow suit, and more intense competition makes those activities peripheral (ibid.). The outcome is a group of countries that are permanently stuck in this intermediate status – the semi-periphery.

After a thorough exploration of the statistical evidence, which suggests that there is indeed remarkably little movement through time during the period in question between the core, the semi-periphery and the periphery, Arrighi and Drangel suggest that industrialisation has failed to change the status of semi-peripheral countries largely because industrial activities have on average become more peripheral in nature. With the advent of vertically integrated transnational corporations, the core now embraces all sectors, but only those *activities* that involve '...strategic decision making, control and administration, R&D...', or in short 'brain' activities (ibid., p. 57).

As their conclusion makes clear, Arrighi and Drangel are cautious with regard to both their evidence and their argument, claiming only to have identified a worthwhile research agenda. The essays in Martin (1990) include a restatement of the argument by Arrighi, together with one sector study (on footwear) and country studies on Chile, South Korea, Argentina, Ireland, Canada, Israel, Malaysia, Nigeria and South Africa. Of these, only the papers by Smith and Lee on South Korea and by Korzeniewicz on Argentina explicitly address the key issue of the developmental prospects for the semi-periphery.

Smith and Lee (1990, p. 80) attribute to WST three specific propositions: first, the existence of the three distinct strata; second, the possibility of mobility in the world-system through dependent development; and third, 'the working hypothesis that countries playing similar roles in the international system...may exhibit similar patterns and mechanisms of development'. While the first and third propositions concur with Arrighi and Drangel, the second surely does not; yet the conflation of the concepts of semi-periphery and dependent development is also a central feature in the earlier, very influential comparative study on Mexico and Brazil by Gereffi and Evans (1981). This conflation has recently been echoed in Wilkin (2008, p. 97):

> WSA [the world-system approach] expects to see movement within the world system. Membership of the core changes over time and the largest semi-peripheral states such as China, India and perhaps Brazil have the potential to move into the core given their relative resources and/or regional dominance.

In his discussion of Argentina, however, Korzeniewicz (1990) follows Arrighi in explicitly arguing that the two concepts are theoretically distinct. While dependent development was based on Latin American cases, its emphasis on the role of foreign capital and its exclusionary alliance with local capital and the state meant that it could not be applied to East Asia, where industrialisation appeared to be linked to a strong state, limits on foreign capital, and a more egalitarian distribution of income and wealth. He suggests that while the concept of dependent development seems to contain equally the relative standing of a country in the world-economy and the nature of its political regime, the concept of semi-periphery 'allows for the two issues to be made analytically distinct, so as to make their relationship an object of theoretical inquiry' (1990, p. 113). In other words, the concept of semi-periphery is essentially an economic concept, a core feature of the world-economy and one that is intrinsically distinct from the political concept of multiple states and the representation of social interests within them. This is the same position as that already noted in outlining the argument of Arrighi and Drangel (1986, p. 15).

Christopher Chase-Dunn deploys the semi-periphery concept in a far more ambitious way.[5] His core definition remains an economic one, with the difference that core activities are defined as 'capital-intensive' (1990, p. 3) rather than by their share of the surplus generated along a value-chain. Semi-peripheral areas fall into two types, those with a mix of core and peripheral activities, and those with 'a preponderance of intermediate levels of capital-intensive production' (*loc.cit.*). However, political agency is the key focus from the outset, notably:

> The idea (is) that the core/periphery hierarchy crosscuts and harmonises class relations in the core, and sometimes in the periphery, but class struggles in the semi-periphery are not so muted, and thus transformative social movements, ones that deeply challenge the

logic of capitalism, tend to form and to be most successful in the semi-periphery.

(ibid., p. 2)

At the most abstract level, circumstances in the semi-periphery are conducive to such a political challenge because its structural location allows of movement up or down, while the core and the periphery are sustained in their relative positions by the hierarchical relationship between them. Capitalist interests in the semi-periphery are divided between those that seek alliances with core powers on the basis of their control over peripheral activities (similar to Baran's (1957) *comprador bourgeoisie*), and those that seek to expand their own core-type activities. The state then tends to hold the ring and become the predominant agent of development; if the *comprador* element is more powerful, a country tends towards a rightist military regime, while the self-reliant element favours a more leftist regime form (Chase-Dunn 1990, p. 5). Unlike poor peripheral countries, semi-peripheral countries have the necessary resources to protect themselves from core countries that seek to block their rise.

Class struggle, for Chase-Dunn, is contained within the political units of the world-system, namely nation-states, and this 'has the effect of reproducing the core/periphery division of labour by producing class alliances that politically stabilise the global mode of production' (ibid., p. 6). In the capitalist world-system, there are two dimensions of exploitation, between capital and labour, and between core and periphery. The periphery is exploited by an alliance between core capital and core labour, while opposition to the core can lead to parallel class alliances in the periphery. Because semi-peripheral countries are pulled in two different directions, there is no stable basis for a class alliance, and as a result the choice between collaboration with and challenge to the core tends to take on a class character, especially in 'type 1' semi-peripheral countries with a mix of core and peripheral activities. In short, within his 'structural theory of the world system' the semi-periphery is the 'weak link' (ibid., p. 25). The collaborationist core workers form a smaller proportion of the working-class, and there is real potential for the class to benefit from a drive for autonomous development that challenges capitalism – although '[t]he matter of transformation to socialism is more problematic' (ibid., p. 27).

Chase-Dunn's work clearly broadens the concept of semi-periphery substantially beyond the original strictly economic argument of Arrighi and Drangel. This allows him to develop formulations that closely resemble other paradigmatic concepts in progressive development theory, such as the developmental state and sub-imperialism. However, the existence of these two very different approaches – the narrowly economic in Arrighi and Drangel and Korzienewicz, and the political agency focus of Chase-Dunn, Gereffi and Evans and Smith and Lee – brings into focus key theoretical issues in the development of an adequate critique of the political economy of global capitalism.

Understanding global capitalism differently

Common to both conceptions of the semi-periphery is the acceptance of an 'analytical distinction' (to use Korzeniewicz's term) between economics and politics. Such a distinction necessarily has effects on more concrete analyses of how capitalism varies in time and space, and what social forces are shaping the present dangers and opportunities that people face. It means that we construct two conceptual frameworks that are analytically independent of each other, even if we follow Poulantzas (1973) in characterising this independence as a relative autonomy of the state. The arguments we develop within the two frameworks take on a permanently partial and self-referential character, becoming 'economics' and 'politics'; we know that at some point in our analysis we need to combine the two – for instance, in trying to understand why a particular economic policy has been adopted in a country – but we find we have great difficulty in undertaking our theoretical enquiry into how to do it. While the amassing of 'concrete' evidence by detailed empirical studies is an essential part of such an enquiry, we need to have an integrated set of tools for our investigation: in short, we need precisely an *integrated* framework of analysis that deploys a common theory and method.

In this respect, the concept of semi-periphery is firmly lodged within the world-systems approach, and that in turn deploys the predominant understanding of political economy in twentieth-century Marxism, one based on a *critique of the market economy*. It is epitomised by Baran and Sweezy's *Monopoly Capital* (1966), Mandel's *Marxist Economic Theory* (1968), and the 'state monopoly capitalism' theory of Soviet economists – all based on the classic works of Hilferding, Lenin, Bukharin and Preobrazhensky. Common to this body of work is a unilinear evolutionary model in which competitive capitalism is succeeded by monopoly capitalism, which engenders increasing state intervention in economic activity. This ensures that regular economic cycles become marked by political conflicts of ever-increasing intensity, which galvanise the proletariat into organising for the capture of state power. This, in summary, is the core argument in twentieth-century Marxist political economy (MPE hereafter).

I do not want to suggest that WST follows this entire conspectus of capitalism's rise and fall; indeed, the school's work as a whole is much more focused on the identification of hegemonic powers and their rise and fall, rather than on the evolutionary future of capitalism as such. But WST does accept from MPE both its analytical distinction between economics and politics, and more specifically its characterisation of class rule as based on market power. These form the basis also for their under-standing of global capitalism as a system in which the core exploits the periphery, *as well as* capital exploiting labour. The central structural feature of 'the economy' in this approach is the division of labour *in society*, rather than in manufacture, to use Marx's careful distinction (Marx 1990, chapter 14 section 4): this division of labour is a feature of all societies from the most primitive, and is therefore not part of the specific features that make up capitalism as a mode of production. The separate sphere of politics centres on the state, which stands outside this social division of labour, and possesses in principle the capacity to shape it into different forms; what these forms are depends on the different economic interests which struggle for power over the state through forms of political representation.

At the global level, there is a social division of labour between activities that generate high shares of the value-chain surplus (or in Chase-Dunn's version, are capital-intensive) and those left with low shares (labour-intensive), which implies a self-perpetuating polarisation of the distribution of global resources. The existence of multiple states ensures that this polarisation takes on a geopolitical form, since those states in which (for whatever reason) a larger proportion of core activities are located will have not only higher levels of consumption and wealth, but also greater power to ensure that they maintain or indeed increase that proportion. As businesses grow into giant transnational corporations, they work with 'their' states to set rules of the game in trade, investment and finance that reinforce this polarisation. At the heart of the process are the concepts of monopoly power and state power.

The MPE analysis of (global) capitalism has been severely challenged by actual developments in the last 50 years. Not only has the 'socialist' challenge of the USSR and the PRC collapsed, but monopolistic control over markets has been dramatically undermined by the expansion of international trade and investment and the effectiveness of anti-monopoly legislation. After decades of stable dominance of 'oligopolistic' markets, many powerful national firms have since 1970 either vanished, or been forced to transform themselves radically. The 'economic' activities of the state have ceased to expand as a proportion of output and employment, as a result of privatisation and the capping of universal welfare rights; the state's focus in economic policy has thus shifted from the direct provision of goods and services and the maintenance of full employment, to an 'enabling' role in underpinning the private sector and ensuring its ideological hegemony. Internationally, instead of the most powerful states continuing the fierce imperial rivalries that led to two world wars, they have fulfilled the prognostication of the 'renegade' Kautsky (1970), and found ways to share power in shaping global institutions of economic governance and political representation, structured according to a neoliberal ideological monoculture.

Other important empirical trends can be noted. First, increased inequality *within* countries, whether core (UK, USA) or periphery (China), has proved to be compatible with capitalism under a variety of stable political regimes. Second, the analytically central distinction between the types of activity regarded as core-like and peripheral no longer runs in parallel with the social division of labour between sectors or product categories. Instead, it is increasingly based on a division of labour within the large corporation, which has become itself a global actor. Arrighi and Drangel (1986, p. 57) accepted this, but without exploring the implications. Most specifically for this enquiry, the empirical performance of semi-peripheral economies *after* the period studied by Arrighi and Drangel (1986) has varied dramatically across time and space, so much so that Arrighi's latest work (2007) posits China as moving from periphery via semi-periphery to core, and shortly on to global hegemony. The question is, then, whether the concept of the semi-periphery actually helps to any degree in understanding these changes. If the MPE approach that underlies the concept has failed to anticipate and explain them, can we do so by reconstructing Marx's critique of political economy, and will the resulting analysis include a revamped concept of the semi-periphery?

The reconstruction needs to begin from Marx's relational concept of capital, *within* which workers and capitalists confront each other as social forces in many different arenas, but most importantly in production, in distribution, in the state and in society at large. Capitalist production is where value is productively consumed and surplus value created; this is a 'hidden abode' in which capital rules through property rights enforced by the state. The preservation of value as it changes form between commodities and money likewise depends upon the enforcement of property rights, and upon mechanisms of market regulation that render the rights of individual capitalists compatible with the reproduction of the social power of the class as a whole. This includes ensuring that the exploitation of workers does not destroy their potential as the source of surplus value, as well as limiting private rights over the supply of key commodities. The fundamentals of capitalism do not include the existence of a multiplicity of states, which is an inheritance from pre-capitalist forms, rather than immanent in the mode of production itself. However, they do affect the necessary features of the state as a social form *of capital*, which is constituted in apparent separation from society and in possession of powers that are accepted as necessary and idealised as natural.

The existence in reality of multiple states undoubtedly needs to be acknowledged as we seek to draw out a more complex and concrete analysis that allows us to understand specific capitalisms in specific times and places. But in no sense can the relation between states be posited, as Chase-Dunn does explicitly, as one of exploitation in parallel with, or analogous to, the exploitation of labour-power by capital. Rather, capitalist enterprises – operating normally from the very beginnings of capitalism across national boundaries as well as within them – seek a wide range of supporting services from those territorial states in which they are economically active. In certain circumstances and to a certain degree, there is an alignment of a given state with a set of capitals firmly rooted in their territory, which enables the adoption of what is now called the 'competition state': this is the form which is most central to WST, as it is to realist IR and IPE. In other circumstances and degrees, states provide reciprocal support to capitals based in each other's territories, as well as coordinating the management of trade, financial flows and relative currency values.

However, what MPE and WST neglect is the significance of class struggle within production as such. They confine class struggle to the realm of 'politics', not realising that the existence of a separate realm of politics is *in itself* a condition of existence of capitalism. And by treating production as a technical realm, they systematically neglect the extent to which the potential for social transformation is contained within the hidden abode of production – contained in an active as well as a passive sense. The reason why socialists throughout the twentieth century have been so incapable of translating their principles and values into advancing a real alternative to capitalism is that they have accepted the dominant definition of politics and the state as standing apart from and above the material existence of society as the collective producer of the means of subsistence.

Instead we can place production at the centre of our analysis. The defining feature of socialism as an idea is not freedom, or even solidarity, but rather *equality*. A free association of producers is incompatible not only with the private ownership of the means of production, but with the grotesque inequalities of *condition* – not 'opportunity' – that characterise society today. These inequalities need to be redefined to include equality of the capabilities required to participate fully in 'the administration of things' – equality of educational attainment, above all.[6] Such an approach directs our attention to the ways in which production and the labour process, considered as material rather than monetary phenomena, have evolved in recent decades. In particular, the barriers surrounding the 'hidden abode' have become far more permeable: rather than capitalist production being directed consciously by an all-powerful managerial dictatorship, it has increasingly been driven towards forms of decentralisation that require the active collaboration of broader and broader layers of employees in management policy choices and decision-making. The impetus for this has come from a variety of sources: most obviously from the far more competitive market environment entailed by globalisation and from the accompanying rapid erosion of cultural differences, but also from the realisation that competitive individualism coupled with purely material rewards neglects the human need for self-actualisation, creative activity and social recognition.

From such a standpoint, WST and MPE more generally have misperceived the changes under way since the 1970s in global capitalism. WST has focused on identifying the next hegemonic power, without appreciating that those conditions for the acquisition and exercise of hegemony as traditionally conceived no longer exist. The greatest difference between the crash of 2008 and the crash of 1929 has been the immediate realisation on all sides that this is a global crisis, to be solved by a coordinated global response: the retreat into autarchy that overwhelmed the fledgling structures of global governance after 1929 is simply inconceivable today. So, too, is the possibility of another 'great power' assuming the role that the USA has exercised since 1945. The great paradox of WST is that an analysis said to be centred on the world-system has locked itself into a methodological nationalism that belies the nature of global capitalism today.[7]

In addition, the uncritical acceptance by WST and MPE of the mainstream's analytical separation of economics from politics has effectively disarmed their analyses from offering any avenue towards the emancipation of society from the rule of capital. What happens at work is treated not as a potential source of radical change, but as a technical matter imbued with an unimpeachable rationality of its own.

In so far as the concept of the semi-periphery is seen as having real theoretical content, rather than being a convenient term of empirical description, its origins in WST and MPE ensure that it too suffers from the same weaknesses. It is certainly the case that global capitalism is characterised by a steep hierarchy of wealth and power when monetary measures of economic activity are aggregated across territorially defined states; and that countries can demonstrate, in the abstract statistics of the World Bank's league tables, movements up or down, or a stable ranking. But those who, like Chase-Dunn, have sought to establish a distinctive role for the semi-periphery as challenging the global order or threatening its incumbent hegemon have not been able to draw from the huge diversity of semi-peripheral experience any clear structural identifiers for the term as such. In the 1990s, it was possible to identify a list of semi-peripheral countries in which rapid industrialisation, often through export-oriented foreign investment, was expanding the numbers and potential strength of the working classes: South Africa, South Korea, Brazil, Mexico, perhaps even China.[8] The last ten years have shown that they have become 'normal' capitalist societies – riddled with contradictions, but possessed of the same robust structural features that everywhere reproduce class rule and its accompanying inequalities. While it is natural to look for common features across the diversity of national experience, the nature of global capitalism today does not dictate any particular dynamic role for those countries that are in the statistical semi-periphery. Critical analysis needs to re-focus on class and class conflict, and away from the idea that the relation between core and periphery provides the core dynamic of global capitalism.

Conclusions

This chapter sought to investigate the semi-periphery as a theoretical concept. The conclusion that it is, *for that purpose,* essentially redundant today is necessarily provisional in two senses. First, circumstances may change radically: just as few people predicted the rise of neoliberal globalisation in the 1970s, the present crisis contains the potential for a wide variety of outcomes in terms of the global order. Second, theoretical investigation is only one phase of this argument: the critique has been largely ontological and epistemological, and it remains to be seen whether this critique can better explain the actual developments of capitalism in the empirically identified semi-periphery.

Equally, there is no question that the concept of the semi-periphery as developed by the WST in the 1980s contributed to the richness of debate on the changing nature of global capitalism. Concepts such as dependent development, sub-imperialism, the developmental state and later the competition state were also developed during this period. Those concepts derived from the same traditions of theory and analysis as WST, and contained similar weaknesses: above all, in their understanding of class and state in global capitalism, and their locating emancipatory potential in the nation-state as such, or a particular variety of it, rather than in society.

Notes

1. For a more general review of developmentalism see Radice (2008), especially pp. 1164–8.
2. The journal *Review* began publication in 1977, while the first volume of Wallerstein's monumental history of the capitalist world-system appeared in 1974.
3. The fact that other writers could characterise some semi-peripheral states as 'sub-imperialist' indicates that the term could equally have been 'semi-core'; see, for example, Marini (1972).
4. In WST the terms 'centre' and 'core' are used interchangeably for the group of most advanced industrial countries. Note, too, that at that time, the intermediate group was exemplified by Argentina, Chile, Brazil and Mexico in Latin America; South Africa; and most of Southern and Eastern Europe including the USSR. The East Asian tigers had not yet come of age.
5. Here I consider only his work on the semi-periphery in capitalism; Chase-Dunn and Hall (1997) undertake a comparative study of different world-systems, including a comparison of the role of the semi-periphery across them.
6. One of the few Marxists to grasp the importance of equal educational attainment was Preobrazhensky (1973).
7. For a careful exploration of the concept of methodological nationalism, see Gore (1996).
8. The case of East-Central Europe could be added, distinctive because their global integration took place after full industrialisation.

3

Globalisation, Accumulation by Dispossession and the Rise of the Semi-Periphery: Towards Global Post-Fordism and Crisis?

Gerard Strange

This chapter is informed by an open and left theoretical 'position' which, contra-*methodological* nationalism, 'takes globalisation seriously' (Radice 1999) as a set of intersubjective and agential processes which have transformed relations of production at the global level and have shifted the balance of class forces 'structurally', so to speak, in favour of capital and (hegemonically) capitalism. While in International Relations (IR) the 'take globalisation seriously' approach is usually associated with Susan Strange's critique of state-centric orthodoxy and her subsequent championing of International Political Economy (IPE) as a distinct discipline, there is a strong case for the claim that it is rooted in rather earlier neo-Marxian critical engagements with orthodox economics (Radice 1975, 1999) and with neo-Marxian engagements with so-called Dependency Theory (see, for example, Wallerstein 1974; Radice 1975; Cox 1981; Lipietz 1982a).

'Dependency theory' itself was never a singular approach. Nor was it ever part of the mainstream, being associated, rather, with a plurality of relatively marginalised sub-disciplines such as the sociology of development, radical anthropology and radical economics, rather than orthodox IR, Economics and Development Studies. In various ways these approaches positively engaged with but also sought to challenge and go beyond the state-centrism of dependency theory. One of the main implications of what has now become radical globalisation analysis is that it forces a very substantial rethink of dependency school (state dominated) and associated conceptual and relational bifurcations such as development and/of underdevelopment, 'north-south', 'core-periphery' and 'first world-third world'. Indeed, as Hoogvelt (1997) and more recently Payne (2005), among others, have argued, it probably means that the 'dependency' approach, in broad sweep, needs to be transcended or even in some respects abandoned (at least in so far as this has represented a *general* theoretical framework) in favour of globalisation.

In fact the need for a radical transcendence of dependency theory has long been recognised by radical theorists of IPE and was notably evident in the early writing of Robert W. Cox, as Hoogvelt and Payne both readily acknowledge. Cox was one of the first radical scholars of *post-imperialism*, an approach that culminated in the late 1990s with the publication of Hart and Negri's seminal text *Empire*. In a hugely influential article first published in 1981, Cox brought together, in what was in effect a general theory of globalisation, critical methodology, IR, political economy, political theory and political sociology. Crucially, this was framed around a *pluralistic* reading of historical materialism (identified primarily with 'critical' as opposed to 'problem-solving' theory). This *open* historical materialism drew *equally* on classical liberal historical realism (notably that of E.H. Carr), historical Marxism and Marxian political economy (notably that of Karl Marx, Eric Hobsbawn and Edward P. Thompson) and Italian political theory (Machiavelli, Vico and Gramsci). In asserting the case for *open* historical materialism as a general method of critical social enquiry (against a backdrop of such a cocktail of influences), Cox explicitly eschewed not only the crass determinism of Soviet ideology but also (and more importantly) what he regarded, pejoratively, as the 'abstract' and 'structuralist' tendencies within western Marxism (Althusser and Poulanzas). Moreover, while recognising its general efficacy, Cox also warned against the 'system-maintenance bias' or 'structural functionalism' of radical systems thinking, notably that associated with Immanuel Wallerstein's world-systems theory (Cox 1981: 127).

More specifically (given the primary concerns of this chapter), Cox shifted IPE beyond IR theory (including dependency theory's IR framework) by focusing on what he referred to as the *internationalisation* of the state and by associating this process directly with the internationalisation of capitalist production through the relatively autonomous agency of *trans*national elites and *trans*national corporations (TNCs) as well as other more direct governance institutions such as the IMF, the World Bank and the OECD (institutions which, for Cox, were both 'more than and less than the state' [Cox 1981: 143]). Cox's primary emphasis on the international, on transnational elite agency and on ideational interventions linked to this agency as key features – alongside states – of contemporary world order, shifted the focus of analysis beyond the 'core-periphery *states*' framework of the dependency school and the conceptualisation of world order primarily in terms of a global hierarchy of exploiting (core), exploited (periphery) and exploited-and-exploiting (semi-periphery) nation-states/regions linked as politico-geographic entities principally through unequal *trade* exchanges associated with the structure of international/regional specialisation and comparative advantage.

One implication of Cox's focus on internationalisation and transnationalisation was that core-periphery were better understood primarily as *class* and relatedly hegemonic *bloc* categories (the transnational capitalist class *and* 'established' workers, on the one hand, and 'non-established' workers *and* other excluded subaltern actors on the other) of an emerging, *global*, capitalist mode of production. In contrast to the state-bound and exchange-focused thinking of the dependency approach, Cox argued for dialectical thinking around the transnational and the national as differentiated but mutually conditioning levels of analysis, as well as associated levels of structures and intersubjectivities. In particular, this meant examining *relations of production* dialectically 'in terms of a [singular] *global* class *structure* alongside or superimposed upon [diverse] national class *structures*' (Cox 1981: 147; emphases added).

This chapter examines the emergence and growth of a capitalist, export-orientated semi-periphery in the context of these transnational/national class and hegemonic categories understood as key elements defining the process of the 'globalisation of IPE' (Phillips 2005). Broadly speaking, there are two phases in this process, the first involving a shift towards global Fordism in mass manufacturing sectors, the second (more recently emerging) involving a shift towards global post-Fordism. The first *stage* of the first phase was associated with the emergence of the so-called newly industrialising 'countries' (NICs) of south-east Asia (South Korea, Taiwan, Singapore and Hong Kong), This occurred from the 1950s to 1960s, becoming decisive in the 1970s and early 1980s. The first phase has since been consolidated in a *second stage* with the emergence of a new wave of mass manufacturing developers focused on the so-called BRIC countries (Brazil, Russia, India and China).

Global Fordism's initial and consolidating stages have in common two underlying processes which taken together have shifted the global balance of class power in favour of capital. The first process has involved the formal freeing up of capital out of the regulative controls and restrictions of the Bretton Woods regime – the Fordist compromise of 'embedded liberalism' (Ruggie 1982). This retreat from social democratic regulation has provided the basis for the transnational agential autonomy of both financial and industrial capital, allowing multinational corporations to expand in number and size as globalising agents of capital accumulation. The second, more neglected, process has been the constitutionisation of global wage labour, described by Coates (2000) among others as 'global proletarianisation'. Taken together, these two processes enable a radical conceptualisation of globalisation in terms of 'accumulation by dispossession' (Harvey 2003, 2004).

Globalisation understood as an on-going process of accumulation by dispossession has now entered a new phase which can be called a shift towards global *post*-Fordism. This takes global convergence beyond liberal productivism in mass manufacturing towards global convergence in high technology manufacturing and in the so-called knowledge economy. While contributing to the rise and consolidation of economic power in the semi-periphery, the globalisation of post-Fordism threatens to undermine the monopolisation of core status by Organization for Economic Co-operation and Development (OECD) countries and radically constrains progressive options for the core in terms of national and regional accumulation strategies.

The remainder of this chapter is structured as follows. First, drawing on Coates, the general process of proletarianisation and its key dynamics is briefly described. Second, turning to Harvey's analysis, the processes and dynamics of accumulation by dispossession (ABD) are detailed. The chapter then turns (third) to a specification of the first phase of globalisation. This section draws mainly on the work of Alain Lipietz (1982a, 1982b, 1984a, 1984b, 1989) describing the first phase as the globalisation of Fordism. Fourth, the chapter examines the second, consolidatory, phase, involving a more decisive shift towards neoliberal globalisation. This section argues that there has been evident a tendency towards convergence in global political economy constituted, politically, around the transnational and national 'competition state' (Cerny 1997), a process described by Gill (2008) as global 'new constitutionalism'. The second phase represents a shift towards global *post*-Fordism. The chapter concludes by examining possible future directions for globalisation and specifically examines possible transnational strategies for confronting what until the recent global crisis appeared to be a deep-seated hegemonisation of neoliberal political economy. It is argued that the semi-periphery is likely to play a critical role in any effective counter-hegemonic confrontation with global neoliberalism.

Global proletarianisation and accumulation by dispossession

According to David Coates (but see also Wallerstein 2005) the past 30 years has witnessed not merely the freeing up of capital from the regulative constraints of post-War embedded liberalism (a system which combined managed trade openness with nation-state relative regulative autonomy). Equally significant has been a parallel process involving the global spread of capitalist relations of production through global proletarianisation. This has seen an enormous growth in workforces constituted as commodified capitalist waged labour notably (but not solely) in Asia and southeast Asia (including India and China) as well as South America. Waged labour is here defined (as in classical Marxism) as the alienation of workers from independent and semi-independent modes of existence and reproduction such that the sale of labour-power as a commodity confronts the worker as a necessary condition of life, that is, the individual is constituted under the proletarian condition. Proletarianisation has also occurred as a consequence of the partial integration of the former Soviet bloc economies into the European labour market. Furthermore, a parallel process of *re*proletarianisation has also occurred in the OECD core.

Proletarianisation has *substantively* expanded the global reach and class power of capital, enabling formerly disembedded MNCs and their financial allies to fully exploit new groups of dispossessed *waged* workers 'where once stood only subsistence peasantries excluded [often] entirely from commodity production and capitalist wage labour systems' (Coates 2000: 256). Proletarianisation is a key process of globalisation, since it is this transformation of production relations, which has enabled capital fully to exploit the new freedoms it has enjoyed as a consequence of neoliberal exchange liberalisation (see also Bello 2007: 1349). As Coates argues, globalisation shifts the balance of class power fundamentally in favour of capital, one-sidedly increasing its substantive mobility relative to labour by giving it 'more proletariats [globally] on which to land' (Coates 2000: 255).

Accumulation by dispossession

Coates's emphasis on proletarianisation as the hidden face of globalisation chimes strongly with David Harvey's analysis of capitalist globalisation through his concept of 'accumulation by dispossession' (ABD) (Harvey 2004, 2005). This concept helps to bring together as dialectics the two sides of the globalisation process identified by Coates – formalised capital mobility and proletarianisation or *substantiated* capital mobility. In essence, ABD expresses what Wallerstein has described as the universalising logic of accumulation and its structural need to commodify and *recommodify* everything. Agentially, this has involved a universal drive by pro-capitalist social forces towards the capitalistic privatisation and re-privatisation of property relations in the periphery, the semi-periphery and the core. The consequence of this privatisation has been the expansion on a global scale of dispossessed workforces. The dispossession of labour has been the means by which capital has sought to break free from *embedded* production relations of all kinds (both capitalist and non-capitalist) when faced by devalorisation and crisis. Equally ABD enables freed up (money) capital to *revalorise* by taking advantage of new opportunities for profitable accumulation created by dispossession wherever such opportunities arise (witness, for example, the takeover and revalorisation of bankrupted and devalued Asian firms by American transnational capital following the Asian crisis of 1997 (Gill 2008: 150–160). Inverting Schumpeter, Harvey has referred to this process as 'destructive creation'. Thus ABD represents a fundamental challenge to both social democratic and state-led developmental/negotiated models of capitalism, reflecting instead a *neoliberal* strategy of 'developmental' restructuring *exclusively* for accumulation. Such processes of ABD have characterised global restructuring since the crisis of the US-led Bretton Woods system of embedded liberalism in the early 1970s (see Radice 1984, 1999, 2006, 2008).

Globalisation phase 1: Global Fordism

The first concerted period of ABD in the post-Bretton Woods era can be broadly identified with the crisis and restructuring of social democratic and developmental forms of capitalism from the mid-1970s, starting with the dollar crisis of 1971–1973, moving to the recycling of the dollar by means of global credit deregulation and debt privatisation and culminating in the debt crisis of the early 1980s. An influential attempt to theorise this crisis in terms of globalisation was provided by Alain Lipietz, a leading member of the Marxist-influenced French 'Regulation School' of critical comparative IPE. Like Cox (1981) Lipietz's main focus was on what he identified as an emerging new global division of labour associated with the 'internationalisation' of production and relations of production. Lipietz termed the new internationalisation 'global Fordism' (Lipietz 1982a). This was seen as a response by multinational capital to the crisis of Fordism both as a factory regime (Taylorism) and as a broader 'mode of [progressive wage and state/Keynesian] regulation' in the OECD core. It marked the end of Fordism as a hegemonic (in the Gramscian sense) 'societal paradigm' in the core and in social democratic developmental states and its restructuring towards a neoliberal version (variously labelled by Lipietz 'liberal productivism' and 'bloody Taylorism'). While liberal productivism was embraced by some social forces in the core labour movement as a way out of the labour productivity and profit crisis of Fordism (hence, for example, the 'new unionism' that emerged in Britain during the 1970s, which gave worker support to the Thatcher-led Conservative Party), this necessitated the stripping away of the Fordist/Keynesian social compromise of 'paradoxical involvement' for most workers. Liberal productivism reconstituted labour as 'core' and 'periphery' workers, with the latter (majority) group being increasingly casualised and subject to a new neoliberal regime of labour discipline. In any case, Lipietz argued, liberal productivism was a transnational regime that undermined core competitiveness.

The new division of labour was marked by the emergence of export-led manufacturing development, first in Japan and then in the newly industrialising 'tiger' 'countries' of Southeast Asia, or NICs as these countries had become known in the development literature. The success of the NICs gave succour to orthodox market economics since it appeared to contradict the 'development of underdevelopment' thesis of Gunder-Frank as well as the 'dependent development' thesis of the broader dependency school. Moreover, NIC success contrasted with the apparent failure of the more inward looking national social democratic models of Import-Substitution Industrialisation (ISI). In fact, Lipietz maintained, the failures of ISI could largely be explained by a careful specification of contingent political interventions (for example, the CIA-led military/dictatorial overthrow of Chile's radical ISI in 1973), and broader negative external/transnational factors (notably the deregulation and privatisation of development financing in the 1970s and the subsequent rise in the price of credit and debt in the early 1980s with the onset of global monetarism; see Lipietz 1984b). On the other hand, the successful industrialisers were those, like the tigers, who for a variety of reasons were able to *combine* protection from import penetration with the strategic development of the export sector. This achieved competitive advantage in world markets from an abundance of domestic cheap labour underpinned by authoritarian state rule and contrasted with the dominant social democratic progressive developmentalism of ISI countries. Crucially, therefore, the export-led model of the NICs was a decisively capitalistic model, underpinned by processes of ABD rather than social democratic inclusion (hence, the enthusiasm for NICs evident in the orthodox development literature). The key social forces engaged in the strategic development of export-led growth were local (usually unelected) state elites and transnational capital, often explicitly underpinned by elite representation and intervention by and for the military-strategic imperatives of the United States (see also Gill 2008: 150–160).

Beyond countering the orthodox critique of the underdevelopment thesis (as well as the celebration of imperialist capitalism as the 'pioneer' of 'development' by some Marxist authors, notably Warren), Lipietz's main point of focus was an examination of the new export-led developing economies industrialisation within the context of the crisis of Fordism. This had seen rising unemployment in the core associated initially with a crisis of over-production and falling profit and had been compounded by a demand crisis associated with the rise of monetarism. Under such conditions, according to Lipietz, the export-led growth model of the periphery, in which core multinational capital was complicit through investment alliances with local elites, had still further destabilising consequences for the core. This was because the new exporters, integrated into the global economy on the basis of a low wage, authoritarian 'mode of regulation' (described by Lipietz as 'peripheral Fordism') undermined core competitiveness in many manufacturing export markets. This led to calls for protectionism from core country producer groups (including many unions) organised around the declining Fordist manufacturing sectors in the core. Most importantly, for Lipietz, the export-led growth of the new industrialisers undermined the Keynesian hegemonic alliance in the core between capital and labour.

Combined with an understanding of globalisation in terms of proletarianisation and Harvey's theory of ABD (as outlined above), Lipietz's analysis of the emergence of global Fordism out of the crisis of welfare capitalism in the 1970s provides a basis for understanding the growth and consolidation of a distinctly *capitalistic* and market-orientated semi-periphery in the developing world over the past 30 years. While initially focused on the tiger economies, as just outlined, the semi-periphery has since grown in a second stage to include, among others, China, Mexico and Brazil, the latter two having abandoned (not, initially, by choice) earlier attempts at domestically orientated ISI while China has abandoned a strongly protectionist, peasant orientated, socialism. What defines these countries as semi-periphery (at least for the purposes of this chapter) are the following characteristics: (1) that while these countries remain relatively and absolutely poor by comparison to the OECD core (especially in terms of per-capita income) they have experienced sustained high levels of economic growth; (2) they have, as just noted, broken decisively with forms of imperialist 'compradore capitalism', social democratic developmentalism, or, in the case of China, peasant socialism, which had locked in forms of pre- or post-capitalist modes of production and regulation; (3) although there are many important exceptions, these countries have achieved economic growth chiefly on the basis of the exportation of manufactured goods to the world market.

Of these factors, it is the emergence of a significant and growing manufacturing capacity aimed primarily at export which decisively defines the semi-periphery. Moreover, as initially identified by Lipietz, this has been associated with a *global* shift of manufacturing towards the semi-periphery where an abundance of labour and low wages has made production more profitable. While for the early wave of successful developers (the tiger economies) manufacturing-based export-led development was achieved on the basis of a varied combination of state protection, subsidised technology transfer and low wage regimes, in the second wave (including China) inward foreign direct investment (FDI) has played an increasingly important role. As Thun (2008) reports, between 1982 and 2005, FDI inflows increased from $59 billion to $916 billion globally. Of this total $334 billion (somewhat more than a third) was to the developing world with 48 per cent ($160.32 billion) going to five 'countries': China, Brazil, Hong Kong and Mexico). China represents the most important example of an emerging manufacturing-based export-led growth capitalist economy. By 2008 China's population was approximately 1.3 billion. In 2000, it accounted for 37.4 per cent of world manufacturing exports. Its manufacturing sector is its most important, accounting for 51 per cent of its GDP in 2002 (agriculture contributed 15 per cent and services 34 per cent) (Payne 2005: 64). However, in line with characteristic (1), above, China has a low per-capita income (US $4,580, ppp; figure for 2002) (Payne 2005: 250). A recent report in *The Guardian* claimed that the average hourly wage for factory workers in China was $0.92.

Although the logic ABD is on-going and universal, it is nevertheless differentially experienced at different places in the global circuit of capital. Furthermore, this differentiation *feeds back* to condition how accumulation develops globally (discussed in the next section). In the semi-periphery ABD has involved a concerted confrontation with pre-capitalist relations of production, specifically, the dispossession of peasantries previously embedded within a variety of 'non capitalist' forms of property relations. China and India represent key areas where this form of proletarianisation has occurred. In the case of China, specifically, it has been associated with the forced removal of peasantries from rural labour and the migration of the dispossessed to the new urban centres swelling the reserve army of labour seeking work in both the labour-intensive sectors of manufacturing (for example, in out-sourced textiles and electronics assembly export processing zones or EPZs). Equally, in terms of 'comprador' imperialist capitalism prevalent in many regions of Latin America and Africa ABD has involved a form of proletarianisation based on the replacement of the semi-feudal/semi-capitalist production chain (in which semi-proletarianised workers 'enjoyed' a contradictory mixture of feudal subsistence land rights and obligations to work for comprador land barons and merchants). The result is a shift towards a full-blown cash-crop production capitalism under which workers are dispossessed of land rights in order to (literally) clear the ground for fully commercialised deals with agribusiness MNCs.

Accumulation by dispossession in the periphery and semi-periphery thus underpins a 'structural' shift from feudal and semi-feudal relations of production, definitive of peripheral 'comprador' capitalism, to full-blown capitalist relations of production characterised by waged labour under conditions of super-exploitation (because dominated by large reserve armies and authoritarian political regimes). This provides the basis for the dynamic development of globally competitive *semi-peripheral* sectors in capitalist manufacturing. The manufacturing sector is split between the labour-intensive and capital-intensive sectors. The labour-intensive sectors are dominated by textiles and increasingly by assembly technologies, notably in computers and electronics. The wage relation in this sector is super-exploitative and typically organised around MNC out-sourced production in what becomes key EPZs. These are underpinned by a massive reserve army and highly authoritarian labour regimes in which free labour organisation is not tolerated but is, in any case, structurally weak.

On the other hand, the semi-periphery has also been characterised by the growth of export-dominated capital-intensive manufacturing sectors, such as steel, ship-building, the car and auto industries and white goods production. This makes use of skilled, semi-skilled and unskilled industrial labour much of which is organised around sub-contracted component production in post-Fordist (just-in-time) urban production chains. While this labour enjoys some wage advantages relative to export zone labour, partly because of the higher productivity of capital-intensive production and partly because – despite post-Fordist practices – it requires a plurality of skilled and semi-skilled 'core' worker groups with relative market and organisational power, it remains subject to intensive forms of absolute exploitation, especially with respect to sub-contracted, semi-skilled and unskilled labour. Again, a combination of the reserve army and authoritarian intolerance of labour organisation combined with the disorganisational logic of post-Fordist sub-contracting underpins the international competitive advantage of this form of semi-periphery manufactured goods production.

Globalisation phase 2: Global post-Fordism

Lipietz later argued that, given the contradictions of transnational liberal productivism, the globalisation of Fordist manufacturing and the related crisis of 'central Fordism' had forced a more decisive '*post*-Fordist' restructuring on the core (Lipietz 1991). This, he suggested could in principle be relatively progressive for the core and periphery. Key, for Lipietz, was the capacity of core countries to maintain a *comparative* advantage in the new global division of labour through the early development of high-end 'post-Fordist' technologies and markets and by restructuring as much as possible around the emerging high value 'knowledge economy'. Despite the deindustrialisation of the 1980s, associated with a tendential shift of semi-skilled and unskilled manufacturing to the semi-periphery, the core remained the core (and a new, higher, 'dependent development' global hierarchy would be reproduced) so long as core countries and regions were able to capture and sustain comparative advantages around, globally speaking, *avant-garde* knowledge and technology sectors (the arts, research and development, design, etc.) as well as cutting-edge manufacturing directly associated with these sectors. Furthermore, such potential for core restructuring around a progressive post-Fordism (labelled 'negotiated involvement') would tend to relax competition in many (especially lower end) global manufacturing sectors (as the core shifted out to the knowledge economy) thereby opening up possibilities for a progressive 'middle way' for the new industrialising semi-periphery beyond low wage and authoritarian modes of regulation.

By contrast, what can be labelled 'convergence thesis' Marxism has emphasised the infeasibility of this 'progressive competitiveness' strategy, *given* globalisation. The consequence of globalisation is that there is a tendency for the core and semi-periphery increasingly to converge in terms of (neoliberal) political economy so that the terms themselves become increasingly redundant. In an associated way, the core's stabilisation around social democratic inclusion and the semi-periphery's pursuit of inclusive forms of relatively autonomous developmentalism are fundamentally destabilised as welfarism and protected development give way to the universalisation of export-led growth and the '*competition* state'. Radice (1999: 7) summarises this position as follows: the shift towards neoliberalism under globalisation has been 'so consistent through the past 20 years and all around the world that it is hard to see [it] as either contingent or the result of independent policy choices by national governments'. For David Coates, the logic of convergence is structural and follows from the contradictions of 'progressive competitiveness' once this becomes a more or less universal rather than nationally distinct competitiveness strategy: countries are either forced back into a beggar-thy-neighbour aggressive mercantilism (which is contradictory since it invites retaliation) or they have to accept the discipline of universal competitiveness, in which case anything other than short-term success is likely to come at the price of labour regime deregulation and austerity (in other words, dispossession) (Coates 2000: 254–259). And this is precisely what is evident according to the convergence thesis.

What, in effect has emerged, according to this view, is a universal shift towards 'competitive *austerity*' around the 'competition state'. In brief, the progressive post-Fordism identified by Lipietz as a basis for continued core prosperity (articulated in policy terms through 'third way' discourses such as 'progressive competitiveness', 'new growth' strategy and 'open economy' macro-economics) will be increasingly undermined, according to convergence Marxism, because newly emerging proletarian workforces in Asia, eastern Europe and elsewhere – where wage costs are low and dispossessed labour is abundant – are themselves increasingly integrated into the new knowledge economy. This has closed the knowledge/skills gap between the core and the semi-periphery upon which the success of 'third way' models as a post-neoliberal core strategy was dependent.

Part of the reason for global convergence towards the competition state is that there has been growing transnational–national elite consensus on and effective agential intervention around this model evident both at important supra-national and nation-state levels. It is the policy congruence and inter-dependence between these two levels of governance and government, which defines the internationalisation of the state (Cox 1981). The internationalised state-system is thus described, on the one hand, by the supra-national technocratic and elite network of transnational economic governance institutions – focused on the IMF, the World Bank, the OECD, the G8 and the WTO. Under the influence of a transnational capitalist class, acting successfully as a class-for-itself, these institutions are said to have sponsored a globalised neoliberal supply-side programme based on price stability, the freeing up of trade, privatisation and the transnationalisation of production processes. Clearly, such a programme can be understood as presuppositional in relation to global ABD. On the other hand, the internationalised state-system is marked by the preponderance of the competition state-proper at the national level, where it subverts more democratic forms of government. Indeed the competition state can be described as such principally *because of* its subordination to the network of supra-national economic governance institutions committed to global accumulation.

The transnational form taken by this nation-state subordination to neoliberal globalisation has been defined in the neo-Gramscian IPE literature as 'new constitutionalism' (see Gill 2008). This is a form of globalised governance which forecloses alternatives to neoliberalism by imposing financially austere rule-bounded monetarist-inspired macroeconomic policies on nation-states. New constitutionalism is thereby said to greatly diminish the state's capacity to undertake discretionary or autonomous forms of governmental intervention and more specifically forms of intervention associated with social democracy and socially inclusive developmentalism. Similarly, Paul Cammack has argued that technocratic elites have used the international state for 'the promotion of a global capitalist economy centred on the logic of competitiveness' (Cammack 2007: 13). For Cammack what is important is that the economic advice offered by the transnational elite is universally the same regardless of where a nation-state sits in the global system and its specific structure of competitive advantage. The advice is, universally, to participate through openness in the world economy; gear the economy to export-led growth; stabilise finance; pursue supply-side policies which enhance competitiveness, for example, invest in education and the knowledge economy, and institutionalise labour-market flexibility. While the impact of the competition state model differs according to local developmental conditions, the shift is universally towards what becomes a self-reinforcing system of competitive labour or 'market' discipline underpinned (because of ABD and proletarianisation) by a global reserve army of labour. Because such a labour regime is largely exclusionary, it has been associated with a general levelling down and/or containment of democracy in favour of authoritarian and quasi-authoritarian state forms.

The spread of third way knowledge economy strategies to the semi-periphery has further enhanced the power of capital. Capital has been able to take advantage of the substantive mobility created for it by semi-periphery proletarianisation. This has seen the emergence of a significant trend towards the global relocation of transnational capital towards the semi-periphery, a trend that is likely to continue. This, in turn, has reinforced an on-going process of ABD, which has been transforming relations of production in the core since the crisis of Keynesian social democracy took hold in the 1970s. The consequence is that the core's 'labour aristocracy' has been dispossessed of the Keynesian-Fordist welfare and full-employment settlement, while being unable to secure a sustainable monopoly over the leading, high-value, sectors of the post-Fordist global economy. Starting from the late 1970s, a large fraction of the old skilled and semi-skilled work-force has been *re*proletarianised through this dispossession. Thus after decades of embedded post-capitalist social democracy core workers since the 1970s have experienced permanent high levels of unemployment, job insecurity, casualisation and de-unionisation. 'Core' workers have often suffered permanent downward mobility into the growing 'secondary' labour market, where they have faced a new neoliberal labour discipline regime underpinned by the same economic and political regime processes operative in the semi-periphery proper – namely, the reserve army and state-led authoritarian policing of labour market competition.

Conclusions: The semi-periphery and possible futures for globalisation

The analysis in this chapter has focused on the supply-side restructuring of the global economy initially out of the crisis of Fordism in the 1970s. It has emphasised the emergence of a distinct semi-periphery/semi-core focused on Asia (and China, in particular) in the context of two processes: the increased formal global mobility of capital and the proletarianisation/reproletarianisation of labour on a global scale. Taken together, these processes constitute a logic of ABD. At least two pessimistic scenarios for the global political economy emerge from the broad sweep of this analysis of tendencies.

In one scenario, an already established convergence towards an austere form of neoliberalism is further consolidated. This would involve a system of partially differentiated 'post-Fordist' competition states (a 'third way' core, based on more or less negotiated inclusion and a semi-periphery focused on strongly authoritarian negative flexibility). Such a spatially differentiated global political economy depends on the capacity of core economies – be these organised around nations or regions – to capture the most innovative and high value-added sectors of the knowledge economy as a basis for export-led strength and comparative advantage, thus maintaining a dominant position in the global value chain. For example, the core might maintain a knowledge advantage in the development of eco-capital and eco-products as new forms of transnational and nation-state regulation aim at producing environmentally sustainable capital accumulation. Such an accumulation *strategy* has indeed increasingly underpinned economic policy in the European Union and the United States.

A second, highly pessimistic, scenario emerges, as we have already seen, from the 'neoliberal convergence' thesis outlined earlier. For those who argue strongly that this is, in fact, the dominant trajectory of global accumulation, the geo/politico-spatially differentiated scenario outlined above is already all but dead in the water. The strength of this approach as a logic of explanation is evident when it is framed in terms of the dialectical logic of capital as globally differentiated *processes* of competitive ABD. Furthermore, this approach appears to be supported by empirical evidence indicating a tendency towards convergence between the core and the semi-periphery as sites for knowledge economy investment and production as well as a fundamental relocation of manufacturing in general to the semi-periphery. Given these trends, it is reasonable to assume that the 'semi-periphery' will dominate the manufacturing sector and conceivably the knowledge economy within little more than two decades.

The danger of this approach is that it becomes a form of reductionist Marxism which seeks to explain too much at the 'capitalist mode of production' level of analysis, breaking methodologically with the rich plurality of approaches evident within critical comparative political economy be this comparative national or regional political economy (I have elsewhere argued for the growing efficacy of comparative regionalism in the analysis of globalisation and development; see Strange 2006). Convergence thesis Marxists are often highly critical of attempts to give careful historical and spatial specification to accumulation beyond the highly abstract level of capitalist mode of production. This is not to argue that the convergence thesis is wrong to give a certain primacy to the mode of production in the analysis of globalisation. Indeed one of its strengths is precisely to emphasise how the project for global competitiveness is anchored around the universalisation of capitalism as a mode of production in order to close off pre- and post-capitalist (including strong social democratic) alternatives.

A more optimistic scenario would involve a reorientation of critical thinking about the global political economy much more decisively towards the demand side – a global reflation *out of* what, commonly for convergence thesis Marxists and neo-Gramscian IPE scholars, has become an increasingly locked-in global competitive austerity, or as Gill puts it a 'constitutionalisation' of neoliberal capitalism. Contra-'new constitutionalism' and convergence thesis Marxism's 'competition state' logic (from which government inaction in the current crisis might be anticipated, allowing market processes to work through the 'crisis' by means of Schumpetarian 'creative destruction') what has in fact been evident in the current global crisis is the extent to which 'big state' capitalism has so apparently, easily and rapidly come back in, tearing up the neoliberal rule book in the process.

While at the global level this has yet to be decisive (at the time of writing), policy intervention at the national level, notably in the United States, has been Keynesian and post-Keynesian-inspired to an extraordinary degree. Far from being locked out by entrenched neoliberal constitutional rules, the new *discretionary* state has plunged headlong into unprecedented commitments to deficit financing and bank bail-outs, expansionary tax cuts, long-term infrastructural spending, historically low-interest rates and – flying in the face of monetarist 'sound currency' orthodoxy – so-called 'quantitative easing' (notably by the Federal Reserve). In the European context, the EU central bank and Finance Council of Ministers have endorsed calls from the OECD and the IMF (following 'crisis' meetings in November 2008) for substantial and coordinated budgetary easing to counter the risk of a global deflation (the European Commission emphatically will not be imposing Stability and Growth Pact rules as it tried (and failed) to do a few years ago against national member-states). This indicates how, during crisis, apparently entrenched ideas and institutions (in this case, those of 'embedded neoliberalism') can be rapidly overturned by counter-ideological pragmatic and discretionary thinking and intervention to meet the needs of macro-economic stability. It is as though supply-side economics and 'new growth' theory, not to mention the broader neoliberal counter-revolution, had never happened. In short, the crisis provides an opportunity for a global re-think around globalisation, one in which institutionalising *demand-side* reform can once again (after 30 years of neoliberal dominance) take priority. To use Coxian language, new intersubjectivities are now being forged which will condition the events and social relations through which life is lived for decades to come.

Given all this, the crisis opens up opportunities for a progressive political economy of globalisation in which, importantly, the semi-periphery is likely to prove a critical global actor alongside progressive thinking within global and regional structures of economic governance. This would involve both a global reflation of demand and the development of institutionally locked in mechanisms for utilising and redistributing surpluses as well as some global mechanism for preventing the emergence of major imbalances between deficit and surplus countries of the sort which have characterised much of the post-Second World War period. Serious attempts to reform the IMF and the World Bank, perhaps along the lines of the original 'Keynes plan' – defeated at Bretton Woods – would be a starting point.

As the largest external recipient of the reserve currency and as the leading political actor within the G20, China structurally speaking is the key semi-periphery state in any such process of negotiated balanced reflation of the global economy. China might undertake an internal recycling of its surpluses to encourage wage and welfare-based reflation of its potentially huge domestic market, with such an internal redistribution feeding through into a Chinese import boom to underpin growth in world demand. The global benefits of Chinese domestic wage expansion might be used to force negotiation of a progressive settlement on global capital especially in relation to the currently super-exploited sectors of labour-intensive manufacturing organised around export zones characteristic of the semi-periphery's peripheral post-Fordist sector. It is here that the surplus value imbalances between transnational capitalist enterprise and labour are at their most extreme. Repatriating TNC super-profits for the benefit of super-exploited labour would feed back into further, sustainable, expansions in demand within the periphery.

To underscore any such global recovery it is also crucial to seek a new progressive supply-side settlement for global labour. This would aim to redress the current class imbalance characteristic of neoliberal globalisation in which the global mobility and ownership privileges currently enjoyed by capital contrast with the manner in which labour remains predominantly locked in at the national level. This imbalance has been critical for reproducing the reserve army in the periphery and semi-periphery and for reproducing the super-exploitation of migrant workers in the core. Reform must aim to tackle this by universalising labour rights in terms of transnational mobility and global minimum wages and welfare legislation. This requires a move towards global labour solidarity and should start from recognising rights equality for migrant labour. There is already considerable support for such a rights agenda, for example, in the United States, where, over the past several years large demonstrations have been held in support of full citizenship for currently semi-legal and illegal Latin workers.

Part II

Globalisation and Change in the Semi-Periphery

4
The South American Semi-Periphery: Brazil and Argentina

Ernesto Vivares

Perhaps in a manner like no other region, South America has been portrayed as a typical and particular case of a semi-peripheral area configurated by decades of populist governments, developmentalist experiences, debt crises and neoliberal adjustments. Reflecting the core assumptions of modernisation studies and permeated by Cold War interests, the central points of reference are the Brazilian and Argentinean experiences. The experiences of these countries nurture a portrayal in which the region appears delinked from the international order, either passive or reactive in its responses to global transformations as a result of persistent domestic problematic. Within this mainstream framework, the academic riddle seems to answer why a region, blessed with all kind of natural resources, lacking racial, religious or serious ethnic differences, has failed to create a stable capitalist order since its independence from Portugal and Spain (Piñera, 2003). Or why has its political economy historically been shifting from inward to outward-oriented experiences of development (Saad-Filho et al., 2007)?

Although the range of explanations varies, certainly two major perspectives rule the mainstream answers, neoliberalism and neodevelopmentalism. Neoliberals perceive Argentina and Brazil's development as subordinated to the way in which free market forces ideally evolve. In this light, the region has reacted to global tendencies through waves of populist governments and developmentalist projects. Similar types of political economic orders in which the dynamic of development seems to be determined by elitist manipulation, fiscal profligacy, welfare overspending and clientelism, and authoritarian efforts at co-optation and regime institutionalisation (Germani, 1956; Dornbusch and Edwards, 1991; Piñera, 2003). Neodevelopmentalists on the other hand, also find the origin of underdevelopment and instability in populist experiences, however their focus tends to lie in the mismanagement of financial globalisation, exchange rate policy as well as the over politicisation of state and economy, and clientelism (Ocampo, 2000; Arestis and Sawyer, 2007; Damill and Frenkel, 2007). In a nutshell, the central characteristic of the South American semi-periphery is its elitist character, the independence of its political and economic spheres of development and its disconnection from, and reactions to, changes in the world order.

In a search for more critical and integral explanations on how semi-peripheral countries have responded to global transformations, this article explores how populism, developmentalism and neoliberalism have expressed different historical responses to a changing world order. In so doing, I examine the changing political and economic nature of state/society complexes, and how they have transformed from being historically integrated into different world orders and subsequently have become disjointed societies (Cox, 1983; Amin, 2006). This paper is a broad-brush critical review which focuses on the semi-peripheral dynamics of Argentina and Brazil with the world hegemons from the colonial times to globalisation.

Similar origins, different configurations and responses

The international history of Argentina and Brazil starts with the Spanish and Portuguese conquest and incorporation of the region in the 1500s as a periphery provider of precious metals to their empires. The region entered into the old world order on the basis of a foundational relationship of Tribute Empire, rather than a mercantile mechanism like that between North Americas and the Anglo-Saxon world. In contrast to the colonial experience of other regions, the Spaniards first subjugated the two most advanced civilisations in Mexico and Peru, and, through exterminating and assimilating largely separate groups in Bolivia, carried this out in Paraguay, Chile and Argentina. Brazil presents a different case since it was the product of Portuguese long-distance trade and defense of national identity defining the Brazilian institutions that would even mark the monarchy, settler oligarchy, landed state and slavery. The beginning of these semi-peripheral areas was a truly catastrophic clash of civilisations that in less than a century, took the lives of nearly 70 million inhabitants in the region (Weaver, 2000: 18).

The Spaniards certainly manifested no interest in settling in the area, but instead aimed to control the access and flow of the finest materials in order to nurture the Crown in Europe and sustain the defence of Catholic Europe from Muslims and Protestants. The colonial policy founded a political order distant from mercantilism, totally in the hands of the Spaniards and the Church, the later operating as an arm of the Crown. Portugal instead acquired a portion of the new world through the Treaty of Tordesillas in 1494. The Portuguese settlement was plagued with hostility, brutality and slavery, with indigenous populations suffering a mass decline. Contrary to the tribute strategy of Spain, the Portuguese adopted a mercantile line to strengthen their position, allowing its planters in Brazil to import African slaves whilst maintaining its tribute peripheral role (Fausto, 2006).

The Tribute Peripheral Empire along both Spanish and Portuguese domains produced conservative-oligarchic state-society complexes characterised by political configurations subordinated to the Crowns, administrated by European elites and exploited by growing local elites of *encomenderos* and landowners. At the bottom, denied of all basic rights, were the indigenous and African slaves while the criollo groups grew in the shadow of illegal trade nurtured by the new free trade era. The fortune of the major regional centres varied according to the availability of natural and human resources and relationships with the core. For Spain, Lima occupied a strategic role whilst for the Portuguese, Brazil was not of major geostrategic importance (Rapoport and Cervo, 2002).

In order to subsist and grow, the social response of these peripheral areas, particularly on the Atlantic coast, was simply to smuggle, whilst keeping the appearances of enforcing and meeting the dispositions of the Crown. Smuggling became a central feature of the real and shared life between the River Plate and Brazil, two peripheries which formally preserved the tribute and conservative oligarchic order and, at the same time, informally became part of free trade imperialism. Smuggling increasingly became a powerful determinant shaping the identity of Brazil and Buenos Aires, and consequently led to the development of powerful trade and oligarch classes on the coast. The new social configurations of criollos were now in strategic position. They were able to mediate and trade on the one hand, with Dutch, Portuguese, French and British traders and on the other hand, they channelled and traded with small centres in the interior of their regions offering them access to new international markets.

The subaltern but dominant social configurations and their informal political and economic culture in Buenos Aires explain, to an important extent, the independence wars and processes. Contrary to the European experience where the development of a capitalist class became the ruling class as already an international force expanding under the liberal state, Argentina's independence war spread a national feeling (*Gemeinschaft*) before a national capitalist class developed fully (Oszlak, 1981). The weak ruling class aimed to keep formal links with the Crown and at the same time to gain access to the new free trade world sustaining their independence from any foreign power. However, facing the prospect of finding no external anchor or political umbrella, in 1816, Argentina declared independence. The new social formation was liberal in its orientations however, not well connected to the new international centres. Liberal groups ruled but were unable to consolidate a path of development and national order. Domestically, the new state was flanked and fluctuated between federalist and unitary forms of national organisations which would mark four decades of domestic conflicts.

In Brazil the situation was exceptionally different, as beyond the gold rush and agricultural expansion, Portuguese commitment to slave-produced agro-export held Brazil as a minor social formation in the map. Brazil was still a slave society and its independence process would not start until the early 1800s, as a result of the Napoleon's invasion and the escape and settling of the Portuguese Crown in Brazil. As liberalism rose in Portugal, the Portuguese declared Brazilian independence in 1822. It was a monarchic, slave and liberal order. Brazilian government remained better connected to the European centres than to its provinces. The reaction to the centralist monarchist government stimulated local autonomy, and political decentralisation became the central organisational principle mixed with an unquestioned slavery.

Beyond the differences, Argentina and Brazil remained weak orders with Uruguay as a buffer between both countries, ruled by different social forces unable by themselves to impose an order without external support, but with a common aim within the era of free trade imperialism. The aim was to gain international integration via export-led development and conservative-liberal rule and to extend geographical control whilst at the same time, always to avoid confrontation with the major rival. Argentina and Brazil entered into the international order as peripheral, rivals and different dislocated state/society complexes marked by liberal-conservative conflicts that would last for several decades.

Both countries found different politically conservative and economically liberal integrated regimes with different positions to the international order, and both countries had to struggle to control their disjointed societies and grassroots pressures for change. In Argentina, the organisation of the state preceded the rise of social hegemonic class whereby the state became the tool of coercion and the space of struggle between opposite social forces seeking to impose different national projects. Conversely in Brazil, the monarchic constitutionalism came about with its institutional machinery already proved and imported from Portugal, making it a unitary national project more capable of organising society. Brazil did not present an anti-colonial liberation struggle but the reorganisation of an empire; a Hobbesian construction (van der Pijl, 2006).

Around the middle of the 1800s, the world order of free trade imperialism began to experience a profound change at its core. In contrast to the English way of industrialisation by competition, a new economic dynamic began to take place in all industrialised nations with deep impacts on the international political economy of the periphery. Finance-driven capitalist industrialisation became the central path for industrialised nations, changing also the way of its expansion. The centre now also exported capital to the periphery. This intensified the centre-periphery relations and opened for the periphery the chance to anchor its external relations to either Europe or the United States, a scenario that would foster a diverse set of peripheral responses.

Top-down development was centralised initially on the basis of the German experience, organised by the state and was seemingly able to preserve and strengthen domestic hegemons and local hierarchies. The new finance capitalist mechanism only required the control of state apparatus, alignment with European nations and protection of foreign direct investment (FDI). Capital was used for railroad construction, ports, public utilities and public works to support export production bringing foreign ownership rather than lending to governments.

At the beginning of the twentieth century, Argentina emerged openly associated with Europe and in particular to the United Kingdom, as a major recipient of FDI and destiny of trade. Brazil seemed to take a different path; more linked to the new emergent international power, the United States, and less reliant on UK financing compared to Argentina. The two South American countries shared their expansionist national interests over Uruguay and Paraguay but with different oligarchic orientations. The politically conservative and economically liberal Argentina would totally commit itself to Europeans, while the monarchic liberal Brazil would turn to the United States in a move to gain independence from Europe, opening the door for a growing and expansive economic and political presence with the growing regional hegemon.

The conservative-liberal stage lasting between the mid-nineteenth and early twentieth centuries would be marked by international and regional rivalries, all preceding a changing international order. In this vein, it is important to note that while the United Kingdom tended to focus on political and economic diplomacy, the United States began to unfold a regional policy of political, economic and even security influence. The United States focused on the creation of hemispheric institutions such as the Pan American Union (PAU), a regional body for South America created in the 1920s and dependant on the US Secretary of State and the State Department (Nef, 1994).

The PAU reflected the hemispheric alliance between the United States and liberal-oligarchic elites and different military and business elites in the region committed to, and were supported by, the United States. In order to keep its influence in the region, the United States was able to play Brazilian and Argentine distrust and rivalry to its advantage. The United States policy favoured Brazil vis-à-vis Argentina, as Argentina was the major competitor of North American products. Beyond the fact that during the populist period Argentina was more prosperous, US support to Brazil gave it the advantage of becoming, in few decades time, the dominant power of the region (Bandeira, 2003).

Populism

By the end of the 1930s and 1940s the changes taking place in the international order would clearly hit the dominance of the agro-export model and its social configurations, triggering unique and independent responses by the two larger countries of the region; two different responses from two different states/societies complexes, with different links to the international order and domestically dislocated social structures. The isolation generated by the Great War and international shocks in trade and finance in the 1930s were rapidly counterbalanced by the rise of a domestic-based industrialisation process and the emergence of the first forms of corporatist welfare state. The oligarchic elites ruling Argentina and Brazil during this liberal stage had comfortably flown the flags of order and progress for decades, order for the subaltern groups and progress for the local aristocratic oligarchies which controlled the economic and political affairs of both nations.

The conservative-liberal order was based on a state class whereby the state was never neutral in relation to the dominant ruling groups and their projects. This includes domestic, international, ideological, political and economic 'neutrality', which simply did not exist. The agro-export-based financing of development, the liberal-positivist state, unequal social structures and social backwardness were all bound together to a peripheral position in the international order (Franco,

2002). The social configuration finally collapsed but not for domestic reasons. Unquestionably, the major hit was transmitted from the international sphere to the domestic. The semi-peripheral orders were literally shaken and brought into question by the long period of international disruption which took hold between 1914 and 1945, and the ascendant working and urban classes.

Free from the constraints of international markets, the domestic and social-led process of industrialisation became domestic-oriented and later grew under the state protection financed through the transfer of resources from primary export sectors and domestic consumption. Domestic-dependent import-substituting industrialisation (ISI) processes shaped complex and different landscapes of social forces, some favouring and others opposing to different economic and social forms of the autonomous industrial capitalism which was then emerging in Argentina and Brazil. The so-called populisms in these countries were in essence counter-hegemonic movements born in the shadow of Liberal Conservative conflicts, adopting components of both but at the same time standing up to the dominant bloc and external link. Initially the populist demands of substantive democracy were not incompatible with the liberal system whereby they adopted the same liberal state, but later adapted them to wider and more differentiated social demands (Laclau, 2005).

By the 1940s, in most of the Latin American countries, national industrialisation had become the path of development. The economic regime in countries such as Argentina and Brazil first generated a strong corporate sector-coordinated system on the basis of an alliance among politicians, bureaucracies, business and workers geared towards a long-run process of inward-looking development, and secondly the creation of a corporatist social regime. Both economic and welfare regimes reflected the centrality within the state of labour and industrial relations (Mesa-Lago, 2000). Production was firmly tied and imbricated with the state apparatus, producing a rigid social stratification which the welfare regime echoed. Welfare production was dependant on class structure, and differentiation, legitimised, institutionalised and expanded by the state as a result of the demands of labour and other social forces.

The Brazilian state/society configuration was rapidly integrated into the North American trade area of influence after being the main contender of the British Empire. As the international crisis in the early nineteenth century unfolded, the centre of social structure also changed. Populism started in Brazil as a local phenomenon that emerged in autonomous municipal governments, characterised by high levels of social inclusion, educational reforms and health measures, elections and market interventions for the common good in the 1920s and 1930s.

The Brazilian state/society populist complex disrupted the liberal-oligarchic order and absorbed the new processes of a top-down revolution. This took place at the very same moment that the country's axe of class structure shifted away from mining, coffee-growing and commercial-financial interests concentrated in the Minas Gerais and São Paulo regions, to the industrial state and family-farmer controlled of Rio Grande do Sul. It was a counter-hegemonic process in the sense that it brought the voice of the people into the political spotlight, which after a decade and a half of unresolved struggles between ruling elites, turned into a developmentalist coalition of social forces behind a nationalist project. The new Brazil had to find its place in the world order as a nation capable of organising its society and developing its capabilities, a conception deeply influenced by its state heritage. It took nearly two and a half decades for Brazilian populism to successfully lay the foundations of state/society complex that would last three more decades, the developmentalist stage.

The Vargas nationalist and populist order ruled Brazil from 1930 to 1954 alternating between periods of democratic and authoritarian administrations, but ever pursuing national interests and technocratic modernisation. National centralisation, economic interventionism, cooling relations with the United States, close cooperation with Argentina, promotion of manufacturing and social control through social co-optation became the defining characteristics of Brazilian populism and of the *Estado Novo* (New State) (Fausto, 2006). Populism became domestically hegemonic, favoured by the external and domestic conditions to make a coalition of social elites and forces. It was state populism with a developmentalist project. Democratic and non-democratic means coexisted (specially controlling union mobilisation) and prevailed since it aimed to create national cohesion rather than social growth. The accumulation model represented the archetype of ISI developmentalist policies addressed to create a heavy industrial sector (mainly iron and steel) using exchange controls to divert resources from the agro-export sector.

The Brazilian ISI process soon led into a macroeconomic division of labour between a domestic capital based on producing non-durable consumer goods and transnational companies producing durable consumer goods and fostering the power of the new social configuration, but re-stringing the political inclusion of popular forces. In Brazilian populism, ISI developmentalism paved the way to a developmentalist and authoritarian political order through the control via co-optation of a new and more radical configuration of social forces emerging in the national life as the direct result of the populist development strategy.

The populist order expressed by Getúlio Vargas presided a true ISI period of massive expansion of heavy industrial production bringing together middle and urban classes, and a fraction of the industrial sector. Strikes were not allowed but workers were allowed to form unions and expected to pay for social welfare. The Brazilian populist order was strongly centralised and intended to create a nationalist regime against the liberal and oligarch structure of the sugar aristocracy, in turn repressing and suppressing revolutionary left and reactionary right-wing forces alike. Those are the cases of the suppression of *Aliança Nacional Libertadora* (ANL) led by the Communist Party, and Integralism, a fascist-style movement.

The dominant bloc led a foundational social reform in the hands of intellectuals aimed at creating an improved and white-centred Brazilian race through social welfare in health and education. Benefits were extended to the population in which racial democracy and welfare regime intertwined unevenly with some cultural racist ideologies and practices from the past legitimising inequalities, which favoured whites and not those from the lower classes (Davila, 2003). Instead, Argentine populism took place in a different regional context and domestic setting, presenting a different configuration and orientation to the Brazilian order. In fact by the 1930s the Argentine industrialisation process was far more advanced and dynamic than that of Brazil, but it was mostly concentrated on the production of basic consumption goods and agro-industrial machinery. The Argentine labour market became international, experiencing a large-scale influx of European immigrants, with a significant influence of anarchism in its labour unions. By the 1930s Argentina had received 4.1 million immigrants and Brazil 2.2 million, four times the proportional impact of immigration in the United States (Weaver, 2000).

A central element of Argentine populism, as a state society coalition of social forces, was that it did have to deal with a liberal conservative state apparatus instead of an imperial state such as the case of Brazil. Populism in Argentina faced a different setting with a different composition of social forces. Firstly, it advanced from emergent social forces into a state controlled by social class alliances, aiming to take strategic resorts of the state apparatus to fund its political order of development. Secondly, the social bases of Peronism were wider than in other populist experiences owed to its anchor over labour unions, industrial actors, federal configurations and factions of different traditional corporations.

By the middle of the 1930s the conservative-liberal order was in complete decline with intense conflicts of interests between elites unable to agree on a common project that would restore the order and co-opt the rapid ascendance of new and organised social actors (Rapoport and Cervo, 2002: 225). Peronism was a counter-hegemonic movement based on a poly-class coalition in which workers and employers were bound together by corporatist arrangements which sought to regulate both the domestic economy and its relation to the international economy (Murmis and Portantiero, 1971). It was distributional and industrial rather than one addressed to developmentalism, and was interested not so much in industrialisation via international insertion but rather in reorganising national labour and industry on a corporative basis in order to sustain incomes, protect distribution and strengthen domestic industry. Peronism was strongly directed towards family welfare and consumption, and gave particular emphasis to its non-alignment with the United States, an external option which played a significant role in its future collapse.

The strategy followed by Argentina constituted a similar option to countries with a similar level of development, such as Australia and Canada, although it took a different approach in its international integration and domestic development. Nonetheless, the Peronist plan was based on an erroneous diagnosis of the post-Second World War international scenario, with a direct impact upon the bottleneck which confronted the Peronist economic strategy: its dependence on external financing for development (Di Tella and Dornbush, 1989: 19). That was because domestic-based ISI and rural sectors were unable to fuel the levels of industrialisation and income distribution demanded by the strategy (Rock, 1987: 262–319).

By pursuing its path, the Peronist administration amplified the pre-existing hostility of the United States towards the Latin American region and its reluctance to support Argentina. Isolated from post-war trade, limited in its conception of economic sovereignty in a hemisphere increasingly falling under US control, and domestically weakened and divided, in the mid-1950s the Peronist administration was left at the mercy of the conservative-liberal opposition. Washington was hostile to key aspects of the Peronist administration, in particular its 'Third Position', challenging US authority over the hemisphere. The Third Position was a pragmatic international response to the US economic and political hostility and a way to make clear to the new Soviet Bloc the independent regional orientation of Argentina. On top of this it firmly refused to join the WB, the IMF or the GATT, avoiding borrowing from the multilateral system, given its massive reserves (MacDonald, 1985: 407).

In 1947, the Argentine government had staked its political destiny on the Five Year Plan, and US financial assistance seemed to be the only option (MacDonald, 1985: 408). In return for financial support, Washington demanded free trade, better conditions for foreign investment and ratification of the Rio Treaty. As the country did not agree, in early 1948 the United States excluded it from the trade benefits of the Marshall Plan (Rock, 1987). In 1950, despite a shift in the Peronist administration towards its final years, there was no guarantee that it would again take up the Third Position, and the United States wanted to make clear to its successors that no middle position would be allowed in the hemisphere. As history manifests, the *Revolucion Libertadora* (Liberty Revolution) and Frondizi administrations responded to this hemispheric policy by enthusiastically joining the Bretton Woods institutions, closely cooperating with the Organisation of American States (OAS) and Economic Commission for Latin America and the Caribbean (CEPAL-ECLAC), embracing Wall Street and subsequently driving the country into a new stage marked by debt and inflation (Rapoport, 1988). It was the time of developmentalism.

Developmentalism and internationalisation of state

The stage known as developmentalism in Argentina and Brazil constitutes one of the most controversial periods given the mixture of outstanding economic advances, expansive corporative social welfare, painful political backward steps and social repression. Three key elements characterised the developmentalist period. The first is the conflictive realignment of Argentina and Brazil to US hegemony, which increased domestic divisions and regional rivalries. Secondly, as a result it was the emergency of a new axe of domestic dislocation which would be at the very base of the intense political and social struggles between the 1950s and the mid-1970s. The domestic line of conflict was between dispersing populist and left-wing forces, on the one hand, and developmentalist, conservative-liberal forces on the other. Thirdly, as the domestic tensions grew, developmentalism under US hegemony came to foster the consolidation of a dominant state form, a military and an authoritarian bureaucratic state. Briefly, if the internationalisation of production was nurturing a historical partnership between democracy, capitalism and Keynesianism in Europe, in Latin America it rendered the consolidation of authoritarian bureaucratic state and national security doctrines assured, in turn, by US military and economic influence (O'Donnell, 1973; Payne, 1996).

The new development recipe for the region's countries constituted a convergence of developmentalism and nationalism processes accompanied by different forms of authoritarian political orders such as the cases of Brazil and Argentina. In an order characterised by the co-optation of popular demands and political repression, the precise form of relations between developmentalism, nationalism and the international hegemony came to depend, to a large extent, on the political and economic relations between elites with the international hegemon.

As the Second World War ended, US attention turned back to the region, mainly motivated by trade concerns, nurturing the growth of an externally dependent industrial sector through its traditional support to US corporations (Bulmer-Thomas, 2003). As US hegemony consolidated, the internationalisation of production became the major external source of financing for development in the region, now regionally determined by FDI and official development aid. The rise of the new order deeply impacted the regional balance of social forces, which shifted in favour to those aligned with the new hegemon.

In less than a decade, a massive surge of external capital reshaped the region and gave way to a new external dependant industrial sector. The new sector provided goods and services to newly well-off people, serving the top of the social pyramid with textiles, chemicals, pharmaceuticals, electrical appliances and transport (Diaz Alejandro, 1970). Shortly, the region became one of the key recipients of US FDI, averaging 40 per cent of all US FDI to the world during the 1950s (Griffith-Jones, 1984: 28).

Noticeably, the process unfolded on the basis of the existing settings built up by populism structured around domestic-dependent ISI sectors and corporate welfare state. The result was the diversification of the production regime, modifying the structure of the regions' urban population and stimulating new political tendencies and conflicts. Hence, unlike the form that Europe had taken, the internationalisation of production in Latin America unfolded in a remarkably different manner, primarily in the shadow of US Cold War preoccupations.

As the United States became concerned with the consolidation of hegemony within the region, the foundation of a regional system that reinforced its political authority was vital. Notably, the task did not require a new system, such as was demanded in Europe and East Asia, but the deployment of more political authority on the basis of both, those regional elites impatient to become partners of the United States and by using the existing institutional framework of the PAU.

Within this framework, two central and inseparable economic and political elements set the nature of developmentalism, to explain its inherent tendency to foster paradoxically both socio-economic development and authoritarian responses to political instability and social mobilisation. The first is its well-known ISI economic model at the base of economic progress while the second was its anchored dependence on US support to contain both the return of populism and the growth of left-wing forces. In this regard, once again the Argentine and Brazilian developmentalist experiences began to share a more common pattern, although presenting different orientations and outcomes. Throughout the developmentalist period Argentina and Brazil's orientations began to coincide more closely, but the attempts of cooperation between Vargas and Peron in the 1960s vanished as the United States assisted the coups in Brazil and Argentina, integrating both countries under its influence. Both adopted liberal-conservative and military dictatorships and began to cooperate closely with the United States on security issues, but this also increased their rivalry (Bandeira, 2003).

Argentine developmentalism

The developmentalist period in Argentina lasted between 1955 and 1975 and has been characterised as a 'hegemonic draw' (O'Donnell, 1973; Rapoport, 1988). This hegemonic deadlock, or the 'impossible regime', resulted from an undefined struggle by the liberal–conservative, civil–military coalition against the Peronist populist coalition and its main organisational pillars, the General Economic Confederation (CGE), the General Central of Workers (CGT), and left wing forces. This stage was characterised by the country's international economic integration within the framework of the Cold War. Domestically, the process featured a hegemonic deadlock existing from the *Revolucion Libertadora* or Oligarchic Restoration up to the dictatorship of 1976 (Franco, 2002: 145).

The international realignment of Argentina began when the Peronist government was overthrown in 1955 by the military forces and the implementation of neoliberal political economic plan created by Raul Prebisch (Rock, 1987; Escude and Cisneros, 2000). The process slowly led into a differentiation between politics and economics, whereby economic progress became incompatible with representative government and social rights, and military rule intervened frequently to sustain the conservative hegemony. The final result was political instability, violence and repression which, by the 1970s, convulsed the country. This stage marks the beginning of the externalisation of the Argentine financing of development, the internationalisation of its economy and the subordination of the state to the guidelines of the major IFIs. Argentina was now within the framework of US global hegemony, pursuing a new developmentalist strategy and the co-optation of popular forces which would lead the country into a profoundly divided society.

The deepening of the external-oriented developmentalist strategy did not take off until the Frondizi administration in 1958. The new strategy was synonymous with developmentalism and industrialisation based on foreign capital to accelerate growth in strategic sectors such as metalwork, energy, heavy chemicals, transport and communications. Overall the strategy led to an expansion of public spending, triggering significant inflation as a result of the struggle around income distribution. The deficit was controlled, with monetary emission and external borrowing transferring resources from primary activities to subsidise the industrial sector and, at the same time, allowing the repatriation of profits for transnational companies, consolidating the external-oriented industrial sector, mainly driven by US and European investments (Rapoport, 1988: 556–559). However, as Europe and East Asia soon become the focus for FDI, the developmentalist administration responded to the absence of capital by accessing official assistance in the form of external loans (Escude and Cisneros, 2000: 31). Pro-FDI industrial policy became a source of national contention but above all, the conditionalities related to foreign borrowing of official loans included cutting government spending, increasing (the already) high interest rates and implementing broad measures directed at liberalising the economy. In 1962 the Frondizi party lost the congressional elections, and fearing a Peronist return, armed forces reacted immediately and illegally declared the national electoral process, dissolved congress and overthrew Frondizi (Halperin Donghi, 1993: 314).

The 1963–1976 period was characterised by an unstable and violent struggle within the dominant military–civil coalition and also by the response to each side from national and popular forces. A prominent feature of this turmoil was the confrontation between conservatives and liberal civic–military elites, seeking to occupy and control the powerful left by the proscribed Peronist movement. Now they were confronting the new generations of Peronist militants and organisations and a wide range of new left-wing groups which were also inspired by the Cuban revolution and the social struggles of May 1968 in France

(Franco, 2000). As developmentalist governments proved unable to deal with social unrest in the region, the new Johnson administration in Washington began to favour right-wing dictators over liberal reformers in an attempt to solve the hegemonic deadlock (Nef, 1994: 408). But far from producing stability and military rule, the free-market policies just made Argentina ungovernable.

By the early 1970s, Argentina was spiralling out of institutional control, and armed struggle arrived with the following four main groups engaged in insurgency: the Montoneros, the Fuerzas Armadas Peronistas, the Fuerzas Armadas Revolucionarias and the People's Revolutionary Army. Civic-military coalitions could not stabilise the country, and the return of Peron in alliance with left-wing forces was seen as a real threat to domestic elites and Washington. In 1973, in the middle of the major political struggles of the country, Peron was elected as President for the third time. After the failed attempt to restore the kernel of past Peronist policies based on income distribution, full employment and social reform, supporting the CGT and CGE and marginalising the allied left-wing sectors of his movement, Peron died in 1974, shattering the political system. On 24 March 1976, the military forces overthrew the democratic government and embarked in historical process of transformation and integration of the country into the world order. The civic–military coalition had the firm objective of dismantling the sources of power within the Peronist state, also breaking up the developmentalist ISI strategy, and imposing a new economic model based on global integration, external financing and export commodities (Rock, 1987: 366; Basualdo, 2001).

The US administration saw the dictatorship as a stabilising factor (Escude, 2000). The new strategy of dictatorship comprised two complementary and inseparable projects, the economic programme and the military war against 'subversion and terrorism', which led to the disappearance and murder of 30,000 people. The dictatorship harvested unexpected support in the country, such as that from the Communist and Radical parties (Rock, 1987). The economic plan, following the monetarist theories of Chicago, which was increasingly adopted by the IFIs, was the first orthodox and monetarist plan aimed at dismantling the state as a source of employment and union power, as well as ending its role as a chief agent in the distribution of resources. The plan rested heavily on foreign loans and investments with international commercial banks, IFIs and Washington willing to support the experiment. Argentina's external debt jumped from 18.6 per cent of GDP – inherited from the times of developmentalism – to 60 per cent in 1982 during the dictatorship, with an important role being played by the re-equipment of military forces prior to the Falklands/Malvinas conflict.

Within a few years, the restructuring initiated by the dictatorship had deeply altered socio-economic conditions in the country. The dictatorship had achieved a diversified, although unconsolidated, agro-export-led model fuelled by financial liberalisation, but one which produced recession, widespread unemployment and an explosive growth in external debt. Salaried workers received 43 per cent of national income in 1974; by 1977 this had shrunk to 31 per cent (Altimir et al., 2002).

By the end of the 1980s the recessive effects of the neoliberal experiment were obvious, and leaving aside the military repression, the weakening of the economy by trade and financial openness, worsened the economic situation and brought the financial system near to collapse (Rock, 1987: 372–374). In the midst of increasing social discontent, the dictatorship hoped that a national crusade for sovereignty such as the recuperation of the Falklands/Malvinas Islands would provide it with the political leverage and time it needed to reorganise its hegemony. But the reality defined a different and paradoxical history, wherein the military's defeat in the Falklands/Malvinas Islands marked the demise of its dictatorship, and soon, in the face of increasing social unrest, the military government was compelled to call new elections.

From a political and economic point of view, it is clear that, despite the fall of the Argentine dictatorship, the dominant sectors and coalitions that emerged during a decade of conservative and repressive policies were capable of articulating new alliances which converged with global tendencies shaping the conditions of the democratic transition. They therefore helped to produce the Argentine *transformismo*, a hegemony based on international–domestic alliances capable of co-opting subaltern sectors and carrying forward the adjustment of Argentine society to the new conditions of accumulation emerging at international and regional levels, within a democratic system (Cox, 1996: 130; Basualdo, 2001). The peculiarity of democratic openness in Argentina was the convergence and alliance of the dominant domestic coalitions and leftovers of the dictatorship with foreign sectors. This international–domestic coalition of forces converged around a similar diagnosis concerning the way a new democracy should facilitate the adjustments necessary for Argentine society to conform to the new global conditions (Rapoport, 1988; Basualdo, 2001). This process gave rise to a particular hegemonic transformist structure, a complex particularly able to align the domestic to the international guidelines of capital expansion via political democratic process.

The post-dictatorship transformation was characterised by its capacity to increasingly subordinate the policies of the main democratic institutions to a new pattern of accumulation and global integration, deepening Argentina's participation in an increasingly globalised economy whilst co-opting the demands of subaltern sectors. Politically, parties (Justice and Radical parties) played a central role in the process of national adjustment to the global economy. They were the first political institutions to experience the effects of neoliberal globalisation, and carry through central alterations of the core base of Peronism and developmentalism, in order to redefine and legitimise the reorganisation of the financing of development.

The bonds between economic leaders and the main political parties became constant themes during a period of ideological change, in which dominant political sectors and economic businesses also integrated with dominant intellectual sectors. As a result of decades of persecution and annihilation, no political body possessed enough power to play a key role in leading the new political system. So it was the dominant economic sectors, those bound to the domestic concentrations of capital and finance, which assumed first place in the task of conditioning the political parties that administered the government, playing a much more important role than external creditors or the IFIs (Basualdo, 2001: 50–51). It is here that neoliberal global ideas finally fitted with the conservative national project, with the latter coming around to the idea that only state re-structuring through privatisations and financial and trade liberalisation could fuel the necessary growth. Conditioned by the new global financial settings, the government could no longer fuel domestic development through managing fiscal deficit.

Brazilian developmentalism

Unlike the Argentine experience, in Brazil the economic option of industrialisation was always at the forefront of the powerful coalition forces' policy, emergent in the shadow of populism. These forces were composed by industrial lobby, conservative and military elites, state-controlled unions and political classes. The difference was the inclusion of export promotion as a central target of industrialisation, with major political economic implications in terms of social repression and exclusion, and the total realignment of Brazil to US regional policy

(Saad-Filho et al., 2007). The first result was to subordinate industrialisation to exportation which would demand a stabilisation programme only possible through a sharp reduction in real wages and deep deterioration in income distribution and social conditions (Bulmer-Thomas, 2003: 316). Secondly, it would demand high levels of control over social conflicts and repression of any political opposition.

Unwittingly or not, the populist legacy was turning into a substantive democracy, but as urban worker and rural protests radicalised, as well as sections of the Roman Catholic Church and left-wing parties, the dominant coalition depicted democracy as a conflictive path fostering revolution from below and alignment with Third World countries (Rapoport and Cervo, 2002; Fausto, 2006). Under a co-optive political order the traditional overlapping between politics, social mobilisation and economics of a unitary society split and triggered a reaction from the dominant economic and military coalition to keep the order, and externally to realign itself within the US area of influence after a short democratic period. President Kubitschek (1956–1961) represented the only expression of a Brazilian democratic and developmentalist administration working cooperatively with Washington. Kubitschek's government strengthened relations with Latin America and Europe (within the US cooperation guidelines for the regions), and targeted Eastern Europe in the search for trade possibilities. Its foreign policy towards the United States favoured a wide access to FDI, and particularly from the United States, which in a short period of time consolidated the external orientation of the domestic-oriented ISI structures as the result of a rapid internationalisation of capital. Domestically, however, the developmentalist government in Brazil continued to be feeble and even naive in relation to the political capacity of the social forces nurtured by the populist process. Regionally, the Kubitschek's pro-US multilateral approach was key in the consolidation of Inter-American system through the creation of the Inter-American Development Bank (IADB) and in President Kennedy's Alliance for Progress in 1961.

In late 1963, as the Brazilian democracy was building partnerships with countries such as Egypt, Argentina and Cuba, Washington reduced foreign aid and diplomatic support to Brazil. In 1964, a military coup overthrew the leftist nationalist Goulart government diplomatically recognised by the United States, which also deployed a naval task force in the port of Vitoria and supplied financial assistance to the new military government. With that, Brazil totally realigned itself with the US to gain regional supremacy and inaugurated 21 years of military rule of a military-developmentalist state aimed at making Brazil a regional potency, free from communism and corruption.

The military administration came with the firm purpose of structurally changing Brazil. Politically, it banned Congress, political parties, jailed or exiled politicians and militants. Labour organisations and universities were penetrated and there was violent repression, torture, summary executions and disappearances. Externally, it froze relations with Cuba, began a process of distancing and renewing rivalries with Argentina, adopted a passive position in the United Nations and started to participate as part of the US-sponsored peace force tasks in the region. Brazilian foreign policy centred now on combating subversion under the US Cold War goals in the region, and was ranked third after India and Vietnam as major recipients of US aid (Davis, 1996; Bandeira, 2003).

Military developmentalists built a restricted political order in which every institution or social actor could remain free as long as they did not oppose the government's internal or external orientation. The country followed industrialisation but at the expense of violent social repression. Yet at the same time, the media, judicial institutions, right-wing political parties, the Catholic Church and even Congress enjoyed a degree of freedom. Until the 1970s, state terrorism had been intensifying, and then outcomes of the economic strategy began to manifest themselves through some kind of industrial miracle and increasing regional primacy (Bandeira, 2003). There was rapid industrial and economic growth paralleled with a deepening of unequal income distribution inherent to the repressive character of the model. Between 1968 and 1973, the average annual growth rate of GDP reached 11 per cent led by industry with 13.1 per cent average but the highly concentrated distribution of income only worsened (CIA, 2008). Now the developmental dimensions of politics, economics, society and institutions overlapped in a small unitary society integrated into the world economy, but with important popular segments of the population excluded from the system.

Deteriorating social conditions, growing social marginalisation, environmental degradation, powerful business communities impatient to absorb state-controlled economic areas in parallel with an increasing external exposure and vulnerability all converged to facilitate a controlled and well-planned democratic transition by the military conservative coalition during 1984 however; it was not until 1989 that a democratic president was elected. The three oil shocks of the 1970s triggered the country's foreign debt escalation, inflation and economic crisis exhausting the military developmentalist order, although not the power of its coalition. Contrary to the abrupt collapse of the Argentine dictatorship due to the sudden withdrawal of international and domestic elite support, Brazil returned to democracy through a managed process by the domestic and international dominant coalitions under the certainty that neither populist nor left-wing forces would threaten the existing power, even under democracy. Furthermore, democracy in Brazil did not return on the ruins of the institutions left by dictatorship, but on a basis of an organised transition managed by military and conservative elites (Saad-Filho et al., 2007: 11). However, elite concern over the lack of external support, international condemnation of human right abuses and decades of repression would facilitate a deal on the basis of the new neoliberal framework with the feeble democratic coalition emerging since 1975. Certainly, democracy would dilute conservative elites' political power; but in an international order marked by a declining US hegemony. With a neoliberal order surfacing it made it easy for elites to control economic power and condition the political order. This explains the absence, within the first stages of the new Brazilian democracy, of political and economic objectives addressed to reduce the massive socio-economic inequalities which demand change in the structures of the political order and income distribution of the country (Saad-Filho et al., 2007). The option was clear and a political programme based on social justice and the construction of a more substantive democracy was left out. For the Brazilian conservative elites, democracy was a means to update and re-legitimise their power, and neoliberalism within the framework of development would help to accomplish Brazil's historical dream, to become an international superpower.

Conclusion

This chapter has explored the changing political and economic landscape of the two semi-peripheral cases of Argentina and Brazil, and in particular, it has assessed their differing response to global transformations. Instead of a recourse to mainstream, ahistorical and top-down interpretations of these semi-peripheries, this chapter has sought to provide a broad-brush and critical political and economic review based on the historical evidence of Argentina and Brazil. In so doing, I have focused on the examination of the changing political and economic nature of these semi-peripheral state/society complexes in the light of the processes of configuration, rise and decline of different social forces and orders, the way they were historically integrated into different world orders, and their subsequent response. Central to this chapter has been the re-examination of the rise, apogee, decline and specificities and lines of transitions between populism, developmentalism and neoliberalism in Argentina and Brazil. Along these lines the central conclusion of this chapter is the normative importance of the international–domestic link and the state society complexes to the re-definition of the notions of centre and semi-periphery. Two central concepts that permit us to avoid elitist and top-down approaches marked by the divorce between the international and the domestic, and politics and economics.

5
Economic Development in the East Asian (Semi)Periphery: Reintroducing Dependency as a Conceptual Tool of Analysis

Jason P. Abbott

The neo-Marxist analysis that gave rise to World Systems theory also provided the ideological and philosophical foundation for Dependency theory. Indeed many prominent Dependency theorists themselves would become leading advocates and proponents of World Systems analyses during the 1970s and 1980s (e.g. Frank, Amin, etc.). Like World System theory, Dependency theories would also come under the same barrage of critique both from traditional Marxists as well as from ideological opponents on the opposite side of the political and philosophical spectrum. Furthermore, the economic dynamism of a whole host of East Asian 'semi-periphery' economies from Taiwan and South Korea to Indonesia, Malaysia, Vietnam and China would lead many to conclude that the structural constraints on growth identified by Dependency theorists had been transitory. Their dynamism did not conform to the pessimistic scenarios projected in the Dependency and World System literature and the inexorable shift from raw material production to manufactured goods ran contrary to the assumptions of much of the literature.

Nonetheless questions about asymmetries of power and wealth between the North and the South have had a profound impact upon the development of International Political Economy (IPE). In particular such questions have been influential in the development of a critical ontology and agenda for IPE that has challenged the positivist and behavioural dominance of the discipline (Abbott and Worth, 2002). Furthermore despite the 'inadequacies' and 'weaknesses' of Dependency theory a large body of literature emerged within IPE that examined and explored the structural power of international capital – both finance and corporate (e.g. Gill, 1990; Stopford and Strange, 1991; Cox, 1996; Strange, 1995, 1996; Klein, 2001, 2007). In much of this literature, and in my own work (Palan and Abbott, 1996/2000), the claim is made that international finance has become ever more important in the pursuit of national economic competitiveness with the consequence that state-firm bargaining is now as important a feature of the study of IPE as bargaining between states. Clearly asymmetries of power exist in such bargains between states and firms, with developing economies generally weaker parties than their developed counterparts. Yet if we recognise such asymmetries we have to ask whether we are simply identifying dependency by another name?

One of the most influential articles in debates on such asymmetries of power and wealth in IPE was a piece by Mitchell Bernard and John Ravenhill which appeared in the journal *World Politics* in 1995. In their article the authors examined the diffusion of manufacturing industry in East Asia during the post-Second World War era. Rather than concluding that what we had witnessed was a smooth emergence of successive waves of economies which had consciously modelled themselves on the Japanese developmental experience, instead they maintained that complex and *hierarchical* networks of production had emerged linking these economies to Japan for crucial technologies and to the United States for markets for finished goods. Crucially they argued that this *dependence* was a source of growing concern among regional state elites but it was not one that was necessarily negative or detrimental. Such dynamics show that even though the most advanced economies of East Asia (e.g. Taiwan and South Korea) continued to depend upon imported technologies, the existence of this dependency, and of a wider regional hierarchy of production, could be mutually beneficial. Pivotal though this research was in provoking a re-evaluation of the relationships between peripheral, semi-peripheral and core states in both their regional and global context much of what they proposed echoed those first put forward by the Latin American scholars Cardoso and Faletto (1979) in their formulation of Associated Dependent Development. What in essence both sets of authors argue is that dependency is not a generalised theory describing a structural and static feature of the capitalist world system, but instead a *process* that has to be conceptualised in a specific socio-economic and historical context. In other words it is the specific *form* that dependency takes that should be the object of enquiry. As Bernard and Ravenhill remark, dependency must be understood in terms of 'the relationship between changes in the global political economy, changes in the political economy of individual states, and changes in the organisation of production' (1995, p. 205).

In this chapter I explore these arguments in order to issue a clarion call to those working in the area of economic development within IR and IPE to revisit the concept of dependency, secondly to return to the empirical examples of concrete situations of dependence such as those I revealed in my earlier study on the automobile industry in Southeast Asia (Abbott, 2003). I contend that examining specific situations and degrees of dependence in developing world economies is crucial to understanding the dynamics of the capitalist world system of the twenty-first century.

Dependency theory: Origins and development

Although Dependency theories essentially emerged as a post-war critique of Modernisation theories such as Rostow's *The Stages of Economic Growth* much of the literature draws inspiration from Marx's writings on the development of capitalism in Ireland and Russia and from Marxist theories of imperialism beginning with Lenin (1916/1993), Hilferding (1910/2005), Luxemburg (1913/2005) and Bukharin (1917). Indeed World Systems theories would draw particularly on Luxemburg's emphasis of exchange relations as an essential feature of capitalism, rather than production, to postulate that the unequal division of the Capitalist World System into core, semi-peripheral and peripheral economies had first emerged with the expansion of European colonialism in the fifteenth and sixteenth centuries rather than a more recent phenomenon synonymous with industrialisation and the late imperialism of the nineteenth century (e.g. Wallerstein, 1974, 1979, 1980).

The defining characteristic of Dependency theories is well known – namely that the world economy is structurally divided into a core industrialised world and a peripheral developing world (e.g. Frank, 1967, 1979). This division, rather than representing different stages in a universal and linear progression from traditional subsistence-based economies to modernity, was instead a necessary product of the capitalist world economy. The core, in other words, only enjoys the levels of development it has achieved as a result of exploiting and expropriating surplus value from the periphery. Thus rather than being *un*-developed the periphery is instead *under*-developed as a result of their insertion into a global system of capitalism.

Although this bifurcation of the capitalist world system into distinct and structurally determined 'regions' would be central to the development of World Systems theory, Dependency theory was always much more diverse than such a summary portrays. Palma (1978), for example, distinguishes three major variants of Dependency theory: (1) dependency as a theory of Latin American underdevelopment, (2) dependency as a reformulation of the Economic Commission of Latin America's analysis of Latin American development and (3) dependency as *methodology* for the analysis of concrete situations of dependence (pp. 899–906).

The first of these variants is most closely associated with the work of Andre Gunder Frank, the Chicago-trained economist who would prove to be one of the most influential of the neo-Marxist scholars of the post-war era, as well as with the work of, for example, Dos Santos (1970) and Hinkalammert (1972). Central to this variant is the construction of a theory of Latin American underdevelopment in which the dependent character of peripheral economies forms the basis on which the whole analysis of underdevelopment is constructed. Most famously Frank illustrates this as a chain of exploitation that both appropriates and centralises surplus value via a series of metropolis-satellite relations from the rural hacienda to the peripheral capital and from there to the core metropolises of the developed world. Such a process for Frank actually retards the development of Third World societies, a process he termed the 'development of underdevelopment'. Development within the system was illusory because of the existence of a 'comprador' class. This class are the principal beneficiaries of the unequal relationship – 'the core of the periphery' – a westernised elite that contributes to the system of exploitation. Thus for Frank the only way for peripheral economies to achieve economic development was through revolution, to break free from the capitalist world system and with it the dominance of metropolitan states.

The second variant, represented in the work of Sunkel (1972) and Furtado (1970) seeks to locate and emphasise the obstacles to national development that arise from exogenous factors. For Palma this variant essentially reformulates the ECLA critique of modernisation theory. Between 1950 and 1953 the United Nations Economic Commission for Latin America, based in Santiago, was headed by the Argentinean economist Raul Prebisch. Prebisch formulated what has become known as the Singer–Prebisch thesis in his 1950 study *The Economic Development of Latin America and Its Principal Problems.*[1] In this work Prebisch stated that in the international economy, peripheral countries were principally producers of primary products which they exported to the developed core, whereas core economies were producers of secondary manufactured goods which they in turn exported to the periphery. Over time international demand and the terms of trade declined for primary products because the demand for manufactured goods was more elastic. In other words as economies developed, their demand for manufactured goods would increase faster than their demand for agricultural goods. As a consequence, over time, exporters of primary products would see their terms of trade deteriorate, requiring such exporters to produce more simply in order to get the same level of manufactured goods. From this Prebisch concluded that peripheral economies needed to diversify their exports away from such goods by championing infant industries using Import Substitution Industrialisation (ISI). Sunkel and Furtado's work, like Prebisch before them, principally focuses on locating and emphasising the obstacles to national economic development that arise from exogenous factors. Furtado, for example, was one of the first economists to express concern over the structural transformation of capitalism and the impact of transnational capital upon the economic autonomy of peripheral economies such as Brazil (1959).

Palma's final variant and the one with which he eventually associates his own work with is a conception of dependency that attempts to avoid the mechanico-formal theory of dependency by instead concentrating on 'concrete situations of dependency'. Many critics of Dependency theories (e.g. Larrain, 1989; Brewer, 1990) argue that much of the neo-Marxist approach, and Frank in particular, treat dependence as an external cause or static phenomenon (see Chapter 1). In contrast the work of Cardoso and Faletto (1979) sought to argue that real development can occur within the periphery despite the existence of dependent relations. Rather than a static unchanging logic, dependency for them is a general condition that is expressed through class struggles, social movements and conflict. In other words, changes in the capitalist world system will not produce automatic and correspondent changes across the periphery but rather find concrete expression through the interplay of *local* interests, state policies and class relations both domestic and external (1979, pp. 10–12).

In their 1979 work *Dependency and Development in Latin America*, Cardoso and Faletto are careful to avoid an abstract theory of dependence. Rather than talk about dependency as a theory they prefer to talk about concrete situations of dependence since for them dependency cannot be conceptualised without the concepts of surplus value, expropriation, accumulation and class relations. In other words, Dependency as a 'concept' must be defined within the theoretical framework of a classical Marxist theory of capitalism. Despite this, the general perception is of a determinist, meta-narrative that for the most part assures the impossibility of the development of the periphery within the current capitalist system (Larrain, 1989, p. 189). Putting aside the theoretical flaws and criticisms of orthodox Marxists (e.g. Brewer, 1990) one of the major criticisms of Frank's thesis of the development of underdevelopment has been that during the past three decades empirical evidence from a growing number of developing countries appeared to directly refute the hypothesis. Nowhere was this apparently more evident than in the 'miracle' economies of East Asia's Newly Industrializing Economies (NIEs). Beginning with the four 'tigers' of Hong Kong, Singapore, South Korea and Taiwan rapid industrialisation and record GNP growth rates spread across a growing number of Asian economies lifting them out both out of poverty and out of the periphery. In the wake of the original four NIEs, Indonesia, Malaysia, Thailand, soon followed, while behind them came communist Vietnam and much more spectacularly the Peoples' Republic of China. Despite this Frank (1984) maintained that such states were effectively exceptions that proved the general rule of his thesis. Their success, he maintained, had not occurred because of *autonomous* industrialisation but because of developments that had taken place *within* the world system.

Principal among these exogenous developments were dynamic changes in the international system that occurred as a result of the economic crises of the capitalist system from the 1970s onwards. As costs continued to rise in the developed world, resulting in a fall in surplus values, multinational capital began to increasingly transfer agricultural, mining and manufacturing processes to peripheral countries in order to reduce the costs of production. While the main reason for this industrial relocation has been to take advantage of cheap labour in the periphery it nevertheless created a *New International Division of Labour* (NIDL).

Furthermore, Frank noted that in the case of the original four tigers there were specific exceptional factors that had contributed to their economic success:

> South Korea and Taiwan clearly were created as 'independent' entities as a result of the Cold War against China and the Soviet Union and have been politically supported and economically subsidised as strategic pawns against them. Hong Kong emerged from history to a similarly peculiar position, and Singapore became a state because of the preponderance of the overseas Chinese population on the Malay peninsula.
>
> (Frank, 1984, p. 217)

Similar arguments can also be made for the development of Indonesia, Malaysia and Thailand. The Vietnam War, for example, provided a particular fillip to the economic development of Thailand. Economic and military aid to Thailand significantly upgraded and developed the country's physical infrastructure as well as providing for significant investments in skills training for the country's bureaucracy (cf. Rock, 1995).

In addition Frank dismissed the 'fruits' of such success. He maintained that export-oriented industrialisation both embraced and depended on authoritarianism and repression (to ensure low labour costs) as well as high levels of international borrowing which made these economies vulnerable to balance of payments crises. In addition technologies transferred to such states were 'the least remunerative and technologically obsolete [producing]…meagre benefits' (ibid., p. 219). Others (e.g. Chase-Dunn, Emmanuel, and Drangel) were unconvinced that the economic growth of the NIEs fundamentally altered the role of the periphery in the international division of labour. Industrialisation in the periphery was simply continuing the periphery's role in low-wage production. The manufactured goods produced were relatively low in value-added and reliant on labour-intensive low-wage industry (c.f. Shannon, 1990, p. 89). Furthermore the NIEs relied on the transfer of the obsolete technologies of industries in decline in the core in order to capture a segment of the world market (ibid., p. 103). Such mobility within the world system was not a refutation of Dependency rather it was precisely the role ascribed to the semi-periphery in the World Systems approach of Wallerstein and others.

As I noted in 2003, comparatively little has been written on Southeast Asia from either neo-Marxist position. Instead the majority of the literature has analysed the region's economic development from either a free-market neo-classical perspective (e.g. Freidman, 1982; Chowdhury and Islam, 1993) or with emphasis on a form of state-led development that has been dubbed the East Asian Developmental State (e.g. Jomo, 1993, 1994; Hill, 1994; Rock, 1995; Amsden, 1995, 2001). Although few and far between there have been some interpretations that closely pursued the dependency approach, of which the most famous is Yoshihara's *The Rise of Ersatz Capitalism in South-East Asia* (1988). Yoshihara echoing the views of Wallerstein and others argued that local capital was insignificant, subservient to international capital because of its limited bargaining power and dependence on foreign technology. Echoing Frank's earlier conclusions on the impossibility of 'real development' in the capitalist world system Yoshihara argued that under the present system, 'it would be impossible for them (Southeast Asian capitalists) to become technologically independent…Their technological dependency is not temporary but, being structural, semi-permanent' (p. 112).

Such arguments notwithstanding, the economic dynamism of the NIEs has continued even after the debilitating impact of the 1998 Asian Financial Crisis. This continued dynamism, coupled with average unemployment levels below the average for Western Europe and the United States, healthy trade surpluses with the United States and most European Union states, and rising levels of GNP per capita all challenge the view that such performances are either exceptions that prove the rule or are somehow entirely consistent with Wallerstein's initial conception of the semi-periphery. Similarly stressing exceptional exogenous factors overlooks the *specific* historic factors that differentiate these states from each other and from other parts of the developing world. Furthermore, supposedly semi-peripheral states such as Taiwan and South Korea have become major sources of foreign investment, both within other Asian NIEs (as world-system theorists predict), but more importantly also in core developed economies such as the United Kingdom[2] and even the United States (see below), while their range of exports has moved far beyond cheap mass produced obsolete manufactured goods.

A variation on the world-system notion of a threefold structural division of the world economy has emerged in the work of a number of scholars on East Asia. This variation stresses the creation of *regional* divisions of labour centred on regional hegemonic states. Cumings (1987) and Bernard and Ravenhill (1995), for example, argue that the continued dynamism of East and Southeast Asia is testimony to the creation by Japan of a regional hierarchy of production. This has been primarily achieved by massive Foreign Direct Investment (FDI) and the relocation of Japanese firms in the NIEs which in turn was the result of rising Japanese labour costs, and the appreciation of the Yen.

Bernard and Ravenhill take Cumings' argument a step further by stating that as Japanese manufactured goods reached the maturity of their product life cycle, rather than simply allowing the production of these goods to be transferred to the industrialising states of East Asia, Japanese capital instead has created a complex network of production that on the one hand allows the production of manufactured goods to occur in the semi-periphery while on the other ensures that crucial aspects of the product's technology are retained under Japanese control. Bernard and Ravenhill, for example, conclude their landmark study by stating that:

> [a]lthough Korea and Taiwan and more recently Malaysia and Thailand may be exporting products in the same industries in which Japan enjoyed success a few years ago; the context in which they are doing so is substantially different, in terms of both industrial organisation and geopolitics...Contrary to...predictions...the industrial exports of those countries remain heavily dependent on capital goods and technologies imported primarily from Japan...[t]his *dependence* on Japanese technology, coupled with the dependence of Japanese corporations on other locations in the region for lower cost for assembly operations, has produced a new *regional division of labour* that is based not on national economies but on regionalised networks of production.
>
> (1995, p. 207, my emphasis)

Consequently, despite much criticism both from within the Marxist tradition and from outside it, the above study clearly demonstrated that dependency analyses can continue to provide a valuable and insightful into the economic development of (semi)peripheral economies. Moreover studies like Bernard and Ravenhill's reveal that such analyses can incorporate very real socio-economic changes and comprehensive empirical data while remaining theoretically sound. To this end my 2004 monograph provided precisely this kind of in-depth empirical investigation of the political economy of Indonesia, Malaysia and Thailand, and sought to investigate whether the kind of technological dependencies highlighted by Bernard and Ravenhill were also a feature of their development. By way of a cross-national comparison the automotive industry was selected for particular scrutiny. What follows in the rest of this chapter is a review and re-investigation of that study of the automotive industry in Southeast Asia in order to demonstrate both the efficacy of such an investigation into concrete situations of dependence and that the specific situations originally highlighted remain evident five years after the initial study.

Examples of neo-dependency: The automotive industry in Southeast Asia

The automotive industry is an extraordinarily complex and dynamic industry, one that has undergone and continues to undergo technological changes that invariably impact upon the wider social organisation of production. Furthermore, it is one of the most global of all manufacturing industries employing in excess of 8 million people directly and 50 million in related sectors including automotive components, research and development, marketing, sales and servicing (OIAC, 2007). It is a sector dominated by a small number of global giants and one in which production has become organised on internationally integrated lines. Consequently, the industry presents remarkable opportunities for empirical investigation into concrete situations of dependency.

In my 2003 study I identified several factors that provide a substantive rationale for closer empirical investigation of this specific industry. Among these were the phenomenon of 'clustering'; the wider socio-economic impact of the industry; and the pivotal role that the industry has played in the post-war economic development of major Asian economies, most notably in Japan and South Korea (Abbott, 2003). The phenomenon of clustering explains why among industries selected by peripheral and semi-peripheral governments for promotion the automotive industry has figured quite often. One thinks not only of the national car projects or targeted ISI programmes in Southeast Asia, but also in Brazil, Mexico, Turkey and more recently in China and India. A modern automobile consists of over 3000 separate parts and components that use different processes many of which are manufactured by supplies in other industries. In addition the industry creates demand in backward-linked industries such as steel, rubber, glass, plastics, etc. and in downstream-linked industries such as oil, consumer credit, sales, maintenance and repairs. The work of Schumpeterian economists such as Chris Freeman have argued that industrial innovation is less of an incremental process and more like a series of 'explosions'. Furthermore when innovations occur rather than being random, they instead appear to be concentrated in certain sectors at certain times because they require many applications to adopt them in order to succeed. This is one reason advocated for why the automotive industry has been the source of so many technological innovations since the need for so many parts and components has created significant industrial clustering (Freeman, 1986).

In addition to clustering, the socio-economic impact of the automotive industry has had enormous ramifications. At least twice since its birth at the turn of the twentieth century the industry has fundamentally changed not only the way in which things are manufactured but also 'how we work... what we buy, how we think, and the way we live'

(Womack et al., 1990, p. 11). The first major shift was brought about by the introduction of the moving assembly by Henry Ford in 1913. Ford's innovation allowed for significant increases in the production of a limited range of standardised goods in large assembly plants using specialised machinery and relatively unskilled labour. This transformation of productive relations would result in improved productivity brought about by the economies of scale realised. The productivity gains would then create the scope for rising incomes which in turn would stimulate demand giving birth to mass consumerism. Such a 'virtuous cycle' of growth would result in the wider socio-economic impact of Ford's innovation being dubbed 'Fordism', a system of production that would have dominated the capitalist world system until the 1970s.

Again the industry would have a wider transformative impact following the introduction of just-in-time systems of production by Toyota. While both Eiji Toyoda, the founder of Toyota, and the engineer Taiichi Ohno drew inspiration from Henry Ford, their collective changes to automobile production would have enormous ramifications. *Toyotaism* sought to rationalise production by minimising stock losses on the one hand and maximising worker productivity on the other. The second aspect of the Toyota System of Production (TSP) has proved more controversial since it resulted in major changes to both the organisation of labour within the factory and to labour relations more generally.

Prior to the Second World War Japanese motor production was principally concentrated in trucks. After the Korean War, however, the industry shifted towards the production of passenger vehicles under the direction of the Ministry of International Trade and Industry. Following this shift Japan went from being an inconsequential world auto producer with less than 2 per cent of world production, to the largest auto producer nation worldwide by the 1980s – a position it continues to retain.[3] Similarly, in South Korea the government actively supported and encouraged the development of the nation's automobile industry (see Amsden, 1989). In 1960 South Korea's auto production was negligible, estimated at less than 0.1 per cent of global production. Even by the early 1980s the industry was still in its infancy producing some 20,000 units annually. However, rapid growth during the decade saw production rise by 1989 to nearly 900,000 units. Today with production of over four million vehicles South Korea is the 4th largest producer worldwide and the largest auto manufacturer outside Europe, Japan and North America (OAIC, 2007). Indeed of particular note for the wider discussion in this study of the semi-periphery is the fact that Korean production has surpassed that of all its European rivals with the exception of Germany.[4]

Dependent development in the semi-periphery? Malaysia and Thailand

Among the dynamic industrialising economies of Indonesia, Malaysia and Thailand government policy towards the automotive sector has varied significantly. While all governments recognised the strategic importance of the industry as part of their wider developmental strategies each nevertheless followed very different specific policies. The common denominator across the three countries was the adoption of Import Substitution policies in line with the analysis and prescriptions of the ECLA. However, by the 1980s policy began to significantly diverge with Malaysia formally adopting a national car project, Thailand opting to position itself as a platform for major global auto producers to export to the wider region and Indonesia largely continuing to pursue a range of policies that resulted in the fragmentation of the sector before launching the ill-fated national car project with Korean producer Kia that would fall victim to the Asian Financial Crisis and to the collapse of the Suharto regime in 1998. Nevertheless, despite these divergent policies all three continued and arguably continue to remain dependent on foreign expertise, foreign technologies and foreign markets. For the purposes of brevity this chapter will examine the Malaysian and Thai automotive industries.

Malaysia embarked on its ambitious national car project in 1983 when the then Prime Minister Mahathir concluded a deal with one of the smaller Japanese auto producers Mitsubishi. In the original deal in return for a 30 per cent stake in the newly created Proton car company, and most of the funds required to construct the plant and operating equipment, the Malaysian government imposed a 40 per cent import duty on Complete Knocked Down kits and raised a range of other tariffs in order to allow Proton to enjoy a 20–30 per cent price differential. Mahathir viewed the Proton project as a cornerstone of his Look East and Vision 2020 industrial strategies that he envisaged would catapult Malaysia into the ranks of the developed world, creating jobs, and stimulating industrial development and technological upgrading as a result of the clustering described earlier.

Initially Proton appeared to be an enormous success. Sheltered behind tariff barriers Proton's share of the national car market rose from 11 per cent on its launch in 1985, to a peak of 66–73 per cent. However, Proton would soon suffer from the classic dilemma faced by developing countries that had adopted a range of ISI policies in the 1960s and 1970s. While the company would exceed output of over

225,000 units the economies of scale reached were not sufficient to make the car globally competitive. In an industry where the top ten producers exceed two million units Proton remained a minnow (*The Economist*, 2006) reliant on domestic sales in a small market restricted in competition. Furthermore Proton's own domestic dominance was also challenged by the launch of a second national car company, Perodua in 1993.

Although ostensibly created to produce sub 1000cc vehicles the logic behind Mahathir's decision to launch a second national car project was to strengthen Proton's bargaining position with Mitsubishi amid growing frustration at the company's reluctance to transfer production of engines and engine parts to Malaysia. The new vehicle would introduce some competition for Proton and Mitsubishi, albeit at the lower end of the market, as well as providing additional opportunities for technological transfer and industrial clustering. Like the original deal Perodua was a joint venture between a local assembler and foreign capital, in this case Daihatsu.

The 1997 Asian Financial Crisis hit the Malaysian auto industry particularly hard with production declining by 67 per cent. The impact led the Malaysian government unilaterally, and controversially, to delay the implementation of tariff reductions it had agreed as part of the ASEAN Free Trade Agreement in a bid to shelter both companies, and Proton in particular, from cheaper foreign models assembled elsewhere in ASEAN.[5] Post-1997 Proton has seen its market share collapse, falling to a low of 24 per cent by 2007. In contrast, Perodua returned to growth and surpassed Proton's market share in 2006 to become the best-selling car company in Malaysia.[6]

In terms of technological development both projects appear to have had notable successes since both manufacturers have raised local content to in excess of 75–80 per cent for most models. However, much of this was only achieved as a result of specific government mandated local content requirements and the introduction of a Mandatory Deletion Programme in 1980 (the former was abolished as a result of the 1992 ASEAN Free Trade Agreement in 2002 while the latter is being phased out). In addition many of the 'local' companies that engage in the manufacture of component parts themselves have a high percentage of foreign capital participation and technical collaboration. Echoing the concerns of Bernard and Ravenhill (1995) and before them Yoshihara (1988) about 'technology-less development' a majority of these component producers are with Japanese partners. A report by AmBank in 2005, for example, noted that:

[g]enerally, local auto parts makers for Proton and Perodua have been slow in venturing overseas due to the bond with the Japanese OEMs that provided Proton and Perodua vendors technical expertise. In return for the technology transfer, these vendors were prohibited from overseas ventures unless *permitted* by or at the *discretion* of the Japanese partners.

(My emphasis)

In particular there have been significant technology bottlenecks in the production of transmission, engines and sub-components crucial to engine assembly (thermostats, insulators, cylinder heads valves, etc.). Although Proton has sought to buy its way out of such technology transfer limitation, e.g. by buying the specialist manufacturer Lotus in 1996, falling sales and increased global competition have led the government to try to secure a foreign purchaser for Proton. Although to date this has not happened, the company did renew its relationship with Mitsubishi in 2008, four years after Mitsubishi had sold its remaining stake in Proton.

What is most noticeable about the Thai automotive industry is that government industrial policy has been more 'liberal' than in Malaysia. After the Second World War, automobiles were still considered luxury items and a limited market was supplied by importation of Completely Built Units (CBUs) from the United Kingdom, France, Germany, Italy and the United States. However in response to the government's industrialisation programme import duties were raised on CBUs, and three companies began assembly of CKD packages between 1961 and 1962 with a 50 per cent import duty reduction (Nawadhinsukh, 1984). At first glance, the size of the Thai automobile market would suggest that it presented a ripe opportunity for the development of an equivalent indigenous automobile manufacturer given the size of its domestic market.

Nevertheless the government in Thailand eschewed the strategy of championing a national car opting instead to target both regulations and duties in order to increase and deepen the linkages between major foreign automobile producers and the Thai automotive industry. Local content requirements were first introduced by the Ministry of Industry in 1975 at 25 per cent for passenger vehicles and between 15 and 20 per cent for trucks and buses. These rose steadily throughout the 1970s and 1980s until in 1986 the MoI raised local content for passenger vehicles to 54 per cent where it remained until their abolition in 2000. Such regulations, and the attractiveness of the domestic market, contributed to local content for pickups, trucks and buses rising to over 70 per cent, with the market leader Toyota close to 100 per cent. In addition to regulations, the Thai government also offered a wide range of incentives to encourage the growth of automobile and automotive component exports including generous tax incentives and the waiving of foreign share ownership rules (Office of Industrial Economics). These were combined with an ambitious regional development programme aimed at turning the country into the 'Detroit of the East'.

The appreciation of the Japanese Yen in 1985 had a marked impact on the development of the Thai automotive industry as the cost of auto imports from Japan rose sharply with knock-on effects on the final price of automobiles. A study by the Thai Farmers Bank (1986) showed that as a result of the appreciation the price of passenger cars rose by US$2000–2500 baht and US$500 for pickups. Faced with such rising cost Japanese assemblers responded by implementing a satellite policy, encouraging their Tier-1[7] suppliers to relocate to Thailand and cluster around their assembly plants. These suppliers in turn established partnerships with local Thai companies boosting local content in the process. The net result has been the creation and development of over 600 auto parts makers making both OEM and REM. These in turn by the mid-1990s had become exporters in their own right. However, it is this author's contention that it was the exogenous factors rather than strategies adopted by the Thai government which was more responsible for the growth in local content and local auto parts production.

After 1991 the Thai government continued to make the auto industry more attractive to foreign investment by liberalising the sector further, for example, the import ban on CBUs was lifted and a new tariff regime introduced that markedly reduced tariff rates. It must be noted, however, that this was also due in part to pressure for Thailand conform to both the GATT and TRIMs to which it became a party in 1993. The net effect of the tariff cuts and more liberal regime proved an enormous stimulus to domestic demand which more than doubled, between 1991 and 1996, from 283,000 units to over 588,000. Both of these factors in turn led existing assemblers, mostly Japanese, to boost their investments and production, and to significant new investment from the 'big 3' US auto manufacturers (GM, Chrysler and Ford).

The story of the development of the Thai automotive component parts sector was very similar, beginning in the 1960s with its initial growth largely the result of government policies on local content. This in turn stimulated OEM and REM manufacturing (Abdulsomad, 1999) which was likewise given an additional stimulus after 1985 with the appreciation of the Yen, which as detailed above led many Japanese Tier-1 suppliers to relocate to Thailand. Toyota, for example, set up its Automobile Family Club in Thailand to supply parts to Toyota's assembly plants, while Ford's major supplier Delphi established a wholly owned subsidiary following the creation of the Rayong plant in 1996. Thus on the eve of the Asian Financial Crisis of 1997 there were in excess of 300 firms supplying OEM components to the major assemblers with a further 250 firms providing spare parts for the REM market (Abdulsomad, 2001) with many others supplying to Tier-1 and Tier-2 suppliers. Nevertheless although Thai companies made the most progress in labour-intensive segments of the industry, principally in simple rubber part, interior components and decorative items, elsewhere Thai manufacturers had made little impact.

The Asian Financial Crisis hit the Thai automotive industry particularly hard. While today over a third of all output is for export, in 1996 approximately 90 per cent of production was for the domestic market. Thus the contraction of the economy in 1997–1998 saw a precipitous decline in sales, down by 76 per cent to 144,000 units (Poapongsakorn, 2000). The decline in domestic demand also hit the automotive component parts sector. Over 200,000 jobs were lost in this sector between 1997 and 1999 as hundreds of local auto parts firms were either forced to close or were taken over by foreign firms (Bank of Thailand, 1999; *Bangkok Post*, 15 April 2000). Of those that survived many were forced to accept greater share ownership by foreign companies in return for injections of capital, often shifting decision-making decisively into the hands of the foreign shareholders. By 2002, for example, of the 700+ Tier-1 firms 40 per cent had a majority foreign ownership (Bangkok Post, 25 January 2002).

However the crisis was not all bad news for the industry. Given that the downturn in domestic demand struck at precisely the time most of the US automakers plants first came on stream Ford and General Motors (GM) opted, rather than moth-ball their investments, instead, to utilise excess capacity by supplying other markets worldwide from their Thai plants. For example, Ford had originally planned to produce over half of its Ranger pickup model for the domestic market. Following the depreciation of the baht the company instead opted to take advantage of lower costs instead producing nearly 80 per cent of all Rangers for export to over 40 different countries. Similarly when the crisis hit GM had to decide whether to abandon its investment in Rayong, or change its strategy. It chose the latter and decided to top-up its European production of the mini-van the Zaphira. Consequently whilst exports constituted only

11 per cent of total production in 1997, this had risen to 42 per cent in 1998 and approximately 49 per cent by 2001. This is increasingly true of component suppliers as well. While many suppliers were bankrupt as a result of the crisis exports of component parts doubled between 1996 and 1998. Again while government policy and strategy to the industry arguably facilitated development this major shift in the development of the industry was brought about by exogenous factors.

Nonetheless successive government policies towards the automotive industry did result in the development of indigenous component parts manufacturers and three major Thai automobile companies (Siam VMC, Thai Rung and Siam Motors). Today the industry as a whole is Thailand's third largest, employing over 200,000 people and producing over 1.2 million units a year. However, as in Malaysia the Thai automotive sector as a whole remains dominated by Japanese industry with a number of significant economic ramifications. Despite the development of indigenous Thai automotive companies and certain segments of the automotive component parts industry, Japanese companies still often direct the 'partnership' by operating satellite policies with their suppliers (Wattanuruk, 1994). Siam Motors, for example, assemble and produce component parts for Nissan and other companies within the group but are unable to sell these parts to other assemblers (Millar, 1995). Furthermore among ancillary firms most have strong connections with the principal assemblers. Nippon Denso (Thailand), producer of electrical equipment, is a division of Nippon Denso (Japan) which is closely related to Toyota and is intimately associated with Japanese assemblers. Such satellite strategies limit the opportunities available to Thai companies because the Japanese assemblers will generally source primarily from the suppliers that they encouraged to invest in Thailand with them. As the Thai government itself comments, 'most of these OEMs are mainly members of Japanese keiretsu groups supplying their own customer base' (Office of Industrial Economics, 2006, p. 17). Indeed these are precisely the kind of observations observed by Bernard and Ravenhill (1995) with regard to sections of manufacturing industry in South Korea and Taiwan.

With the liberalisation of the industry from the mid-1990s there has been an influx of investment from multinational Tier-1 suppliers. Denso (Japan) has significantly boosted its investments as has the US supplier Delphi. While such firms purchase parts from Tier-2 suppliers and below, their presence has led to significant restructuring and consolidation in the auto parts sector as a whole with the result that foreign companies now dominate it. In 2005 a study by Price Waterhouse

Coopers predicted that as a consequence of this trend by 2005 the number of Tier-1 suppliers would fall from 600 to 20. However to date this projection has not been realised. Indeed in 2006 there were over 709 companies involved in component supply in Thailand. Nevertheless of these approximately 40 per cent were foreign owned and a further 10 per cent had foreign participation.

Another major problem facing the Thai automotive industry is that it lacks the research and development capabilities necessary to compete in the global market. A study of the industry conducted in 1995 ranked the production technology of the industry as only C+ (UNICO, 1995) while the Thai Development Research Institute found that Thailand only had a revealed comparative advantage in the production of parts for trailers and trucks. More recent studies continue to express concerns about weaknesses in research and design, as well as infrastructure (Teoh et al., 2007).[8] Also highlighted as recurring weaknesses of the industry are the lack of skilled labour, poor managerial capacity and the weak technical base of the labour force as a whole. Prior to the Asian Financial Crisis only 3 per cent of the country's engineers worked in the automotive sector (Poapongsakorn, 2000), with many medium-sized having to operate with little engineering support.

Like Malaysia, the lack of technology transfer is a major complaint by the Thai government. While Thai firms have made successes in component parts manufacture, production of items such as: wire harnesses, alternators, motors, electrical signal lamps and spark plugs are virtually controlled by Japanese or Japanese-related factories. Although European and US companies appear less concerned with technology transfer and origin than their Japanese counterparts, the problem for these companies is that the dominance of the industry by the Japanese, and the brand loyalties that have developed over the decades has meant that their Tier-1 and Tier-2 suppliers have similarly had to relocate in Thailand. As a consequence the industry as a whole is faced with an uphill struggle to break both its technological and skill dependency and to move beyond basic assembly operation (Millar, 1995; Asiaweek, 2000).

Concluding remarks

The review of the current situation of the automotive industry in Southeast Asia demonstrates that the technological dependence continues to be a salient feature of the political economies of Malaysia and Thailand despite their continued macro-economic dynamism. The continued existence of specific dependencies in specific industrial sectors does appear to be a feature of East Asian development. For example, Sasuga (2008) also demonstrates that similar trends are present in the automotive industry in China. In this way it demonstrates how (i) the automobile industry occupies an important example of the type of production central to the development and character of the 'Asian tigers' and most poignantly of the character of the semi-periphery itself and (ii) demonstrates how a form of neo-Dependency can be understood and applied to the region's economic positioning within the overall global economy.

The review of the auto industry in this chapter has demonstrated that situations of dependence continue to be a feature of economic development in the capitalist world system. However, such dependence is neither a static phenomenon nor a simple process. Thus while dependency is a common feature of development in the East Asian semi-periphery the specific nature of that dependency, of how it is manifested, is a result both of the complex and dynamic relationship between state, local capital and foreign capital, and of changes and processes occurring in the regional and global economies. Furthermore the economic and technological development that has occurred is both real and substantial. Arguably such levels of dependent development have greatly exceeded those envisaged by Cardoso and Faletto in their concept of Associated Dependent Development. Nevertheless for all its dynamism development in the East Asian semi-periphery continues to remain dependent; dependent on foreign capital, foreign technology and foreign skills. Such 'situations of dependence' then present serious economic questions for governments and policymakers, and reveal that dependency remains a necessary conceptual tool of analysis despite the theoretical flaws of generalised theories of dependency.

Notes

1. Singer formulated his variant of the thesis in his 1949 publication *Post-War Relations between Underdeveloped and Industrialized Countries*. In this Singer explored the impact on wages and investment of unequal trade. Singer argued that core economies were able to retain greater savings through higher wages and profits than peripheral economies so that over time the terms of trade shifted in favour of 'investing' countries and away from 'borrowing' countries.
2. In 1995, for example, the Korean *Chaebol* Samsung chose Teeside in the Northeast of England to be its European headquarters. Since then other Korean and Taiwanese (Lucky Goldstar) investments have followed.

3. In 2006 Japanese automobile production stood at 11,596,327 units, approx. 16% of the total world output International Organization of Motor Vehicle Manufacturers.

4. At 4 million units Korea's production is almost 1 million units higher than France and three times that of Italy (OAIC, 2007).

5. This delay has continued throughout the recovery from the crisis with tariff reductions also offset by increased government subsidies to Proton.

6. Between 1999–2006 Proton's sales collapsed dramatically to post-crisis low of 115,000.

7. The automotive industry is for the most part organised into a supply chain consisting of various tiers. At the top of the chain the Original Equipment Manufacturer (Ford, Toyota, etc.) designs and assembles the car. Tier-1 suppliers manufacture and supply components directly to the automaker, and often exclusively for that OEM (e.g. a fuel pump). Second tier suppliers produce some of the simpler individual elements of the component the Tier-1 supplier manufactures (e.g., the housing of the fuel pump), while Tier-3 and Tier-4 suppliers are mainly involved in the supply of raw materials. Generally speaking the further down the supply chain you go the lower the technological sophistication of the components and the lower the value added.

8. A review of the industry by the Office of Industrial Economics in 2006 noted that because of such weaknesses many Thai-owned companies have to opt for foreign technical and research support on a product-by-product basis (2006, p. 18).

6
China and India – The New Powerhouses of the Semi-Periphery?

Gerard Downes

This chapter argues that if the South American/East Asian or state socialist model captured the post-war 'model' of the semi-periphery, then the post-Cold War states of China and India embody a new 'globalised' form. Rather than opting for a version of neo-mercantilism or protectionism, India and China have both based their economic strategies on globalising their economies by attracting multinational investment and Foreign Direct Investment (FDI). As a result both states, whilst different in terms of their overall economic output have maintained high economic growth through the emphasis on manufacturing and on facilitating cheap labour for MNCs. As a result both countries have become increasingly competitive not just in the global market, but also in organisations such as the WTO, where they have both become important regional players in terms of their influence. However, these moves have also served to merely consolidate their role as being dependent upon western investment and companies and both China and India remain severely underdeveloped in terms of their internal institutional development and in terms of living standards and marked inequality.

The semi-periphery as explanatory model

World Systems theory emphasises that the contemporary world system is a structure with an origin and trajectory that develops over time and within which there are fundamental qualitative social, political and economic developments, while also providing a compelling account of the causes of inequality and uneven development within the world system (Wilkin, 2008: 93). The concept of the semi-periphery is regarded by many analysts as the most constructive contribution of World Systems theory to our understanding of the global economy (see Peschard, 2005).

In his structuralist challenge to modernisation theory, Immanuel Wallerstein contended that the semi-peripheral zone has an intermediate role within the world system displaying certain features characteristic of the core and other characteristic of the periphery. As Griffin Cohen and Clarkson (2004) outline, the condition of semi-peripherality, whether it is defined as primarily social, cultural, economic or spatial, can be understood as having the both the consciousness of subordination and the means of resistance in contrast to the core which may lack the consciousness, or the periphery, which may lack the requisite means. Semi-peripheral countries such as China and India therefore, while conscious of their (apparent) subordination to the hegemonic power(s) at the centre of the global system, are endowed with sufficient resources to resist domination. Being in the incongruous and conflicting position of the semi-periphery in turn, distances actors from the deterministic assumptions of the centre while still being close enough to have an insider understanding of those assumptions and the state capacity to ameliorate them. This results in a scenario whereby the semi-periphery is a provocative environment from which to observe and study the dynamics of enhanced global integration and, in particular instances (which are far more numerous in India than in China), resistance to globalisation (ibid.).

While dependency theorists tended to focus on how various forms of subjugation and exploitation changed as the worlds capitalist economies became more integrated (see Arrighi, 1995), their approach appeared to condemn countries on the periphery to perpetual impoverishment without proposing a mechanism, other than violent revolution, to bring about significant improvement in their respective situations. Dependency theory was also limited by its rudimentary generalisations and the determinism of its economic analysis. In response to dependency theoretical inadequacies, Wallerstein (1979) offered a recognised 'semi-periphery' of countries, in particular the so-called Asian Tigers, that had radically ameliorated their respective positions within the world system since the early 1960s, and exhorted that their example offered other states on the periphery the hope of extricating themselves from the stasis of underdevelopment.

Nevertheless, the model of a semi-periphery remains empirically and theoretically problematic, particularly with regard to how it is delineated and measured. For example, the conception of a semi-periphery is almost entirely absent from dependency analysis, while it is treated by others as a residual category in which 'semi-peripheral' states are assumed to be eventually pulled towards either the core or periphery (Arrighi, 1985: 245). Outlining the respective cases of China and India as occupying the 'semi-periphery' is therefore inherently problematic as both states occupy an ambiguous position with the global political economy and also demonstrate notable characteristics of both core and peripheral states. In much of the literature pertaining to the economies of India and China since their respective liberalisation or marketisation processes began in 1978 (China) and 1991 (India), the performances of two rising powers are oft-times portrayed as symbiotic, a depiction which negates an essential element of their respective growth patterns and which leads to simplistic comparative analyses. It is instructive therefore to heed the obvious yet prescient words of one of globalisation's pre-eminent disciples when attempting to examine both China and India in tandem, namely that 'India is not China' (Wolf, 2008). Likewise, it is important to reflect as economic historian Angus Maddison (2007) states, that 'in many respects China is exceptional as it is and has been a larger political unit than any other' (Maddison, 2007: 15).

The development paths undertaken by both China and India have been very different, while the disparities between the two economies' integration into the world system are extensive. Any analysis of the economies of India and China must therefore be cognisant of their divergent developmental strategies and their differing degrees of integration into the global economy. When China began its process of economic liberalisation in 1978 it had a class structure and wage level congruent with those of a peripheral state, but an economic structure which resembled that of a semi-peripheral state (Li, 2005). As regards India, it can be asserted that within the context of the inter-regional flow of labour and high-tech skills, that it has graduated to 'core' status in the context of regional globalisation (see Adapa, 2007) Yet, paradoxically, despite an annual per capita income of less than US$500, a ranking below that of Sudan and Somalia on the Global Hunger Index (BBC, 2008) and an adult literacy rate of barely 50 per cent, India is one of the world's leading sources for human-capital intensive service products such as information technology software and biotechnology (Balasubramanyam, V. N. and A. Balasubramanyam, 1997).

Today, both China and India have the potential to advance into the core group of states given the extent of their resources and/or regional dominance (Wilkin, 2008), as well as their respective abilities to take advantage of the flexibilities offered by the cyclical depressions and other downturns in economic activity afflicting core states.

Nevertheless, it can be proffered that, in terms of productive activities, both states currently conform to Wallerstein's definition of semi-peripheral states as 'in part they act as a peripheral zone for core countries and in part they act as a core country for some peripheral areas' (Wallerstein, 1976: 463).

China as a semi-peripheral state

Wide-scale predictions of a great re-convergence in the global economy with China regaining its former pre-eminence are more indebted to historical determinism than coherent reasoning. While the tendency of many analysts to extrapolate from current growth rates and observe that China will supersede the United States as the world's largest economy by 2040 not only disregard the obstinacy of American hegemony, but are based upon the premature assumption that China's current upward economic trajectory will continue unabated. Pronouncements on the inevitability of China's resurgence as the globe's primary economic leviathan have tended to overlook the important question of whether China was ever an economic superpower, at least by contemporary standards. For hundreds of years, China was beholden to a cycle of growth without development, in which the only impetus behind the expansion of the economy was an increase in population, the majority of whose lives rarely rose above subsistence levels. This demographic shift intensified competition for limited resources, inflated the mortality rates from episodic famines and natural disasters and compelled the government to expend ever greater energy on social control.

While Andre Gunder Frank (1998) contends in his devastating critique of anti-historical and anti-scientific Eurocentricism that there existed a single global economy or world system with a world-wide division of labour complemented by multilateral trade from 1500 onwards which was dominated by Asia, and in particular China, until at least 1800, his analysis is not supported by economic historian Angus Maddison, who maintains that China's decline began long before the eighteenth century (Maddison, 2007). What is incontrovertible however is that between 1820 and 1952 as world product rose eightfold, China's share of global GDP fell from one third to one twentieth, while its real per capita income fell from parity to a quarter (Kynge, 2006). While many Asian countries were afflicted during this period by the twin impediments of moribund indigenous institutions which hindered development and foreign colonial domination, in China these problems were exacerbated further by internal disorder and civil war which had deleterious demographic and economic welfare effects on the Chinese population (Maddison, 2007).

China's gradual re-emergence from this economic devastation has led some observers to predict that a new 'commonwealth of civilisations' will emerge in the early decades of the twenty-first century. Giovanni Arrighi and Beverly Silver (1999), for example, in their analysis of the crises of British and Dutch hegemonies, assert that in both instances system-wide financial expansion preceded system-wide social conflict. In order for a non-catastrophic transition to a new 'commonwealth of civilisations' to take effect, adjustment and accommodation by the United States to its less-exalted status is a sine qua non, as is the emergence of a new global leadership from main centres of 'the re-emerging China-centred civilisation' which is willing to provide system-level solutions to system-level problems left behind by US hegemony (Arrighi and Silver, 1999: 289).

A central question to examine in the context of the contemporary global political economy therefore is what impact the economic re-emergence of China and striking growth of India will have upon the underlying dynamics of the extant world system, particularly if, as Wallerstein (1998) retains, the capitalist world economy has passed through its structurally temporal moments of genesis and development and has moved into its current moment of structural crisis? If this is the case, then the historical system is unlikely to witness the full acting out of another hegemonic cycle. Instead of greater modernisation and enhanced upward mobility, we may instead be entering an era of 'bifurcation' during which the world-system will be in disarray with many simultaneous possible solutions proffered to all the equations of the world system, resulting in a lack of predictability about short-term patterns. Emanating from this system, however, will be a new type of 'order', which according to Wallerstein, will be absolutely indeterminate, in the sense of being impossible to predict, as well as being subject to much agency, in the sense that 'even small pushes may have enormous impact on the path of the system in crisis' (Wallerstein, 1998).

The global economy at the end of the first decade of the twenty-first century can therefore be mapped along the 'B' or downward phase of the fifth Kondratieff long wave (The Age of Information and Telecommunications) wherein capital within the global economy is shifted from declining sectors into 'sunrise' industries leading core states to establish new leading sectors or monopolies in order for profit margins to return to levels that pertained during the expansionary phase of the current Kondratieff wave (Li, 2005). In order for capital to move from those declining sectors into new or expanding monopolies, the declining sectors must be re-located from the core to the periphery or semi-periphery thereby providing a historical moment in which opportunities for upward mobility within the system are fomented (Wallerstein, 1979: 69–72).

India and China are excellent exemplars of states that have exploited altered market structure to engage in upward mobility within the world system. For example, the downward phase of the current Kondratieff wave has coincided with China becoming the pre-eminent locus for FDI among countries of the periphery or semi-periphery. By early 2006, FDI in China had climbed to US$640 billion, leading to a scenario in which 60 per cent of exports from China in 2005 emanated from foreign-funded enterprises within its borders (Zhibin Gu, 2006). By 2002, China had overtaken the United States as the primary recipient of FDI on a global basis despite accounting for only 4 per cent of the world's Gross Domestic Product (GDP) and 5 per cent of global manufacturing exports (Li, 2005). China's investment-driven, export-oriented model vindicates Cardoso's (1973) contention that policy makers in countries of the periphery (and latterly semi-periphery) attract FDI by predicating growth upon low wages and providing myriad other incentives to potential investors resulting in dynamic, but uneven, growth.

The capitalist global economy has, in historical terms, been able to defer structural or terminal crises by means of expansion into overseas markets which are replete with reserves of cheap labour and natural resources, thereby preventing labour and environmental costs rising to the point of effectively endangering accumulation (Li, 2005). However, the limits of geographic expansion have now been superseded, a scenario which renders any further 'systemic cycle of accumulation' in the global economy inimical to existing reserves of labour and environment. In these circumstances, those populous countries with large reserves of cheap labour and underdeveloped or exploited natural resources, such as the bourgeoning economies of China and India, may prove to be the final repository for the expansion of the global economy and lead to a dramatic increase in labour and environmental costs in the early decades of the twenty-first century.

China's nationalist trade policy strategy has sought to meld Japanese-style mercantilism with 'soft totalitarianism' and has brought in its wake both environmental degradation and a chronic waste of resources through reckless investment (Prasad, 2008). Overall, this model of development remains one in which access to Chinese markets is impeded, and cheap labour, involving in certain instances children and prisoners, undercuts labour's ability to bargain for higher wages and benefits in competitor countries such as the United States (Johnson, 2000). China's model of economic development therefore highlights how the semi-periphery provides a source of labour that counteracts any upward pressure on wages in the core and also provides a new home for those labour-intensive industries that can no longer function profitably in the core, for example textiles and car assembly, as well as playing a fundamental role in stabilising the political structure of the world system (Hobden and Wyn Jones, 2008: 148). China's long-term economic strategy is to transform its state-owned enterprises (SOEs) into versions of Japan's vertical and horizontal *keiretsu* or South Korea's *chaebol*. By amalgamating profitable and financially precarious businesses together into developmental conglomerates and supplying them with credit, China hopes to create its own versions of corporations such as Samsung, Mitsubishi and Hyundai. Inevitably, consolidation on this scale will divide the labour force into an aristocracy of labour on the one hand, working for strategic corporations and ordinary workers on the other, in medium and small enterprises selling intermediate goods to the developmental conglomerates (Johnson, 2000).

China's marketisation process was initially ignited by the Communist Party's sense of self-preservation and maintenance of political command which resulted in mere modification of existing economic institutions and minimal political reform. The myth of a finely orchestrated reform project devised assiduously by the National Congress of the Communist Party of China delivering structured, gradual 'free-market' reforms is a forceful, but ultimately erroneous, one. As James Kynge (2006) highlights, many of the key events, and occurrences that propelled reform were, in fact, 'unplanned, unintended or completely accidental, in which much of the crucial impetus... sprang not so much from the implementation as from the miscarriage of central government policies' (Kynge, 2006: 14). Similarly, Chalmers Johnson (2000) asserts that 'China has never tried to become a "free-market economy" but rather to engage and exploit other market economies to become a great power' (Johnson, 2000: 173). Ultimately, China's process of economic reform or marketisation was a development to re-orient towards markets and to open up China to foreign capital. As Robert Weil (1994: 11) observes:

> All of China is engaged in a massive gamble, to see if it can reach a permanent level of higher development through what the government calls 'reforms' to achieve market socialism or 'a socialist system with special Chinese characteristics', while retaining national control

of the economy, preserving some degree of social ownership and planning and avoiding the worst dislocations normally associated with Third World capitalism.

(Weil, 1994: 11)

The economic reform process within China was triggered not by ideological reorientation but rather by a seemingly innocuous payments predicament that emanated from an abortive attempt to implement Deng Xiaoping's 'Ten-Year Plan for Economic Development'. Deng had gambled that his strategy could be paid for by the discovery of big new oil deposits and that China's planning apparatus could administer a massive programme of industrial plant import and construction (Naughton, 1996: 67). However, a negligible number of oil deposits were discovered meaning that many of the Ten-Year Plan's provisions had to be jettisoned while those that already been paid for left a sizable deficit in the Chinese state's finances. Deng therefore had to improvise in order to cajole some modicum of growth from a moribund economy that was only just beginning to recover from the excesses of Mao's disastrous Great Leap Forward (Kynge, 2006: 14; Peoples Daily, 2008).

China's phenomenal levels of growth since 1978 and its concomitant wide-scale integration into the global political economy has been largely predicated on exports by state-owned enterprises or foreign companies. Tellingly, at the instigation of the economic reform process, virtually all of productive assets in the Chinese economy were state-owned. Thirty years later, 70 per cent of China's productive wealth remained concentrated in the state. The decision to keep productive resources in state hands was a prescient one as it permitted the state to mobilise those resources during the rapid industrialisation of the 1980s and 1990s, while also serving the vital developmental purpose of creating infrastructure and expanding industrial capacity.

Another intrinsic element of China's developmental model was the creation of Special Economic Zones (SEZs) from 1980 onwards in which special tax incentives were given to foreign investments, commercial tax rates halved and import duties waived completely. The creation of the SEZs within China represented an attempt to replicate the strategy for economic success of Asian Tiger economies such as South Korea and Taiwan. The dismantling of China's commune system between 1977 and 1979 which destroyed the only rudimentary public health system in China, boosted agricultural production and led to a radical reform of the food sector and also freed up enormous reserves of labour for the manufacturing export sector. Subsequently, millions of rural peasants flocked into the SEZs, where low-wage labour in tandem with liberalised trade and investment, acted as a huge enticement for foreign technology and capital.

The location of the initial tranche of SEZs was no accident of geography as three of the first four zones – Shenzhen, Zhuhai and Shantou – were established in the southern province of Guangdong bordering Hong Kong, and in close proximity to Taiwan. However, in contrast to South Korea and Taiwan where the introduction of Export Processing Zones (EPZs) presaged rising wages, technology transfer and the introduction of a taxation regime; by 1990, average factory wages within the SEZs in Guangdong were a mere 50 cent per hour as opposed to US$4 an hour in neighbouring Hong Kong. In order to exploit this enormous discrepancy between the value of labour power in the two areas, by 1991 twenty-five thousand Hong Kong denizens had taken ownership of factories in Guangdong employing 3 million workers (Nema and Pokhariyal, 2008). The combination of low-cost labour, technology transfer, enormous reserves of capital and large incentives to foreign investment led to an export boom predicated on labour-intensive manufactures such as garments, textiles, footwear, plastic, toys and electronic assembly parts (Sachs, 2005: 161).

The marketisation process in China was given its greatest impetus by Zhu Rhongji, who acted as deputy prime minister from 1993 to 1998 and as prime minister from 1998 to 2003. Rhonji's avowed admiration of Thatcherism manifested itself in his dismantling of over 40,000 of China's SEOs from 1996 to 2001, a retrenching move which resulted in the loss of over 53 million jobs. In many cities of northern China half the workforce was made redundant overnight (Hutton, 2007). The drive to transform the majority of China's SOEs into share-holding or limited-liability companies was initiated at the 15th Chinese Communist Party Congress in September 1997 in response to claims by party apparatchiks that the continued subsidisation of loss-making SOEs, state control over certain input and output prices, rigid labour laws, easy access to bank credit and monopolistic market practices, had acted as strong incentives for SOE management to operate their firms inefficiently (Gabriel, 2006).

The rapid development of China's economy has led to intense degrees of urbanisation and proletarianisation which, hypothetically, should create favourable conditions for labour to organise, thereby presaging a concomitant increase in the protection of economic, political and social rights. Beverly Silver (2003), for example, contends that the pattern whereby the size of the industrial working class is declining in high-wage economies and simultaneously increasing in low-wage countries replicates labour shifts identified for the automobile and textile industries on a global scale. As a result of these combined processes the mass-production industrial proletariat has expanded speedily in both size and centrality in many low-wage economies and has led to a scenario in which, since the mid-1980s, Asia, and especially China, has been the key site of industrial expansion and new industrial working-class formation (Silver, 2003: 106).

However, the secular trends of rising real wages and taxation which have marked the entire life span of capitalism as a historical system (Wallerstein, 1979) do not necessarily correspond to China's developmental path and neglect a notable tendency whereby, as inter-state competition intensifies to lure investors to EPZs, labour costs and environmental standards are held low, resulting in extensive social dumping. Pakistan, for example, in response to a complaint from the International Labour Organisation (ILO) admitted that it had exempted its EPZs from certain labour laws because of requests from Daewoo, while the governments of Namibia and Zimbabwe retained that choosing not to apply certain national labour regulations would be decisive for the success of their respective EPZs (Moran, 2002: 82).

Within China, while wages of migrant workers have risen since marketisation began in 1978, particularly for those working in factories along the east and south coasts, in historical terms they remain risible. Chinese workers are unable to form independent trade unions and must rely upon the Communist Party-controlled All-China Federation of Trade Unions, which has proved readily compliant to the demands of foreign investors and inimical to the interests of its 134 million members (O'Brien and Williams, 2004: 253). The fact that over 700 million people in China live on less than US$2 per day provides an enormous pool of reserve labour willing to work at wage levels below those which prevailed at the start of the Industrial Revolution in Britain. For example, when the wages of a modern-day semi-skilled migrant worker in the bourgeoning municipality of Chongqing are adjusted for time and converted into Chinese renminbi they are less than half the wage levels demanded by handloom operators in the Weavers' Minimum Wage Bill rejected by the House of Commons in May 1808 (Kynge, 2006: 30).

While there are well-documented accounts of labour discontent within China (see for example, Solinger, 2003; Cody, 2004, 2005) many of these protests have been against job losses as well as unpaid pensions and wages resulting from the dismantling of China's welfare state and state-owned industrial enterprises amid the country's movement towards greater integration with the global self-regulating market. Labour unrest within China therefore has been accompanied by a significant Polanyi-type counter-movement for the self-protection of society against the disruption of established ways of life and livelihood (Arrighi and Silver, 2003: 354).

India as a semi-peripheral state

In contrast to the development path undertaken by China and states which have adopted the classic Asia strategy of exporting labour-intensive, low-cost manufactured goods, India's growth has been driven by large-scale service-sector exports in capital and knowledge-intensive manufacturing such as information technology. Despite triumphalist pronouncements that India's success in high-end capital-intensive sectors is indebted to the 1991 New Economic Policy (NEP) which initiated a wide-scale series of liberal market reforms, it was the nakedly neo-mercantilist decision by the Janata government to effectively expel IBM from India in November 1977 for non-compliance with the country's 1973 Foreign Exchange Regulation Act, which proved to be the catalyst for the boom in India's indigenous software sector.

The radical re-orientation of the India's developmental strategy from Import Substitution Industrialisation (ISI) since independence to liberalisation in July 1991 derived from an unprecedented series of crises encompassing a severe balance of payments emergency, exchange rate management, fiscal and monetary policies, domestic resource allocation trends and public sector management (Singh, 1997: 58). India's overhaul of its ISI strategy also needs to be set within the context of growing interdependence throughout the global political economy. By the early 1990s, transformations in the financial structure were manifested through policies of deregulation and privatisation, which led to increased capital mobility on a global scale. In the production structure, the increased diffusion of existing technologies led to greater technology transfer to developing economies. The rise of international regimes and the increasing characterisation of the international system as a 'plurilateral' structure (Cerny, 1995) helped to place economic concerns more centrally on states' international agendas, while the demise of the Soviet Union enhanced competition between developing country markets, such as Brazil, China and India, for FDI, bank credit and government aid, market shares and for multinationals' capital and technology (Strange, 1996).

In contrast to the extraordinary economic success of China's SEZs, India's experience of EPZs indicates that since the first zone was established in Kandla, Gujarat in 1965, the EPZs have had considerable difficulty in attracting both FDI and domestic inward investment for multifarious reasons. Overall, the extent of FDI into India while substantial (US$15.7 billion in 2006) lags a long way behind that of China's FDI of US$69.5 billion the same year (**Global Business Policy Council, 2007**). One of the primary reasons for this disparity is that while SEZs operate with lax labour and environmental standards in China, resistance within India has grown to the concept of the provision of specific laws and regulations which prioritise EPZs at the expense of development in other sectors and regions. For example, in 2005 the Indian National Congress-led government sought to introduce a series of retrenchment reforms which endeavoured to establish a large degree of labour market flexibility within the EPZs. These measures were successfully resisted by elements within the governing United Progressive Alliance (UPA) coalition who were opposed to the further diminishing of labour protection for workers in India (Sharma, 2006). The development of India's EPZs are further inhibited by the lack of a natural conduit for capital and the movement of goods redolent of the manner in which neighbouring Hong Kong and Taiwan act as gateways for capital and goods emanating from the EPZs in China's Guangdong province.

Notwithstanding the inherent difficulties of initiating labour-intensive manufacturing on the kind of scale witnessed in China, India has latterly become a net exporter of FDI and retains a capacity to attract capital which confers upon it a degree of economic power commensurate with that of a regional power. Through its flagship Indian Institutes of Technology and the Indian Institute of Sciences, India annually produces hundreds of thousands of scientists and engineers who have enhanced India's reputation in knowledge-intensive sectors such as information technology, biotechnology and the space industry (Perkovich, 2003: 131). Nevertheless, while lucrative in terms of accentuating levels of GDP growth, these high-end technologies are relatively risible as employment providers, a scenario that has led to criticism that the government's emphasis on supporting high-technology and service industries has been undertaken at the expense of helping the overwhelming majority of India's population that is reliant on small-scale agricultural production (O'Brien and Williams, 2004). For example, while India's software companies such as Tata Consultancy Services, Sycamore and Infosys Technologies have been hugely successful enterprises, the information technology industry as a whole employs a mere one and a half million people amid a labour pool of 470 million people (Prestowitz, 2005). Moreover, the geographic disparity in the location of India's software firms is reflected in the fact that almost 80 per cent of the industry is concentrated in the cities of Bangalore, Mumbai and Delhi (Balasubramanyam, V. N. and A. Balasubramanyam, 1997; Perkovich, 2003).

Despite the panoply of economic statistics that gushingly depict twenty-first century India as an exemplar of social and economic mobility, the country lags significantly behind even lesser resourced countries of the semi-periphery and periphery in terms of other key developmental indicators. In conjunction with rising levels of inequality since the initiation of the NEP, child malnutrition is twice the level which pertains overall on the African continent (Hunter Wade, 2008: 393). In spite of its booming information technology and biotechnology industries and the embrace of neo-liberal economic norms since 1991, per capita income within India (US$530 in 2003) adjusted to purchasing power parity [PPP] (US$3000 in 2003) compares very unfavourably with China (US$6800 adjusted to PPP) (Srinivasan and Tendulkar, 2003). According to the UN Human Development Index (HDI) which accesses how states provide their citizens' basic needs by measuring four variables (life expectancy at birth, adult literacy rate, school enrolment and GDP per capita), India at the beginning of the twenty-first century ranked 115th out of the 162 countries for which data were accessible (The Hindu, 2001). India's infant mortality rate in 2004 (62 per 1000 live births) was greater than that of neighbouring Bangladesh (56.4 per 1000 live births) (World Bank, 2005). Three hundred million Indians live on less than a dollar a day; 45 per cent of children are malnourished, while less than half of India's 500,000 villages are connected to an electricity grid (Guha, 2007). Similarly to China, enormous regional disparities exist within India: the neighbouring north-eastern states of Bihar and Uttar Pradesh, for example, account for 42.5 per cent of India's poor (Prestowitz, 2005).

Notwithstanding the structural impediments to transformation which have plagued India since the colonial era, its international status has been latterly enhanced as evidenced by India's forthright membership of several of the institutions of global governance such as the World Trade Organization (WTO). India has long-established status as a regional leader and its role in the vanguard of highly influential alliances such as the G20[1] group of developing countries which emerged in August 2003 prior to the WTO Ministerial Conference in Cancun, Mexico and the G8+5 provides it with far greater authority at multilateral level than many other semi-peripheral states.[2] Whereas India's trade negotiators proved supine in the Uruguay Round from 1986 to 1993, the country's growing economic competitiveness, in tandem with that of China, was reflected in the crucial talks on the Doha Development Round in July 2008 where both countries were able to face down the United States' negotiators and effectively scupper any potential deal due to objections voiced by the two countries over the contentious issue of safeguard mechanisms used to stymie import surges.

In contrast to India which was one of the 23 founding Contracting Parties to the General Agreement on Tariffs and Trade (GATT) that was initiated in October 1947, China only joined GATT's successor organisation, the WTO, in September 2001 after 15 years of oft-times fractious negotiations. The primary goal of the China's trade representatives throughout the negotiations was to gain admission to the WTO for China with the status of a developing country, a move which would exempt the country from certain provisions of WTO agreements such as subsidies for domestic industries and the granting of unimpeded market access to foreign competitors (Johnson, 2000). The debate as to whether China would join the WTO with the status of a 'developed' or 'developing' country is indicative of how the country's position has not been clearly defined within the global political economy.

China's membership of the WTO has already proved highly contentious. For example, when its highly successful textile industry was opened to further global competition after acceding to WTO membership, it led to the invocation of a raft of anti-dumping clauses and import quotas by the United States and the European Union, both of whom threatened China with a trade war in the wake of the abolition of the Multi Fibre Agreement in January 2005. The accession of China into the WTO will in the long term have a significant impact on the current regime of accumulation as it marks the first time in its history that China has agreed voluntarily to open up its markets according to a set of rules and principles set down by an extra-territorial body (Kynge, 2006: 117). China's trade negotiators in the WTO have given more than 600 market-access commitments in the accession document, excluding other market-access commitments made on specific products and sectors in the goods and services schedules. Restructuring and retrenchment will be required under WTO rules of, for example, China's capital-intensive automobile industry where 125 car companies are to consolidate into between three and six firms in order to resist competitive pressures from foreign manufacturers (Zhibin Gu, 2006).

The necessity of profound structural changes within the Chinese economy as its economy becomes further embedded within the processes of globalisation highlights how many of the pronouncements acclaiming a resurgent, behemoth China often fail to analyse many of the internal, often contradictory dynamics which have the potential to produce enormous social dislocation and alienation. For example, China's pattern of growth has been geographically distorted towards coastal regions while many inland areas have either stagnated or regressed, leading to enormous migration (estimates emanating from the unreliable National Bureau of Statistics range from 150 million to 200 million people) from the interior to the coastal regions.

Consequently, patterns of inequality between the regions are higher than for any other comparable country in the world. To take one example, the ratio of the average income of China's richest (Guangdong) to poorest province (Guizhou) rose to 4.3 per cent by 1993 and remained at that rate in the period 1998–2001. Corresponding figures for India and the United States in the late 1990s were 4.2 and 1.9 per cent, respectively (Hunter Wade, 2008: 393). A further predicament that China's economic policy makers must overcome is the wild vacillations in the rate of growth which have stimulated sharp booms wherein rapidly rising prices give way to periods of stagnation. In attempting to extricate its economy from cyclical downturns, China risks becoming embroiled in a classic crisis of over-production, particularly as the global economy further stagnates.

The perennial question of political reform and the sustainability of political authoritarianism will be one of the most exigent issues to be resolved in China within the next decade. China's centralised apparatus is no longer compatible with the dynamism of a decentralised and diverse market economy, which depends on migration, multiple bases of power, strong growth rates and a high degree of regional, cultural, ethnic and linguistic diversity (Sachs, 2005: 167). Part of the reason for China's economic success has been the greater empowerment of provincial and local governments to experiment by allowing for diversity, creating a more complex division of labour and enabling mobility. However, extensive corruption in local and regional governments resulting from the systemic inadequacies that have accompanied China's transition to marketisation is undermining the legitimacy of the one-party system:

The overarching contradiction of an omnipotent, single-party regime that combines the characteristics of state capitalism with a market orientation and endowed with the ability to bankroll its systemic inefficiencies is not maintainable in the long term. China's political system fails to permit the checks and balances necessary to administer a market economy so that each organ of government and each economic entity are regulated by an external or independent body (Kynge, 2006: 186). The Chinese Communist Party has recognised the incongruity of this paradoxical situation by pouring enormous energy and resources into attempting to create a system of self-regulation in politics, law and the economy, under which 'all parties are equal but the Party is more equal than the others' (ibid., 2006: 187).

An additional problem faced by Chinese policy makers which may serve to underline the country's social fragility is that the dismantling of China's commune system, which destroyed in turn the only pubic health care system within the country, means that, since the 1980s, China's rural poor have had to depend on out-of-pocket payments for their health expenses. This development has had catastrophic consequences such as rising infant mortality rates in some rural areas while wide-scale epidemics, such as the SARS pandemic in 2003, highlight further how China no longer has a functioning public health system in rural areas capable of surveillance and control of epidemic diseases (Sachs, 2005).

Similarly, while India does not face an impeding crisis of political reform, it will undoubtedly encounter other long-term structural problems certain to undermine its developmental capacity. Since independence in 1947 India's policy makers have failed to initiate any worthwhile mass literacy programme or a modicum of significant land reform. As a result, India has singularly failed to repeat the example of East Asian developmental states such as South Korea where the landed aristocracy was emasculated by land reform and the peasantry atomised into smallholders (Heller, 1999: 32). A further structural difficulty that must be confronted by India's legislators is that while the country boasts world-class information technology and biotechnology sectors, these industries' respective impacts on long-standing structural unemployment is almost negligible. Furthermore, India's recent economic success has complicated the conduct of macro-economic policies. For example, the rising levels of FDI into India have stimulated a rapid appreciation of the exchange rate, in turn harming external competitiveness and stimulating a stock market boom with many similarities to the speculative 'Dot Com Bubble' which lasted from 1995 to 2001.

Conclusion

Wallerstein's assessment that semi-peripheral states are an important mechanism for restructuring the world economy has particular resonance with regard to the burgeoning economies of China and India. China, for example, has now displaced Japan as the principal US creditor and has become the new focus of Asian economic regionalism (Cox, 2004: 313). Furthermore, as semi-peripheral states China and India are imbued with the capacity to 'protect' the world system in that they 'partially deflect the political pressures which groups primarily located in peripheral areas might otherwise direct against core states' (Wallerstein, 1974: 349–350).

Nevertheless, China and India are structurally deficient in certain key areas and face several of the common problems encountered by erstwhile peripheral countries such as weak financial markets and regulatory structures as well as extortionate levels of income and equality disparities which threaten to undermine social stability, particularly as the impact of globalisation renders the semi-periphery ever more vulnerable to widening inequality. China also faces the problem of lacking an independent judicial and legal system and being beholden to an authoritarian political elite which tolerates excessive levels of corruption, particularly at local and regional governmental levels (Zhibin Gu, 2006: 47). Political reform within China is inevitable as the country engages in ever more rapacious forms of marketisation. Whether this reform will lead to movements of the left and right finding fertile ground as such movements tend to do in semi-peripheral and second-tier core states due to the contradictory location of semi-peripheral areas in the larger world-system (see Chase-Dunn, 1998: 213) is unclear.

Hypothetically, those aspects of globalisation, for example internationalisation of production, which have altered market structure and resulted in the concentration of the bulk of the material production facilities and organised working classes in the countries of the periphery and semi-periphery should provide those states with an unparalleled degree of bargaining leverage against core states (Li, 2005). Such an alteration empowers semi-peripheral states such as China and India to utilise their leverage in order to transform the world system from one based on highly unequal exchange and monopolistic profits and to provide system-level solutions to the system-level problems left by the world market economy. However, the evidence so far encountered regarding the possibility of such a transformation emanating from those two states is dispiriting in the extreme.

Notes

1. Although the number of members of the G20 fluctuates, the number 20 has been retained by the group to signify the date on which the grouping was founded, 20 August 2003.
2. India forms part of the so-called G4 leadership of the G20 along with South Africa, China and Brazil.

7
'Upper Volta with Gas'? Russia as a Semi-Peripheral State

Rick Simon

Speaking in respect of Russia's energy conflict with Ukraine at the end of 2005, Aleksandr Lebedev, millionaire businessman and erstwhile deputy of the Russian State Duma, referred to Russia as 'Upper Volta with gas' (Parfitt 2006) in a deliberate echo of the widespread suggestion that the Soviet Union in the early 1980s had become 'Upper Volta with rockets', a third world state that just happened to have nuclear weapons. Like the Potëmkin villages of the eighteenth century, which were all façade and no substance, the Soviet Union had become a Potëmkin state. Now, Lebedev was saying, the changes that had taken place since 1991 had left Russia essentially unaltered – the nuclear façade had simply been replaced by energy.

Although amusing, Lebedev's comment is, however, as inaccurate as its Soviet-era equivalent. In reality, Russia has never been on a par with a peripheral state like Upper Volta (now Burkina Faso), but neither is it a leading player in the capitalist world-economy. Instead, Russia displays many features characteristic of the semi-periphery. I will argue, however, that Russia is a not a typical semi-peripheral state, however, having undergone a process of industrialisation essentially outside of the capitalist world-system and, more recently, a transformation that I would characterise as a form of passive revolution.[1]

Under Yeltsin, Putin, and now Medvedev, Russia has been reintegrated into the global capitalist economy, joining the IMF and World Bank and pursuing membership of the WTO. After the disastrous economic collapse under Yeltsin, Putin's Russia experienced growth rates averaging 6 per cent per annum, lifting it to seventh in the world in terms of GDP. Windfall incomes from rapidly rising energy prices have enabled foreign debt to be substantially paid off, average income to be increased, unemployment to be reduced, and leverage to be exercised.

The euphoria generated by such a recovery has been dampened, however, by the financial crisis of 2008 which has revealed inherent weaknesses deriving, in particular, from dependence on energy exports. In this chapter I will discuss the nature of Russia's contemporary status but this needs to be done in the context of development in both the Tsarist and Soviet periods. After establishing briefly the key features of a semi-peripheral state, I will, therefore, discuss Russia's historical development as a semi-peripheral state and the specificities of the Soviet Union's relationship to the capitalist world-economy before moving on to examine the nature of contemporary Russia's semi-peripherality. In the conclusion I will assess Russia's prospects and potential directions for further development.

What is the semi-periphery?

The contemporary world-system is characterised by a single, capitalist, mode of production combined with a fragmented system of nation-states. Over several centuries, the capitalist world-system expanded from its west European core to encompass ever greater areas, creating a global division of labour through a process of 'combined and uneven development' in which each state embodies a particular mix of core (capital-intensive) and peripheral (labour-intensive) production techniques. This seemingly technical 'division of labour' conceals a hierarchy of power through which the advanced capitalist core exploits the periphery, enabling it to further the accumulation of capital. Between core and periphery there exists an intermediate zone, the semi-periphery, which includes those states, Wallerstein (2000 [1974]: 89) argues, with an approximate balance between core and peripheral activities.

The semi-periphery's intermediate relationship produces conflicting pressures which have implications both for the behaviour of semi-peripheral states in the world-system and for their internal economic and political structures. First, the capacity of semi-peripheral states to attract declining industries from the core leads to a 'symbiotic and self-perpetuating' relationship between core and semi-periphery, the latter acting as a kind of 'safety valve' and thereby extending the core capitalists' capacity to maintain the profitability of a particular production process (Babones 2005: 32). Chase-Dunn suggests that the semi-periphery can, therefore, act 'to depolarize the core/periphery hierarchy by providing intermediate actors whose very presence reduces the salience of potential conflict along the core/periphery dimension of inequality' (1998: 211). Second, and potentially disruptive to core-semi-periphery relations, is the fact that a semi-peripheral state looks in two different directions – on the one hand, to the core and, on the other, to the periphery, promoting a contradictory and potentially highly conflictual social structure as different elements of the nascent capitalist class are linked either to the core or periphery and the working class is also divided between those working in industries constituting a link in core-dominated production networks, and those in peripheral industries and agriculture. Such potential conflict makes the semi-periphery, according to Chase-Dunn (1998: 341), 'the weak link in the capitalist world-system' and thus the primary locus of revolutionary and counter-revolutionary movements and regimes. Third, the desire to overcome underdevelopment and re-order relations with the core and periphery, the weakness of the bourgeoisie, and the frequently heightened nature of class conflict, pushes the state apparatus itself into a more prominent role than is usually seen in either the core or periphery.

The hierarchy in the global economy is not fixed but neither is it very fluid. Semi-peripheral states become dependent on particular forms of activity, for example the exploitation of natural resources, which skew their economic structure in such a way that they become locked into a particular pattern of development from which extrication becomes almost impossible. In these circumstances, Giovanni Arrighi argues, a semi-peripheral state can follow two basic alternative paths of development: it can struggle either against exclusion from the world-system or against exploitation by the core. The former entails becoming more integrated into the global division of labour in order to gain a secure niche, but at the same time being subjected to more intensive exploitation by core states and excluded from the most rewarding economic activities. Any industrial development results from local elites taking advantage of world-systemic forces that they themselves have not initiated (Arrighi 1990: 17–18, 29). The alternative is to limit exploitation by creating a division of labour autonomous from the axial division of labour of the capitalist world-economy. This approach entails, first, undertaking a broad range of economic activities, self-exclusion from relations of unequal exchange with core states, and active involvement in unequal exchange with peripheral states supplying high-wage labour commodities in return for low-wage labour commodities. Success in this particular undertaking leads, however, to self-exclusion from the wealthiest markets and sources of innovation (Arrighi 1990: 17–18). As we shall see, Russia, during the Soviet era, followed the latter strategy but has been pulled between these two strategies under Yeltsin and Putin.

Russia's historical semi-peripherality

Prior to the late eighteenth century, Wallerstein argues, Russia constituted its own world-system in the 'external arena' to the burgeoning capitalist world-system. As capitalism began to develop in its core areas in Western Europe it required resources and markets leading to geographical expansion into, and the absorption of, these external areas. Russia, which had undergone industrial, state and military development especially from the reign of Catherine the Great, was thus integrated into the emergent capitalist world-economy as part of its semi-periphery (Wallerstein 1989: 137, 2000 [1974]: 94).

Russia's integration was enabled not through industrial production, however, but primarily through the export of grain (Wallerstein 1989: 162). Pressure from Western Europe transformed Russia's domestic production and, thus, the composition of its exports. Russia's iron industry, unable to compete with developing British technology, collapsed in the early nineteenth century. Exports of iron were replaced by wheat, raising the proportion of primary products and foodstuffs in Russia's exports by the mid-nineteenth century from 71 to 95 per cent, while that of manufactures decreased from 20 to 2.5 per cent (Wallerstein 1989: 141–142). Russia survived total deindustrialisation by maintaining an internal market for textiles through high tariff barriers and imports of technology. The strength of its army and expansion eastwards and southwards also enabled Russia to play an enhanced role in the world-system, ensuring its semi-peripheral, rather than peripheral, status (Wallerstein 1989: 152, 187). Overall, however, Russia's comparative backwardness was reinforced, its technological shortcomings being cruelly exposed by the Crimean War (1854–1856).

In the late nineteenth century, foreign investment and the latest technology flowed into extractive industries, infrastructure, and some manufacturing sectors, accelerating industrialisation and drawing the Russian economy into global circuits of capital and promoting the emergence of capitalist relations of production. Agriculture, on the other hand, continued to utilise primitive production techniques prompting Trotsky (1977: 25–33) to argue that the Russian economy was characterised by 'combined and uneven development', which served to buttress Russia's semi-peripheral position in the capitalist world-system rather than overcome it.

The opportunity for breaking away from the imposed pattern of development arose with the global crisis precipitated by the First World War, the consequent crisis of the Tsarist system, and the Bolshevik seizure of power in October 1917. After the destruction and enforced nationalisation and centralisation of the Civil War period (1918–1921), the New Economic Policy (NEP) was introduced to stabilise and rebuild the Russian economy. Through the NEP, Russia re-engaged with the capitalist world-economy, exporting grain and oil to finance industrial development. Such dependence on global markets proved crucial to the timing of more radical economic transformation. Kagarlitsky (2008: 277) argues that international grain prices declined precipitously in the late 1920s threatening the entire industrialisation strategy by reducing Soviet capacity to purchase the latest technology. In the face of deteriorating terms of trade across the board, anything of value was exported in the pursuit of scarce foreign currency and the Stalin leadership switched to a policy of forcible extraction of the necessary resources from the peasantry. Through the state's monopoly of foreign trade and exploitation of its own resources industrialisation was advanced, domestic production substituted for imports, and the Soviet Union was able to cut itself off from the capitalist world-economy. Thus, under Stalin, industrialisation occurred, crucially for the character of Russia's contemporary semi-peripherality, *outside* of the capitalist world-system.

Soviet industry was developed by meeting plan targets rather than generating surplus value in a competitive market environment. Moreover, the political priorities of defence and industrialisation fostered the emergence of an economic and ministerial structure geared towards heavy industry and the promotion of sectoral interests. The elite which emerged from this environment could not develop the forces of production or change Soviet economic priorities towards more consumer-oriented production and industry increasingly lagged technologically behind the more advanced capitalist states.

By withdrawing from the capitalist world-system and embarking on a form of industrial development substantially different from that of the capitalist states, the Soviet Union and other 'socialist' states ceased, however, to play the role traditionally associated with the semi-periphery or periphery. Furthermore, the Soviet Union's relationship with Eastern Europe was in many respects the reverse of that typical of capitalist core-periphery relations in that the USSR provided predominantly energy and raw materials, at well below world market prices, in return for finished products.

This is not to say that the 'socialist' bloc's parallel development was unaffected by the capitalist world-economy – far from it. The Soviet Union had always engaged in limited trade with non-socialist states but, again, it was not the pattern typical of a core-semi-periphery relationship. In 1950, the structure of Soviet exports was one where consumer goods (4.9 per cent) and industrial goods (12.3 per cent) made up a substantially greater proportion of exports than energy (3.9 per cent) (Robinson 2004: 6). By the 1960s, however, the political unity of the 'socialist' bloc had been rent by the Sino-Soviet split and the incapacity of the Soviet model of socialism to promote sustained long-term growth necessitated the implementation of economic reform across the Soviet bloc and re-engagement with global capitalism on a much larger scale. Against the background of Détente between the two superpowers and developing recession in the capitalist world-economy, the Soviet Union began to revert to forms more typical of a semi-peripheral state as exports of energy rather than finished industrial products predominated. By 1987, the USSR was the world's biggest producer of oil and energy sector products constituted 46 per cent of exports. In the same year, the export to primarily peripheral and semi-peripheral states of the Soviet Union's most globally competitive manufactured products, armaments, also reached a peak when weapons worth $31 billion were exported (Lushin and Oppenheimer 2001: 271).

From the late 1960s, the East European states also began to feel the squeeze. Most states increasingly sought to sell their more desirable commodities on the world markets for hard currency in order to pay off their rapidly accumulating debts while supplying their Soviet comrades with goods of ever poorer quality. By reorienting towards the capitalist world-economy, Eastern Europe became more and more of a burden on the Soviet Union, hindering the latter's own capacity to restructure its economy.

The capitalist world-economy was increasingly dominated from the late 1970s by neo-liberal ideas and practices which emphasised free markets and the rolling back of the state. In the United States and the United Kingdom, this combined with an aggressive, anti-communist foreign policy (the Second Cold War), designed to dismantle communism as an alternative world-system, which fed into the USSR's domestic political and economic crisis.

Against this backdrop, Gorbachev initiated *perestroika*, creating the conditions for what Gramsci termed as 'passive revolution' – a top-down transformation of Soviet social relations and reintegration into the capitalist world-economy (Simon 2010). Through *perestroika* the state monopoly of foreign trade began to be dismantled, enterprises gained more autonomy, and the communist party ceased to exercise control over production.[2] As opportunities arose, officials utilised the differentials in domestic and world prices, especially of raw materials, to export for handsome profits, and managers made the most of a changing legal framework to begin privatisation of their own enterprises. This enabled the emergence of an alliance between sections of the Soviet elite (*nomenklatura*) and nascent capitalists which utilised the embryonic Russian state to dismantle the USSR from above. Such an alliance could not establish, however, the hegemony of the bourgeoisie over the rest of society because, on the one hand, the bourgeoisie was non-existent as a social class and, on the other, the *nomenklatura* was itself not a social class but a highly differentiated elite with no coherent world-view other than to maintain its grip on its own particular power-base in the security/military apparatus, industry or the regions (or some combination of the three). After the brief flowering during the perestroika period, civil society has also proved incapable of playing an autonomous role enabling the state itself to become the key actor in promoting the development of capitalism and Russia's reintegration into the capitalist world-economy as a semi-peripheral state (Bedirhanoglu 2004).

The nature of Russia's semi-peripheral status

Since the collapse of the USSR, Russia has become a semi-peripheral state, albeit an atypical one, because the 'passive revolution' has entailed the retention and recombination of significant components of the Soviet system at the same time as reintegration into the world-economy primarily through the medium of energy and raw material exports. In addition, Russia's past as the central element of a former super-power with a very clearly defined periphery or 'sphere of influence', and membership of international bodies, gives it a global presence unlike that of any other semi-peripheral state with the possible exception of China.

Russia's transformation has taken place in two phases, which are broadly co-terminous with the Yeltsin and Putin administrations. Under the former, the absence of clear social relations of production, social forces capable of leading the transformation and the rules of the political game, created a chaotic situation with both a weak economy and weak state. Under Putin, on the back of improving economic conditions, the state was able to assert its autonomy and promote a form of bonapartism to establish some unity between contending social forces. Rapidly rising energy prices have also enabled the state itself to become a major locus of capital accumulation and to utilise its control of energy supplies to assert Russia's regional power.

Russia's transformation under Yeltsin

A coalition of heterogeneous social groups brought about the downfall of the USSR, but only a narrow clique of neo-liberal ideologues, close to Yeltsin and linked to the interests of Western and especially US capital, was in a position to further Russia's reintegration into the capitalist world-economy. It was confronted with a number of obstacles: the inherited industrial structure; lack of a bourgeoisie; the absence of market relations; potential opposition from industrial management.

Russia's industrial structure was not conducive to reintegration into the world-economy because, as Maurseth (2003: 1165) notes, compared to the geographical concentration typical of capitalist development, 'Soviet economic development resulted in a highly dispersed economic landscape with mono-industrial towns scattered around the country.' As Hill and Gaddy (2003: x) put it, '[p]eople, cities and factories languish in places communist planners (and the GULAG) put them, not where market forces and free choice would have attracted them'. As a consequence of Soviet planning, Russia emerged with a more uniform industrialised economy in which the gap between rich and poor was comparatively small, geographical differences were diminished but not eliminated, educational attainment was high, and the agricultural sector had been considerably reduced in size. Russia was, therefore, quite unlike 'organic' semi-peripheral states, which have been subjected throughout their existence to the pressures of combined and uneven development, producing highly differentiated regions, industrial sectors and social classes.

Changing Russia's industrial structure and addressing the other potential obstacles to capitalism required re-subjecting Russia to combined and uneven development. To achieve this rapidly the neo-liberal team led by Egor Gaidar implemented 'shock therapy' in January 1992, desiring to eliminate the remnants of the Soviet system and move Russia from a centralised, planned economy to a capitalist market economy through price and trade liberalisation, considerable reductions in state expenditure, and privatisation of state assets. Shock therapy was designed to produce economic, social and psychological trauma creating a 'blank slate' on which the new socio-economic system could be built from the top down. The belief was that such an ordeal would be short-lived and output would soon begin to recover as the market, both domestic and global, began to assert its magical powers. The strategy certainly delivered a devastating shock to the Russian economy but the recovery was a long time coming: GDP fell 50 per cent between 1990 and 1995 – the largest drop recorded by any state in peace-time; liberalisation of prices generated an inflation rate of 2500 per cent in 1992 stripping ordinary Russians of their savings and rendering them incapable of meaningful participation in the privatisation process; the absence of new rules of the game and opportunities elsewhere encouraged capital flight of the order of $130 billion to offshore accounts between 1992 and 1997 and enabled the emergence of organised crime as a significant player in the economy.

Shock therapy not only had a major impact on Russia's economy and citizens but also drove a wedge between the nascent bourgeoisie and enterprise management. Bitter divisions between former allies in 1992–1993 manifested themselves in an institutional conflict between presidency and parliament which was only resolved by the use of military force and the imposition through the 1993 constitution of a presidential system. This created the paradox of a strong presidency but a weak state unable to generate sufficient revenue to meet its obligations which after December 1994 also included war in Chechnya. It thus soon found itself prey to the emergent 'oligarchs'. From a base in the embryonic banking system, the oligarchs were able to offer money in return for shares in the most lucrative sectors of the economy at bargain-basement prices (the so-called loans-for-shares scheme), a process that Goldman (2008: 63) considered 'the biggest and most controversial transfer of wealth ever seen in history'. The oligarchs transformed themselves in the process into billionaires with considerable political influence and gigantic holdings (financial-industrial groups, FIGs) especially in finance, energy and raw materials. Under their aegis, these sectors began to be integrated into global circuits of capital.

Competition between the oligarchs over the division of Russia's riches was fierce but, faced with a potential communist victory in the 1996 presidential election against a backdrop of economic collapse and war in Chechnya, they achieved a limited unity to ensure Yeltsin's re-election. A combination of control of the media, almost unlimited resources and unanimous support from Western governments steamrollered the communist candidate, Gennadii Zyuganov.

After 1996, the relationship between government and big business became ever more complex as the oligarchs returned to bitter rivalry fighting for control of Russia's resources and most profitable companies and developing alliances with government figures able to effect desirable outcomes. On the one hand, the apparent restabilisation of the political situation masked a fiscal crisis brought about by the giveaway of state resources to buy support for Yeltsin's campaign and which prompted an extension of state intervention into the economy to squeeze revenue out of the raw material and financial sectors (Reddaway and Glinski 2001: 534–535). On the other hand, privatisation continued with success in obtaining major state assets being determined by the oligarchs' relationship to key figures in government. Central to this process was Anatoly Chubais, the architect of the earlier mass privatisation programme and the conduit for the influence of Western financial institutions into the Yeltsin administration. Chubais used his position as vice-premier to ensure that favoured oligarchs like Vladimir Potanin's Oneksimbank, which derived its income from its relationship with the Treasury, was successful in obtaining Svyazinvest, the key to Russia's communications industry, and Norilsk Nickel, the world's largest nickel producer. Thus, Reddaway and Glinski (2001: 559) argue that 'the money that Oneksimbank received thanks to oligarchical access to political power was spent to buy new and more effective levers of power for itself'.

During the late 1990s, the interrelationship of business and political power deepened into the formation of 'clans', mutually supportive networks of oligarchs, politicians, bureaucrats and security service personnel. The most influential of these developed around Yeltsin himself and was dubbed 'the family'. As well as the involvement of Yeltsin's daughter, Tatyana Dyachenko, and future son-in-law, Valentin Yumashev, who became Yeltsin's Chief of Staff, the 'family' was notable for its links to the oligarchs, Boris Berezovsky and Roman Abramovich. In 1998–1999, revelations of the corruption endemic in the regime became commonplace but attempts to impeach Yeltsin in May 1999 foundered on the incapacity of the communist-led State Duma to achieve the necessary two-thirds majority.

While the oligarchs battled over the real spoils of the Russian economy, enterprise managers had, by and large, achieved their goal of transferring the bulk of manufacturing industry into their own hands through the mass privatisation process of 1992–1994. Unable to compete with foreign companies, however, manufacturing failed to integrate into the capitalist world-economy, prompting Gaddy and Ickes (1998) to argue that 'Russian companies, especially in the manufacturing sector, have indeed changed the way they operate, but to protect themselves against the market rather than join it.' Lack of competitiveness and the steep decline in production did not lead, however, to a raft of closures and mass unemployment but, more frequently, to short-time working. Soviet-era practices, such as the employment of more workers than were needed and the provision by the enterprise of a range of material, social and cultural benefits, combined with the management's desire to keep the source of its power operative. Shortage of income also ensured that relationships between enterprises and between enterprises and the state were conducted through the medium of barter, continuing the Soviet-era practice of non-monetary transactions. It also meant, however, that the wages of millions of workers went unpaid.

Thus the result of these cross-cutting influences from the Soviet past, on the one hand, and integration into the capitalist world-economy, on the other, was a social formation based on different relations of production in different sectors of the economy generating contradictory pressures which combined with those created by being pulled between core and periphery. Its chronic weaknesses were exposed by the financial crisis of August 1998 which resulted from a combination of the state's fiscal crisis, in particular the collapse of short-term bond (GKO) pyramid, and the crisis of the Asian economies. It dealt a major blow to the oligarchs' interests, forcing some out of business and others to restructure by shifting away from financial concerns to production especially in raw materials.

Russia's transformation under Putin

Having recovered somewhat from the 1998 crisis, the oligarchs wished to guarantee that Yeltsin's successor would not reverse the privatisations of the 1990s and would maintain the existing regime. In choosing Putin they hoped for someone malleable and manipulable but his background in the security apparatus and lack of ties to any of the emergent politico-economic 'clans' gave him a degree of autonomy which enabled him to promote a more genuinely 'bonapartist' solution to the problems confronting the Russian state, by rising above the contending elites.

Putin's overarching aim has been to re-establish the 'power vertical' with the Kremlin at its apex. With a strong domestic state Russia would then be in a much better position to assert its interests at a regional and global level, reversing the humiliations suffered under Yeltsin. Putin's strategy entailed acting on a number of fronts simultaneously in order to end the fragmentation of the political and social order. It was necessary to end the oligarchs' political influence, subordinate the regions, which had become increasingly autonomous, to the centre, unify the disparate elites that continued to exist from the Soviet era or had emerged from the new relations of production. Key to this whole process was reversing the catastrophic economic decline.

Putin's first act as President was to grant immunity from criminal prosecution to Yeltsin and his family thereby indicating that the privatisations of the nineties would not be reversed. This did not mean, however, that the political influence accruing from those privatisations would be tolerated. Having re-launched the war in Chechnya amid considerable popular support and thus re-asserted the capacity of the Russian state to defend its integrity, Putin set about addressing the power of the oligarchs. At a meeting in July 2000, Putin and those oligarchs present agreed that the latter should confine themselves to managing their economic resources, that they should exercise influence through the established lobbying channels of the Russian Union of Industrialists and Entrepreneurs (RSPP), and that failure to observe these conditions would bring severe penalties. Leading oligarchs, Boris Berezovsky and Vladimir Gusinsky, were hounded from the country for not agreeing to this new modus vivendi.

Ending the regions' de facto autonomy required a number of measures that could only be implemented over a prolonged period as the state gradually asserted its dominance. The first act was the creation of seven super-regions (federal districts), headed by Kremlin appointees, to oversee the actions of regional administrations. Second, the composition of the Federation Council (the upper house of the Russian parliament) was altered to give the Kremlin more influence over the regions' representatives. Third, the crisis surrounding the Beslan school siege in September 2004, provided Putin with an opportunity to shift from the election of regional leaders to their appointment by the Kremlin. In Chechnya, Putin pursued the war against separatist forces with great vigour, linking it to the wider 'war on terror' to avoid the opprobrium heaped on his predecessor for abuses of human rights. Despite having subdued the Chechen resistance and installed the pro-Kremlin Ramzan Kadyrov as the new president, the North Caucasus as a whole remains unstable, however, as ethnic conflict has spread into the neighbouring regions of Ingushetia and North Ossetia.

These measures have all contributed to a greater cohesion between elites, a process enhanced by the creation of a political party ('party of power') in the shape of United Russia. This organisation, of which Putin is now technically the leader, controls two-thirds of the State Duma and an overwhelming majority of regional assemblies. Its success has been assured by the Kremlin's control of the mass media, re-captured from Berezovsky and Gusinsky, manipulation of the party and electoral systems to reduce the competition, and blatant ballot-rigging in some regions to produce the desired outcome. Nevertheless, economic recovery has also given Russian voters a reason to support the status quo.

While Putin has centralised the state, civil society continues to exercise little influence on decision-making except through officially sanctioned channels. A recent law placed restrictions on the capacity of NGOs to operate effectively, a Public Chamber was inaugurated to bring together favoured representatives of civil society organisations, and the trade unions belonging to the dominant Federation of Independent Trade Unions of Russia (FNPR), have essentially been incorporated into state-led bodies. At a local level, unions in enterprises inherited from the Soviet era continue to collaborate with management to obtain the best conditions for the enterprise as a whole, reducing industrial action to very low levels. Strikes and other activities have been more evident in the factories of Western companies such as Ford near St Petersburg where labour relations are more characteristic of core states and the workers have been able to take strike action and establish their own organisations autonomous from the FNPR.

It was Putin's desire to re-establish Russia's economic power that has had the most impact both domestically and on Russia as a global power. Since 2005 a number of strategic resources and enterprises have been designated not only to ensure state control but also that they remain in Russian ownership (Hanson 2007: 878). Even before this official step had been taken, however, Mikhail Khodorkovsky, Russia's wealthiest businessman and owner of its most successful oil company, Yukos, had fallen foul of the authorities. Khodorkovsky was imprisoned, allegedly for tax evasion, but in reality he had committed two cardinal errors: first, breaking the oligarchs' agreement by materially supporting opposition political organisations in the run-up to the 2003 parliamentary elections; second, intending to sell Yukos to foreign companies. Either through outright confrontation or by cajoling owners to sell, the state has taken control of considerable economic resources, especially in the energy sector, or government ministers have been placed in leading positions on boards of directors. Thus, in Sakwa's opinion, 'Putin's new rules of the game opened the way for Russia's oligarchical (or comprador) capitalism to be transformed into a new system' (2008a: 150).

Nevertheless, re-establishing Russia's power could not be done without favourable conditions in the world-economy and, in this sense, Putin was a very lucky president, enjoying considerable good fortune on the economic front. Under Yeltsin, energy had continued the trend apparent in the late Soviet era as the leading export product although by 1999 oil production had slumped like the rest of economy to 40 per cent below its 1987 peak. Oil prices were also low encouraging oligarchs to strip valuable assets rather than invest in production. This situation began to change after the 1998 financial crisis as the southeast Asian economies began to recover and, in particular, the rise in demand for energy from China and India began to outpace even their own impressive rates of GDP growth. From less than $20 a barrel, the price of oil began to rise steadily through the 2000s to an unprecedented peak of $146 a barrel in 2008. At the same time, European countries, concerned at the political instability surrounding energy supplies from the Middle East, increasingly saw Russia as an attractive alternative, particularly with its capacity to supply oil and gas directly and in large quantities via an expanding network of pipelines. Putin thus came to power just as the Russian economy was entering favourable new circumstances.

Under Putin, Russia's economy grew strongly at an average of 6 per cent per annum, lifting Russia to seventh in the world in terms of GDP. As Table 7.1 indicates, however, it still took until 2003 to achieve the levels of output of 1990 and was also insufficient to raise Russia beyond that of a middle-ranking economy. Moreover, as Goldman (2008: 80) has demonstrated, GDP decline and growth can be correlated almost perfectly against falls and increases in oil production.

Russia produces 11 per cent of the world's oil, with the second largest reserves after Saudi Arabia, and 25 per cent of its natural gas with the largest gas reserves in the world. By 2007, oil and gas accounted for approximately 64 per cent of the value of Russia's entire exports, making the Russian economy, in the eyes of the Economist Intelligence Unit (EIU) (2005: 44), 'even more dependent on volatile international commodities markets than it was before the 1998 crisis'.[3] To try and offset such fluctuations the Russian government instituted a stabilisation fund in 2004 for windfall oil receipts (80 per cent of oil revenue above $27 a barrel). With the price of oil rising steadily from 2004 to mid-2008,

Table 7.1   Russian economy: Selected indicators

Category	1990	1995	2000	2003	2007	2007 World Ranking
GNI per capita (PPP$)	8400	5890	7050	8950	14400	68
GDP per capita (PPP$)	8340	5930	7240	8230	14600 (est.)	73
FDI (per cent GDP)	0.0	0.52	1.04	1.84	2.2	81

Source: http://globalis.gvu.unu.edu; World Bank

the stabilisation fund grew rapidly, reaching $157 billion, in January 2008, and then being divided into a Reserve Fund to cushion the budget against a fall in revenue and a National Welfare Fund to be invested in Russian blue-chip companies (Sakwa 2008b: 304). By December 2008, the balances of these funds were $132 billion and $76 billion respectively. Unlike the stabilisation fund whose income came entirely from taxation and customs revenues from oil, the two new funds will gain from the taxation of both oil and gas. Russia has also accumulated the third largest reserves of foreign currency after China and Japan.

Russia's liberal finance minister, Alexei Kudrin, has promoted a policy of using the windfall profits to pay off debts rather than spending on other projects. Government external debt has been reduced to one of the lowest rates in the world from around $158.4 billion (80.9 per cent of GDP) in 1999 to $76 billion (6 per cent) in 2008 (RIA Novosti 15 November 2008). While state debt has been considerably reduced, however, Russia's greatly improved credit rating has enabled companies to borrow more easily raising the overall level of debt in the Russian economy to $210 billion by October 2006 and increasing the ratio of debt to GDP to 23 per cent in 2005 (Goldman 2008: 81). The improved business climate also promoted a dramatic rise in foreign direct investment (FDI), around half going into the energy sector. As Cyprus is the largest single source of FDI, however, much of this is actually the repatriation of capital that had been exported in the 1990s rather than fresh investment from foreign companies.

In addition to oil and gas, Russian companies provide more than 25 per cent of the world's diamonds, a third of the world's nickel, 40 per cent of its platinum and around 12–13 per cent of its aluminium. Altogether, Hanson (2007: 874) considers export dependence on raw materials-based industries to be around an enormous 80 per cent. The production of such minerals and semi-finished goods is, however, highly energy-intensive and their competitiveness will decline as domestic energy prices rise. Increased integration into the global economy and orientation away from domestic markets has also altered the structure of another major sector, steel, where there has been a shift to lower value-added products providing inputs for US and European steel production and for which there are fewer trade barriers.

While the raw materials and non-ferrous metals sectors have prospered, output of manufactured goods has declined considerably since the early 1990s. The share of exports of machinery and other equipment in 2003 was only 8 per cent compared to 20 per cent in 1991. This figure would have been worse if arms exports had not recovered from an earlier fall. While manufacturing has grown since 1999 the level of production is still below that of 1990. A recent report suggested that there are considerable disparities between sectors in terms of productivity and capacity to export, rendering only 20–25 per cent of manufacturing industry competitive (GU-VShE 2007: 8–9). Despite its increasing importance for Russian GDP growth by 2008, manufacturing suffered from a lack of and, indeed, a declining proportion of investment.

The energy sector and raw materials have thus been the primary channels through which Russia has become re-integrated into the capitalist world-economy. As they have attracted high earnings and investment, other sectors have declined. Thus, combined and uneven development has once again begun to have a profound effect on the Russia's socio-economic structure. Regional disparities in wealth have increased considerably as those regions with highly profitable extractive industries have attracted investment and Moscow has become the largest city in Europe by drawing in investment into the financial sector and its booming construction industry. Agricultural regions, on the other hand, have generally declined with little inward investment.

Russia's social structure has also changed with the development of a widening gap between rich and poor. In the Soviet period personal wealth could not easily be accumulated and income differentials were comparatively low although those in the upper echelons of the party and state had access, dependent on political 'rank', to goods and services unavailable to ordinary citizens. From 1992–2007 the income differential between the top 10 per cent and bottom 10 per cent increased from 6.6:1 to 15.6:1. Poverty, generally considered almost non-existent in the Soviet period, increased dramatically during the 1990s to affect 30 per cent of the population. By 2007, however, this had fallen back to 15 per cent as wages increased significantly and were generally paid on time, and unemployment was reduced (Sakwa 2008b: 327–328). While for those not in paid employment life can still be very hard as state benefits have been monetised, for most Russians the stark contrast with the Yeltsin era generated massive support for Putin, enabling his comfortable success in the 2004 presidential election and that of his successor, Dmitrii Medvedev, in 2008.

Putin's drive for unity and to establish the 'power vertical' implies a recognition that the Soviet legacy and global processes have profoundly influenced the character of contemporary Russia. Rather than the hegemony of a dominant class in a system characterised by consensual relations, the state has had, in the absence of any dominant class, to play a much more coercive role. The state is constantly being undermined, however, by Russia's semi-peripheral position. Within the regime itself different 'clans' or factions have emerged with varying strategies for Russia's engagement with the capitalist world-economy and the degree of state control. While the seemingly increasingly marginalised St Petersburg liberals, of whom Kudrin is the major remaining figure in government, have promoted greater integration into the capitalist world-economy, a more 'statist' faction, usually referred to as the *siloviki* (deriving from the Russian word for power) with backgrounds in the security services, and frequently closely linked to Putin, has emerged. According to Daniel Treisman (2007: 143), the latter now 'occupy key positions in the oil, gas, defense, transport, and nuclear power sectors', enabling them to dominate political and economic decision-making at the highest level, as well as providing access to sources of considerable personal wealth. Such a picture provides a rather simplified view of a very complex reality in which different economic and state sectors vie with each other for influence and resources and the presidency acts essentially as a power broker.

Conclusion

Russia's semi-peripheral status has been illustrated in various ways as 2008 draws to a close. First, the invasion of Georgia indicates Russia's desire to establish a dominant relationship with weaker semi-peripheral and peripheral states on its borders and to disrupt relations between those states and more powerful core states. Second, the global financial crisis has revealed the inherent weakness of the Russian economy: the main stock market lost two-thirds of its value, wiping off almost $1 trillion in share value, Russia's 25 richest men have seen their wealth tumble by a staggering $230 billion, and capital flight is in excess of $12 billion a week (MacDonald 2008). When combined with falling oil prices which have now dropped to around $50 a barrel, significantly below the $70 a barrel needed to balance the budget, the Russian state might appear to be heading into dire straits. For the time being, Russia has some insurance against worsening global conditions through the reserves created from the earlier high price of oil but a full-blown global recession would signify declining demand for oil and a consistently low price. While natural gas prices are not as volatile as those of oil, they will still follow oil's downward trend, exposing the reliance on energy exports as a profoundly weak foundation for economic development.

The current crisis will thus enhance many aspects of Russia's semi-peripherality. The conflict between different 'clans' will be exacerbated as the frailty of many of Russia's oligarchs and entrepreneurs will be revealed. This will serve to strengthen the autonomy of the state even further as the latter decides which to bail out and which to let sink. Nevertheless, if the crisis is prolonged and energy revenue is substantially diminished, the capacity of the state to broker deals will be eroded, enhancing the political struggle around the succession to Medvedev. Second, Russia's economic prospects might have been severely dented but the core states are themselves facing serious economic difficulties and the situation of many other states, especially those in the former Soviet Union, will be even worse, strengthening Russia's capacity to enforce its regional hegemony. Capitalism's crisis might not entail a wholesale re-ordering of the world-system but Russia will continue to play a significant global role while remaining a semi-peripheral state for the foreseeable future.

Notes

1. For a more detailed discussion of the concept of passive revolution and its application to Russia's evolution since *perestroika* see Simon (2010).
2. Gramsci developed the concept of passive revolution as a materialist critique of its conservative origins the Italian political philosopher Vincenzo Cuoco initially termed it as a feasible strategy for political transformation. Previous examples of Gramscian analysis to post-Communist Russia that engage with passive revolution include Lester (1995), Bedirhanoglu (2004) and Worth (2005).
3. According to the US Government's Energy Information Administration (EIA), 'a $1 per barrel change in oil prices will result in a $1.4 billion change in Russian revenues in the same direction' (www.eia.doe.gov).

8
Turkey in the World System and the New Orientalism

Phoebe Moore and Charles Dannreuther

Turkey's integration into the world system of capitalism after the collapse of the Ottoman Empire is usually understood from the restrictive perspective of a Western 'Orientalist' view. This perspective presents the Ottoman Empire either as a Feudal Mode of Production (FMP) or as an Asiatic Mode of Production (AMP). Although Turkish and Western contributions to World Systems Analysis (WSA) have challenged both these views (Keyder 1987), the shift from the Ottoman Empire to the Turkish Republic and the associated implications for Turkey's role in the current world system of globalising capitalism are often restricted to a Christian, post-Enlightenment view of progress: that after a period of peripheralisation followed an impressive story of upward mobility culminating now in the civilising process of EU accession.

This chapter argues that the semi-periphery is no longer simply a place of unfulfilled promises or one in which the desire for progress is exploited to balance the structures of the capitalist world system. Today the semi-periphery challenges the system itself. Turkey demonstrates its anti-systemic aims in the political challenge that it presents to the world system. The new transformative semi-periphery is not interested in simply 'developing' according to the pre-ordained sets of institutional structures to then achieve 'core' status amongst battling hegemons. Rather, its potential today is its ability to challenge and perhaps alter the entire system. South America's socialist strategies and the democratisation of the Western European countries have demonstrated the political drivers for systemic change. What makes Turkey interesting is that it is not challenging the political and economic expression of global capitalism through the socialist or democratic routes so often associated with the semi-periphery. The Turkish government is now using a very interesting critical technique called Ottoman Orientalism to challenge the arguably hegemonic civilising processes of EU integration. This chapter discusses the way in which Turkey is doing this, and argues that the transformative semi-periphery cannot cohere to one set of ideological, political, or identity-oriented principles, but now enjoys an anti-systemic status not seen in the theorisations of the semi-periphery in the traditional WSA.

The chapter questions whether the current debate on Turkey's membership into the EU is a symptom of a prolonged Western Orientalism. In doing so it explores whether Turkey will be allowed to become a full member of the EU, or to perhaps gain core status despite Turkey's stubborn refusal on certain issues and will look at what a unified authority in the form of the EU means more widely for the role of the semi-peripheral states. The chapter argues that the definition/identity of the semi-periphery itself is changing, as political relationships become increasingly complex in the climate of post-Soviet restructuring of loyalties, with the exigencies of globalisation, and with the ambiguity of development.

While the semi-periphery was historically 'needed' as a producer for the core and as an envoy for the periphery, it has become an increasingly necessary political portal for the core for an increasing range of economic, social and political reasons. Turkey can thus become more powerful than it may have previously been. Wallerstein (1979: 75) pointed out that the political role of some semi-peripheries in creating conflicts for core countries distinguished these entities from others which played a predominantly economic role in the world economy. The United States, for example, saw Turkey as a route to a powerful presence in the EU, as well as a link to the Arabic states. Furthermore, Turkey, as the cultural 'other', or the perceived non-European contender for EU accession, does not maintain the same characteristics as supposedly underdeveloped post-Soviet nations, and its accession is not universally seen as a prerequisite for the reuniting of Europe. Turkey provides an ideology of opposition that holds power to change the dominant mode of accumulation. This chapter thus defends the need to update the concept of the semi-periphery both to re-assess its significance and to describe a force for a potentially very influential subversive power in the contemporary political economy.

First, differing from Hoffman (2008: 378–9) who argues for the (geo)political character of the transformation from Ottoman to national rule, we present WSA as an effective way to study the division and exploitation of labour and capital accumulation on a world scale. Then we turn to an analysis of Turkey as a new semi-periphery through setting the stage of its own history as well negotiating its current political role in the world system of EU capitalism. The chapter argues that surrounding post-Soviet Europe has been unwilling to release its Western Orientalist view of Turkey. As a result, the government has returned to an Ottoman Orientalist view, which was originally a retort to the Western assumptions of the exotic other, and now continues to buttress Turkish policy in a way that moulds a completely different species of the semi-periphery. Culturally and politically, this nation is adopting an Ottoman Orientalist position that refutes the Western Orientalist view and poses a real anti-systemic challenge to the current status quo. So, in summary, the semi-periphery as it is noted today, boasts a number of unprecedented characteristics. It is not going to accept its position as a mouthpiece for the core, nor as a purgatory for the periphery. It is no longer a circumvention of resistance, but *is* resistance, as it becomes increasingly powerful transnationally.

World systems

World Systems Analysis emerged in the 1970s as a response to the inadequacies of *Dependencia* theories, which had not been able to explain the development of the periphery. This form of analysis has seen a resurrection in contemporary Marxists circles due to its ability to theorise international divisions of labour simultaneously to rejecting the deterministic and path-dependent aspects of mainstream development theories. The rebirth of WSA is a response to the developmentalist idea proselytised by the United Nations Development Programme (UNDP), the International Monetary Fund (IMF), and the World Bank (WB), which is the idea that all states would and must develop according to a set pattern, one that is set by developed countries with industrialised trajectories. Wallerstein and others refuted the 'catch up' thesis this kind of thinking advocates, and depicted a model for understanding the relations between states that was not restricted to the patterns proposed by developed countries. WSA, introduced in the work of Wallerstein, Arrighi, Amin and later Silver, Chase-Dunn, Abu Lughod, and Gills among others emerged in the 1970s as a response to the inadequacies of *Dependencia* theories. Perhaps the most important WSA innovation is the treatise that without the semi-periphery, the capitalist system would not exist. Divisions of labour are consolidated across different spatial categories, so in the contemporary context of globalisation and increasing international divisions of labour, the models of core, semi-periphery and periphery are being re-explored.

How do World Systems theorists highlight the pertinence of the semi-periphery for a capitalist system? The reasons are political and politico-economic. Politically, as the world system is by its very nature based on inequalities between the core and the semi-peripheral states, rebellion is always a potential issue within the core, who have not only to worry about resistance in colonial areas but whose own citizens are usually not benefited on the ground by the typically exploitative relations with the periphery. High-income, high-status sectors polarised against low-income sectors often lead to the formation of class identity and class struggle in both the core and the periphery. The semi-periphery balances these extremes by circumventing or at least managing this struggle through the formation of a middle sector that sees itself as better off than the lower sectors.

But there is an economic dimension to the importance of the multiplicity of states as involved in the single political economy of a capitalist world system. The system is singular, in that there is no single authority. Profit-driven actors are not confined to legislative mechanisms and are given the free reign of share seeking. Wallerstein points out that the state machinery can be organised according to the needs of capitalists around the 'artificial restraints on the operation of the market' (Wallerstein [1979] 1997: 69–70).

Arrighi writes about the layers of capitalist integration and claims that the top layer is the least researched, as it is least transparent and least accessible avenue for analysis. The 'top, middle, and bottom' layers he refers to in the market economy fall distinctly within the realm of core, semi-periphery and periphery, within a systemic cycle of accumulation. The market economy's middle zone is possibly the most widely researched, as its activities are most observable through volumes of quantitative data that is produced by a variety of capitalists.

The transparency of activities that constitute the activities of the market economy and wealth of quantitative data that these activities generate in the middle zone have made this intermediate layer the privileged arena of social science and economics. The layers above and below the market economy are the shadowy zones (*zones opatiques*). The bottom layer of material life is 'hard to see for lack of adequate historical documents'. The upper layer, in contrast, is hard to see because of the actual invisibility or the complexity of activities that constitute it.

(Arrighi 2002: 24)

The semi-periphery took a new form with the onset of both state socialism and dependency-inspired forms of neo-mercantilism. So, the *Dependencia* school and then WSA revised this category, and introduced a model of an international division of labour, including a core–semi-periphery–periphery of dependence in the Cold War era of western Marxism.

World Systems Analysis does not support the notion that an international system can be explained only with a look to individual states, and defines a world system in terms of ownership of production and capital accumulation. Most importantly, within this model, emphasis was placed upon the role of the semi-peripheral state as both a buffer zone between the core and the periphery, a crisis-manager for the core, and a 'mother' for the periphery. However, we argue that the semi-periphery is now importantly seen as an agent for transformation (Frank 1966; Chase-Dunn 1989; Wallerstein [1979] 1997).

The reading of the semi-periphery as depicted in WSA must be rewritten to account for globalisation as well as the spatial limitations for the expansion of capitalism. Cultural and identity-based elements likewise need to be established. As Wallerstein notes, the assumptions that Marx made regarding the 'natural' transition from feudalism to capitalism must be re-written, because these events are not necessarily historically contingent and are 'not continuous but occurred in historical spurts' ([1979] 1997: 145). Wallerstein writes that 'by about 1900, these expansions had more or less come to an end, as the capitalist world economy could be said at that point to cover the entire globe' (ibid.). The Paris regulation school of Lipietz and other recent post-Marxist writers such as David Harvey are seen to have rejected the spatialised equilibrium theory characterising the work of Wallerstein et al. in favour of an interpretation that looks at structurations of global flexible accumulation. While Lipietz looks at the rise of post-Fordist flexible accumulation of the 1970s and 1980s in the core, and theorises the strengths of this model, the growth of flexible accumulation patterns are now stronger in the semi-peripheral nations, and as these accumulation patterns become stronger, the role of the semi-periphery must be re-assessed (see Strange's chapter in this volume).

Ottoman empire as world system

Until the seventeenth century, the Ottoman and the Russian world-empires could be seen as world systems in their own rite. But as the capitalist state became hegemonic through states' competition to build the biggest armies, to create the strongest bureaucracies, and to diversify economic and trade activity, the capitalist world system prevailed and remains 'almost impossible to unbalance' (Wallerstein [1979] 1997: 26). This period saw the emergence of the Ottoman Empire as an international player and then its subsequent decline into relative peripheralisation. The Empire's consolidation into the capitalist world economy occurred with the reduction of state distribution of resources and the rise of commercial farming, in the context of the emergence of the circulation of commodities and exchanges of capital. This was complemented by the restructuring of the control over labour to capture the increased surplus value of labour and profit for the burgeoning capitalist classes. These elites were often located abroad and provided a solid transnational network of elites. The rise of interstate politics replaced inwardly focused state decision-making and constructed a capitalist world system based on unequal exchanges, with increasingly, states becoming actors in this system at varying degrees of prosperity (Wallerstein and Kasaba 1987: 336).

However, in analysing the significance of the Ottoman Empire before its integration into the capitalist world system and the contemporary Turkey's role in the world system, the evolution of historiography and the leftovers of Orientalist assumptions can be observed. Leopold Ranke challenged the elitist authoring of history to represent things *wie es eigentlich gewesen ist* (as they really did happen), and encouraged the readings of documents actually authored during the period of time when relevant events occurred. But even that practice could not prevent assumptions of historians presiding in the dominant countries. Since historians were typically linked to ruling political structures, discriminatory assumptions prevailed among social scientists regarding the characteristics of modern states and of primitive groups. Studies during the period of Enlightenment were full of racist and patronising undertones such as Montesquieu's *Persian Letters*; supposedly penned by the exotic and passionate Orientals. A memorandum from British Ambassador Stratford de Redcliffe to the Earl of Malmesbury in 1856, presumed that Ottoman modernisation would never take place, since 'Europe is at hand, with its science, its labour, and its capital. The Koran, the harem, a Babel of languages, are no doubt so many obstacles to advancement in a Western sense' (Makdisi 2002: 52). The primitive, exotic 'other' was described in direct contrast to the civilised 'us'. As Edward Said influentially noted (Said 1978), the discursive construction of a social, ideological, military, artistic, and scientific is a political project to maintain a relationship of domination and/or hegemony over perceived weaker groups (Buchowski 2006: 463).

Anthropologists became the missionaries for mediation between dominant modern states and the colonized primitives, in a way that legitimized the colonisers' manner of administration. But there were areas in the world that did not suit the criteria for primitive or modern identities, such as the Arab world, China, Persia, and India. What these areas had in common was their histories as world empires, and thus within the areas, people still had shared languages, customs, and non-Christian religions. However, because these areas could not demonstrate the same level of military capabilities as the pan-European world, they were not allowed the title of 'modern', but were seen as the 'higher civilisations'. As a result, a new type of analysis emerged, that of the Orientalists, who specialised in philological skills to tackle the question of why these areas seemed to be 'frozen' in their history and could not match the seeming superiority of European modernity. So, anthropologists began to busily analyse 'primitive' tribes, and the Orientalists studied the 'higher civilisations', sharing the epistemological commitments to understanding cultural specificities and idiosyncrasies of the areas they researched (Wallerstein 2006: 4–8).

The positioning of Orientalism when looking at Turkish history is complex, since usually, this idea is used to understand Western stereotypes and discriminating perspectives towards non-Western entities. The Ottomans, at the end of the empire, embraced elements of Western Orientalism by accepting the enlightenment themes of progress and the 'logic of time' (Makdisi 2002: 3) and by absorbing the tenets of European definitions of development (Deringil 1998, in ibid.), while denying political/colonial insinuations. The biggest difference of course with 'Ottoman Orientalism' was the conviction that Turkey and the rest of Europe could and should be able to institutionalise the region without acclimatising all of the related factors towards Europeanisation. At one level these included the heavily Christian overtones and behaviours and beliefs embodied in Weber's protestant ethic of capitalism. But it also included the more current institutional requirements of Europeanisation associated with public sector reform and pre-accession. While Western Orientalism implied the backward East and the prolific and superior West, a group of historians have taken the initiative to revise the restrictive and derogatory portrayal of the East in showing how the late Ottoman Empire in fact revised Orientalism itself to include both modernisation and Islam, and in a way that could preserve the integrity of Turkish identity and culture, and in a way that hoped to move European speculators to revise their view of the Turkish 'sick man of Europe'. While the Ottoman area was once perceived as the 'exotic other' it is now becoming a 'stigmatised brother' (Buchowski 2006) and the Balkans are 'neither fish nor fowl' (Todorova 1997). This new version of Eastern Europe is seen by the rest of Europe as 'semi-oriental, not fully European, semi-developed, and semi-civilised' (Buchowski 2006: 464). But even in the latter days of the Ottoman Empire, a form of 'Ottoman image management' (Deringil 1998) informed constitutional advocates and reformers who aimed to locate Western principles within Islamic ideals, to demonstrate that this Empire was the founding father of civilisation in the East as well as in Europe. Both Western and Ottoman Orientalism have remained into the present, where we see a sceptical EU as well as a sceptical Turkey. Despite the fact that Turkey has indeed embraced 'rationalism, secularism, commercial activities and industry' (Buchowski 2006: 464), it still maintains an 'otherness' in a relationship of alterity (Fabian 1983; Taussig 1993; Nealon 1998; Strong 1999; Cooper 2007).

More recently, analysis of the significance of the Ottoman Empire has enjoyed a reappraisal of its significance in the history of Europe. The responses of the international community to Turkish inclusion into the European Union still reflect, however, an Orientalist conjecture, and the thesis common to European Marxist historians of socio-economic deterioration in the period of the Ottoman Empire and via centralist power requires re-consideration (Inalcik 1995: 22). The Empire's incorporation in this sense involved a total re-structuring of production processes, as well as the restructuring of a 'political system of an area such that the incorporated area becomes an integrated part of the axial division of labour and a functioning part of the interstate system' (Wallerstein and Kasaba 1987: 336). The Ottoman Empire was a large and bureaucratised system with many trade links across Europe and particularly in the later 1700s became involved in commercial relations. Wallerstein and Kasaba make the following claims with regard to the original formation of the capitalist world system:

- There has existed since the sixteenth century a social division of labour which we may designate as a capitalist world economy.
- Processes internal to the operation of the capitalist world economy require it periodically to seek to expand its frontiers.
- Starting from a European base, the capitalist world economy has in fact constantly expanded its frontiers, eventually 'incorporating' all areas on the earth of itself (including the Ottoman Empire) (ibid.: 337).

The AMP is a concept that is being revised to 'inject subtlety' into the AMP's rigid and immobile definitions and looks for a distinctive identity of Ottoman society and social formation which is not restricted to either the AMP or the FMP. Turkish social scientists are looking at how the Ottoman state reserved control over agricultural land not simply through absolute rule, but through a specific social formation.

Similar to the way in which Marxist historians have revised their generalisations in the light of historical data available since Marx, Turkish social scientists are modifying AMP in light of the research on historical knowledge. The outcome is more than a revision; it attempts to 'inject subtlety' into rather rigidly defined AMP elements leading to new questions and hypotheses for a better understanding of a social structure which had otherwise been characterised as 'immobile'. In essence this has been an effort to identify the distinctive nature of Ottoman society and the result had sometimes been to define Ottoman social formation outside both the AMP and the FMP. During Ottoman expansion, land was taken from landlords rather than from the peasants, a factor that Turkish authors believe to demonstrate a kind of collusion between the state and peasant labour against feudal warlords (Inalcik 1995). Furthermore, much of the land was being transformed by the dominant class into *wakfs,* or land used for charity or for public services, as is reserved under Islamic law. So these factors, according to Divitcioglu, mean that the Ottoman social formation was not exclusively bound to either the norms of the AMP or of the FMP. Urbanisation, economic integration between the rural and the urban and specific advances towards commerce and monetisation point towards modernisation of the Ottoman Empire in a manner that does not exactly match either of these models. So, in light of this discrepancy, Islamoglu-Inan and Keyder suggest a marriage between the AMP theories and Wallerstein's peripheralisation analysis to understand both the internal dynamics and the external relations. A true peripheralisation process and the end of the Ottoman 'world empire' came about with the formation of commercial *ciftliks* (private estates) and the commercialisation of agriculture as well as a view to the external realm (Islamoglu and Keyder 1987). The final underscore for the direction of the new Turkish Republic was created by the Young Turks likewise, who encouraged secularisation, free education, and wealth-driven policy from a distinctly nationalist angle.

Contemporary Turkey

Into the nineteenth and twentieth centuries, agriculture and manufacturing were surpassed by the services industry in Turkey. At the same time greater political relationships with the international called the role of the semi-periphery into question. Rising domestic consumer demand and the privatisation and commercialisation of industry generally allowed full integration into the capitalist world system, with Turkey ascending to semi-peripheral status due to its political and economic relationships. Over time, the secularisation of Turkey, the relationship with the Kurdish population, a developing relationship with the United States, the roller-coaster political economy of inflation and eventual IMF involvement in economic restructuring, and the questions of EU accession have given Turkey an increasingly prominent although at times controversial role in the global political economy. Turkey became a semi-peripheral state in the classical world systems theorisation, with many state-controlled characteristics despite the neoliberalisation of this economy. But its role following the Second World War has developed most prominently with membership of the North Atlantic Treaty Organisation (NATO) beginning in 1952, its associate membership of the European Community in 1963, and a renewed interest in making ties with the Western world as a 'ticket to long-term peace and prosperity' (Rittenberg 1998: 3). The incorporation of Turkey into the world system as a political and economic player has led to its incorporation as a new manifestation of the semi-peripheral state as it manages the complex economic and political affairs that surround it. This militant but secular state has described a new and important form of resistance to the now neoliberal-dominated European Union agenda.

In the 1980s and 1990s, inflation was the biggest problem for the Turkish economy. Several programmes to fight inflation were designed, but public finances were not strengthened sufficiently. Turkish domestic consumer demand increased dramatically. Consumption by the private sector increased in real terms by 13.1 per cent, and real private investment expenditure increased by 19.4 per cent in 1990. In June 1980, the Association Council made a decision to cut customs duties on agricultural products to zero, to be put into place by 1987, and in 1986, the Turkey and EEC Association Council made steps to re-establish an 'association process', as Turkey applied for full EEC membership (Euractive 2004). By 1989, the Commission was prepared to endorse Turkey's membership, and by 1997, at the Luxembourg Summit, Turkey was granted full-candidacy status. Every Turkish government since the fall of the Berlin Wall has sought full EU membership, but has not succeeded. However since the 1980s when Turkey began a mass liberalisation programme, it began to form strong economic ties with Europe, and as a result Turkey has become increasingly competitive as a potential full member. From the 1980s to 1990s, a fascist Pinochet-like martial regime originally led by General Kenan Evren in the shape of Turkey's third coup d'etat, led the economic reform that was intended to introduce the country to the global economy with the deregulatory and neoliberal projects seen in international projects across South America and East Asia. Alongside mass secularisation, trade unions were banned, as were political parties. The year 1980 marks the shifting of government from import-led policy to export-led growth along the lines of the Washington Consensus model. In January of that year, the IMF and the WB worked closely with the Turkish bourgeoisie to stabilise the economy, and to plant the seeds for market-driven policy that included privatisation and liberalisation of finance (Aydin 2005). These policies also allowed the flexible specialisation style of small and medium enterprises (SMEs) in Antalya to take root, the ties for which were developed in the Islamic schools and which became an economic powerhouse in contemporary Turkey and the support base for the Justice and Development Party (AKP).

The external deficit in 1990 was at an all time high, and in 1991 the economy became classified as entering a growth recession (Selcuk 1998: 19). The IMF was consulted again when in 1994 the financial crisis really took root and GDP fell by 4.7 per cent but 'it soon became clear that the [IMF] programme was destined for failure' (1998: 17). Politically, after the collapse of the Soviet Union, Turkey's political and economic roles in the area have become increasingly important, despite its predicted rise in importance to the East, simultaneous to falling importance to the West for the containment of the Soviet Union, were mildly overstated forecasts. Turkey was quickly seen as a good investment opportunity for international capital. The Black Sea Economic Cooperation project was a regional effort that in fact complemented the surrounding countries' globalising efforts rather than challenging or overcoming them (Sayan 1998), and Turkey became a site for multinational corporate presence, as well as seen as a channel for resources in the region. Twenty two out of fifty corporations researched in 1997 were using Turkey as a middle ground for investment in this area.

Nonetheless, Turkey's 'neighbourhood' is potentially volatile and the influence of the West is seen as a calming mechanism, despite historical evidence demonstrating the opposite. Turkey's alliance with the United States was seen as a coalition against Saddam Hussain, and America's use of the Incirlik Air Base, as well strategic ties with Israel by way of a free trade agreement and a stated commitment to the peace process make its Westward commitments obvious. The world began to believe that Turkey could be the first Muslim democracy. Put another way Turkey could become the first Muslim state which makes friends with the United States and so can be granted democratic status or a 'full member of the modern world' (*Economist* 1991, in Rittenberg 1998: 12). The 1991 *Economist* describes the area surrounding Turkey as one that appears as a 'large stretch of the world notably liable to produce turmoil and mayhem on a large scale in the coming 15–20 years, the appropriately crescent shaped piece of territory that starts in the steppes of Kazakhstan and curves south and west through the gulf and the Suez to the north coast of Africa' (ibid.), and sees Turkey as the possible leader and stronghold for this area for geographical reasons as much as historical. However, Russia has also maintained a definite presence in the area, so the Turkic hegemon did not completely emerge as was originally expected. The Turkic countries do not actually maintain homogenous populations either, so social harmony was not immediately evident, and as EU membership has increasingly been debated, various issues have come to the fore.

In 1997, the Turkish government threatened to stymie expansion of NATO and to challenge Western Europe's use of NATO weapons if the EU continued to prevent membership and in the same year, Turkey was granted candidacy status. Around this period, Turkey began to adopt many of the EU institutions, but on its own terms. Boatca writes about the changing role of the transformative semi-periphery, from a calming antidote between the core and the periphery as well as a challenging force in economic mobility to challenge the hegemony of the core, to a far more crucial role of overthrow and one of 'engendering anti-systemic strategies' (2006: 328). Turkey will never fully embrace the Anglo Saxon model of reform, and its secular approach to all political activity is a culturally specific approach that has been successful in maintaining a distinct identity while also taking chosen aspects of development.

By 2001, the EU Council of Ministers entered an EU-Turkey Accession Partnership, and the government of Turkey created a National Programme of Turkey that would work towards bringing Turkish law up to the standard of EU laws, and 30 amendments were adopted by the parliament to meet all of the criteria agreed at Copenhagen for membership into the EU. The following year, the Turkish parliament worked to pass reforms that could address human rights criteria required for membership, though this has been an ongoing issue for consideration. Nonetheless, also in 2002, it was decided that if Turkey could demonstrate, by 2004, its fulfilment of the Copenhagen political criteria, which includes a commitment to adhere to democratic governance and commitment to a market economy as well as a human rights agenda. In 2003, the EU Council of Ministers made a final decision on the Conditions for the Accession Partnership, and part of the response to this was Turkey's complete banning of the death penalty in 2004. In the same year, the Council of Europe decided that monitoring should be reduced and finally eliminated, and created a progress report that led to the EP Foreign Affairs Committee to state that the EU should open negotiations with Turkey, but that all conditions had not been met, so would need further consideration. On 6 October, the MEPs decided that the process would not be closed but rather:

> The opening of negotiations will be the starting point for a long-lasting process that by its very nature is an open-ended process and does not lead 'a priori' and automatically to accession; however (...) the objective of negotiations is Turkish EU membership but (...) the realisation of this ambition will depend on the efforts of both sides; accession is thus not the automatic consequence of the start of the negotiations.

The main point of contention had to do with Turkey's breaches of human rights as understood by the Commission, and the idea for a privileged partnership rather than full accession was overturned. So in 2004, negotiations were permitted, but with 'strings attached' (Euractive). In 2005 the Council reminded the EU of the desire to include more states, and in June the Commission entered into a framework for negotiation with Turkey that led to the declaration of a new member state: Cyprus. Turkey declared that it did not aim to regard Cyprus as a full member, and this was very quickly met with a counter-declaration from the EU on 21st September the same year. A series of meetings occurred over the next three years that indicated Turkey would not simply ingest all policies handed to her, but that this once-empire has its own agenda and interest in maintaining a relationship with the Middle East as well as forming new relationships with the EU member states and maintaining a relationship with the United States. Turkey's flirtations with EU institution building are just one of the indicators that this semi-periphery is strategically preserving its exclusive identity, rather than simply 'servicing' the core as might be expected in WSA. Recent developments show the complexity of Turkey's re-negotiation with Europe as the 'other' through the secular mechanism of the Accession process and demonstrates how these international negotiations dramatically influence and affect the balance of relationships between Turkey's secular and Islamic leaderships through the positions that they have taken in relation to the EU.

Turkey and the EU's semi-periphery

Turkey's unique relationship with the EU demonstrates how balancing this part secular part Islamic society in a global division of labour creates contradictions in both core and semi-periphery. Turkey is closer to EU accession than would have been conceivable ten years ago and it is worth noting that no country that has begun accession talks has failed to join the EU. But popular and elite EU opposition to Turkish accession, a Customs Union agreement that serves the EU well and an unsympathetic attitude from key EU institutions to the challenges facing the Turkish political reformers has contributed to growing popular opposition to the accession process in Turkey. In many ways Turkey's position as poised between the core of the EU and the periphery of Eurasia re-asserts the centrality of the semi-periphery in the management of the uncertainties of the global political economy.

Turkey's position in the international political economy has changed dramatically over the past decade. The financial crisis of 2001 contributed to an economic reform process that elevated Turkey's status in the eyes of the International Monetary Fund (IMF 2004). Although Turkey has enjoyed preferential trading status with the EU since the Ankara Agreements of 1963, the Customs Union signed in 1995 created 'the deepest economic and trade relationship that the EU has ever had with any third country' according to Enlargement Commissioner Olli Rehn (Rehn 2008). Prior to the current (2007–) financial crisis the dramatic fall in inflation encouraged unprecedented waves of foreign direct investment (FDI) into Turkey. EU FDI in Turkey has made up almost two thirds of total FDI flows over the past six years and has increased 20 fold from €450 million in 2003 to almost €9 billion in 2007. Indeed EU FDI has increased from an average 0.5 per cent of Turkish GDP between 1990 and 2004 to about 3.5 per cent of GDP in 2006–2007 (Commission 2008).

The Turkish economy has therefore moved towards a more central position in the global division of labour through its greater proximity to the economic core of the EU. But the costs are not insignificant. Despite the high levels of growth in the Turkish economy, unemployment is high especially in the young population. Wealth generation is also concentrated geographically in the large cities to the Western side of the country with large migration flows moving east to west. Turkey's domestic economic reforms and large nationalised pension sector have helped it ride the credit slow down in the 2007–2008 recession, but its exposure to international credit and investment markets has left the economy vulnerable. The IMF's recent prescription is to maintain reforms that keep reducing the debt to GDP ratio, to impose stricter rules on local government finance and tax administration and to keep lowering inflation (IMF 2008).

The pressure from economic organisations such as the IMF to keep pace with demanding economic reforms has been accompanied by a parallel agenda for social and political reform associated with the EU accession process. Politically Turkey has maintained its attractiveness as a bridge between East and West for the political core of the Western alliance. NATO membership forged Turkey with the West during the secular divisions of the Cold War but its key attraction to the political core today is as a link to Islamic states in a religious divide. The Islamic AKP control of the Prime Ministry and Presidency has enabled it to promote a reforming agenda that is at least superficially orientated towards western agendas. Despite refutations of Huntingdon's doom laden and essentialist 'clash of civilisations' thesis, the War against Terror has provided a powerful logic for Turkish accession to the EU. In the technical terms of the accession process this means that most of the screening reports have been approved and eight of the accessions chapters on specific policy areas have been opened with one closed (Commission 2008). The UK's government is a leading advocate of Turkish accession and the reforming agendas proved that Turkey need no longer be seen as the sick man of Europe. The House of Commons Foreign Policy Select Committee has recognised that the pace of reform in Turkey has outstripped the expectations of its critics noting that:

> 34. There were expectations that Turkey would struggle to harmonise with the *acquis*; its better-than-expected progress has meant that Turkey's opponents have had to find other 'reasons to frustrate accession'.
>
> (House of Commons Foreign Affairs Committee 2007: 8)

Opposition to Turkish accession is indeed widespread in the EU with key figures across the EU policy elite opposing Turkish accession. In the EU's Commission ex Internal Market Commissioner Fritz Bolkestein edited a book of interviews with high profile European politicians all agreeing that the accession of Turkey represented the geographic limit to

European integration (Bolkestein and Eppink 2004: 14). Previous and current Presidents of France and German Foreign Ministers have made similar remarks at politically sensitive times. The European Parliament has twice criticised Turkey for the slow progress of its reforms. In its November 2008 proposal for a resolution the EP criticised the slowing rate of reform of Turkey's political elite and its lack of action across areas of democracy and rule of law, human and minority rights (EP 2008). Euro barometer poles also have consistently been against Turkish accession with a recent one expressing 55 per cent of the survey 'against' (EUROBAROMETER 5 2008: 28). Turkish accession is a divisive issue for the core leadership of the EU stalling the closing of key negotiation chapters as well as lower levels of EU financial support for Turkey in comparison to other pre-accessions states. The ambitions of Turkish elites to accede to the EU and to promote the reform agendas associated with accession are therefore constantly frustrated.

It is in this context that the shifting nature of the semi-periphery is most clearly expressed. The semi-peripheral role played by Turkey is as central to the EU's accumulation as it was in previous periods. Turkey still provides attractive investment opportunities for EU capital able to exploit the supply of cheap nearby labour and the demand of growing young markets while the benefits of the Customs Union are asymmetric, favouring the EU's higher value-added labour processes over Turkey's (Adam and Moutos 2008). The textile sector clearly demonstrates the benefit to the EU of a supply chain that adds value through knowledge economy services to low value-added production activities.

But just as important are the social conflicts that the semi-periphery can contain as an economic and cultural hinterland. The public sphere in Turkey is undergoing similar challenges to those that the EU faced in the 1990s with significant debates ranging over the constitutional nature of the polity, the role of key political positions in the executive and parliament and the representation of societal interest in the political system. These issues are far more deeply rooted than the debate over EU accession and strike to the heart of how Turkish society is organised into a political system. The rise of the AKP specifically challenges many of the core secular beliefs of the Turkish state forcing a decision by the constitutional court in 2007. Turkish identity politics do not necessarily draw from the same experiences as those shared by the Founding States of the EU; or those that acceded after the Central and East European Countries enlargements. The complexity of the battle for Turkish identity is far more complex as it addresses the role of secular and religious politics in addition to other traditional issues that accessions states have to address in relation to national identity and self-determination.

These representations of Turkish society have been evident in the media since the liberalisation of the 1990s with conservative and religious iconography matching with secular images into such diverse media outlets as political cartoons. The politicisation of these issues is made very real through the use of the Constitution's Article 301's to prosecute anti-Turkish statements which has in turn presented problems for Turkish elites both in relation to the EP's demands for a free press and in the embracing of the internet (You Tube was banned in Turkey for a video that insulted Kemal Ataturk). Yet Turkey has not enjoyed equal treatment in these areas. Diez, for example, argues that human rights infringements were seen as reasons for the accessions of Spain and Portugal as membership would help to entrench the rule of law and democracy (Diez 2007). What has happened instead in Turkey has been a proliferation of identities developed in opposition to EU accession as conservative sections elements bemoan the lack of consistency of EU actors and nationalists see EU interference in areas that are not sufficiently explored and/or understood.

The promise of Turkish accession therefore has a divisive effect on Turkish domestic politics in that it maintains the heat of politically dividing issues while offering neither their resolution through domestic means nor guaranteeing a convincing alternative that could provide a European-inspired compromise. Initiatives that bring Turkey closer to the core political and economic heart of the European Union, through introducing Lisbon Agenda style policy reforms, have to be introduced without explicit reference to the EU as the association sours any benefit to an increasingly Euro-sceptic public. While the controversies have precipitated high levels of popular engagement in EU accession discussions and sustained them over a long period of time they also reveal a difficult reality that the EU needs to address. While the EU places special emphasis on the need for human rights and the rule of law in Turkey, its lukewarm reaction to the reforms that have already taken place across Turkish society fail to acknowledge how much has changed in such a short amount of time. That the EU further fails to acknowledge the need to provide stability in a rapidly changing society only serves the conservative secular and religious causes that are so often presented as being not 'European'. In the meantime Turkey plays a semi-periphery role in absorbing the uncertainties that surround the boundaries of the EU and providing markets for EU surplus and capital investment.

What has changed in Turkey's position is that the core is no longer such an attractive proposition. The instability in credit supply that had sustained the EU and USA's knowledge-based economies could place Turkey in an advantageous position. High levels of demand, fuelled by credit generated in rapidly innovating capital markets, depend heavily on trust (Dannreuther and Petit 2008). The supply of trust through state regulators setting standards, advertising agencies developing brands, lawyers defining contractual obligations and accountants defining good corporate governance practices has been at the heart of the EU's economic expansion since the mid-1990s. But it is an expensive process and one that has clearly demonstrated its vulnerability. With the removal of easy credit supply there is no market for high-quality products, expensive advertising campaigns, or high-risk activities no matter how much legal certainty or risk management is provided. In this situation the fundamentals of a large market that makes real products and that has a labour force growing in age, skills, and potential prosperity places Turkey as an economically more promising environment than the ageing, service-based economies of the EU. Furthermore the trust that comes from shared moral and ethical positions or from the belief in the need for a strong system of secular laws both provide a powerful apparatus within which economic development can emerge.

Towards a conclusion?

The Ottoman Empire and the later Turkey became a player in the expansion of global capitalism beginning in the seventeenth century. We have not outlined in great depth the trajectory of the peripheralisation of the Ottoman Empire and the emergence of a semi-peripheral Turkey but have theorised that the fall of this Empire was a characteristic of the emergence of a modern capitalist world system. What we have shown is that the subsequent rising power of Turkey as a new breed of the semi-periphery has not and need not, in its rise to core status, adhere to the Anglo-Saxon neoliberal policies that have been advised.

Now, Turkey is at a critical juncture with regard to its future in the uncertainties of membership and the unclear direction of its identity across Europe. Prime Minister Recep Tayyip Erdogan is extremely pro-EU and has promoted institutional changes and held several talks to incorporate Turkey into the EU agenda. He has also made it clear that he promotes the foreign policy of the EU, and that Turkey's Strategic Depth Doctrine as piloted by Professor Ahmet Davutoglu (Davutoglu 2001), now chief foreign policy adviser to Erdogan, recommends a balanced and potentially authoritative geo-strategic relationship with neighbours as well as the West. This has overtones of a rightful inheritance of the Ottoman Empire's legacy and with a continued control of the Bosporus. This doctrine is at the pinnacle of new Ottoman Orientalism, a perspective that will challenge the view of Turkey as an exotic 'other' but rather one that will potentially take a leading role in Europe and to answer to the accusation that Turkey does not 'fit':

> Turkey no longer solely represents a geographic barrier against communism, but rather is transforming itself to meet the various threats emerging from its new geopolitical environment. In this context, Turkey's global role has shifted from a Western geo-strategic military deterrent to an exemplary model of a Muslim-majority, secular, and democratic nation. By broadening its horizons and seeing the positive role that it has to play in Europe, the Middle East, and Central Asia, Turkey is beginning to realise its full potential as a versatile multiregional and increasingly powerful international actor.
>
> (Walker 2007: 2)

This quote demonstrates what is becoming a mainstream perception of the changing role of Turkey in the region. The supposed 'Turkish model' allows a secular republic with a Muslim majority to operate as a functional democracy. While the country has extensive ties to Central Asia and has recently offered aid to this region, it has been an ally to the United States as well. Turkey's positioning in the contemporary world, however, is in crisis as the government's desire to become a fully accepted member of the EU clashes with an overtly authoritative strategic foreign policy. As a result, it is impossible to read this nation as a semi-periphery in the WSA sense. Instead it must be understood as a particularly important and transformative entity in the new Europe, with a new role for the contemporary age that was not characteristic of the semi-periphery Wallerstein and others have envisaged. While Turkey gains influence as a sought after ally and economic member by the United States and of the European Union, it has transformed the category of the semi-periphery itself. Its power has mounted through economic and strategic means, and therefore the concept of the role of the semi-periphery itself must change.

Part III

New Semi-Peripheral Developments and Possible Futures

9
CEE as a New Semi-Periphery: Transnational Social Forces and Poland's Transition

Stuart Shields

Central and Eastern Europe (CEE) has been a region that has been historically considered as semi-peripheral, a characteristic that was highlighted during the authoritarianism of the state socialist era (Martin 1990). The post-communist region has always been considered as 'backwards' part of Europe. As Daniel Chirot puts it, the region 'was in some sense economically backward long before it was absorbed into the broader Western world market. This backwardness had roots in the very distant past, not in any distortions imposed on Eastern Europe in the past few centuries' (Chirot 1989: 8). Consequently, attempts to understand the contemporary transformation need to explore the historical trajectory of crucial issues like CEE's semi-peripheral development. Since the end of the Cold War, the formal re-integration of CEE into the global economy has achieved the restoration of semi-peripherality through two main processes, first that associated with the initial neoliberal transition period and second, a similarly neoliberal Europeanization likewise completed under the auspices of the mobilization of transnational social forces. The focus of this chapter is not to re-engage with previous theoretical usages of the semi-periphery, but to show how such semi-peripheral regions have been integrated into the contemporary world order.

Using the example of Poland as a case study within CEE, the chapter explores how the policy of neoliberalism has become the abiding feature of transition, best seen through Poland's initial engagement with shock therapy. In the first part of the chapter I seek to develop a theoretical/methodological perspective which is critical of traditional perspectives on transition and International Relations (IR)/International Political Economy (IPE) that tend to buy into an inside-out/outside-in dichotomy. This involves the chapter establishing the key features of the global structural transformation that occurred since the 1970s and then identifying the agents of said transformation in the context of the Polish transition to a market economy. Although mainstream perspectives pay lip-service to considering transition as a complex, multi-faceted and global process they rarely overcome the dualism of global/national and continue to isolate parts from the totality. To achieve this, the chapter is divided into three main sections and the argument unfolds in the following manner. First, I propose a transnational historical materialist account of the processes associated with globalization. This facilitates a discussion of 'transition' that emphasizes the transnational social forces engendered by the neoliberal accumulation strategy of the emergent new order in post-communist development. Second, the chapter launches an interrogation of the transnational context for transition and links this to the emergence of a transnational capitalist class by identifying the social relations of production which in a particular combination have provided the foundations of the social process. The final substantive section then considers a series of events across the time span of transition where transnationally oriented agents have been implicated in significant interventions into the transition process in Poland. This section offers an account of the historical conditions of the rise and ideological disposition of these candidate ruling classes and the particular conditions under which they come to reproduce the social relations of production under their control.

Transition and globalization: A transnational historical materialist perspective

At its simplest, the defining change in the global political economy has been the successful mobilization of neoliberal social forces. There are four points to highlight. First, that the emergence of neoliberalism is embedded in the restructuring of capital on a world scale following the economic crisis of the 1970s. Second, neoliberalism needs to be understood as a set of processes that operate transnationally rather than as a set of discrete national events. However, I stress here not just the 'international' or 'global'; rather neoliberalism works as a multi-scalar economic discourse, establishing market deference as a necessary (pre)condition, re-naturalizing and thereby insulating economic relations from politics (Ashley 1983). Since the 1970s certain aspects of discursive sequestration have come to be most effectively achieved at the 'global' level.

The orthodox literature on transition has generally failed to account for the new (unequal) integration of the CEE into the global economy. This leaves us to turn to other areas of analysis where the material dimensions of the global economy are taken more seriously. In IR/IPE a number of scholars inspired by the work of the Italian Marxist Antonio Gramsci have begun to provide a suitable lexicon to productively frame questions concerning neoliberalism and the transnationalization of capital (Bieler and Morton 2001; Cox 1981, 1983; Gill 1995, 1998; Morton 2003). For those interested in the external and global facets of transition, Gramscian IPE has provided a 'number of innovative concepts that promise to illuminate the mechanisms of hegemony at the international level' (Germain and Kenny 1998: 3). The chapter is therefore an attempt to examine the complexity of historical development in which the political conditions of economic change, social structures and relations of force within a particular national state are clearly at the forefront. The chapter articulates one of the central concepts of a Gramscian-inflected IR/IPE – the emergence of a transnational capitalist class – and its application to the historical case of transition Poland. Using this position as a starting point, I argue throughout the chapter that changes in the global political economy constitute the beginnings of the transnationalization of the state; the shift both upwards in scale (to the regional and global) but also and downwards in scale (to the local and urban) from the post-war scalar predominance of the national-state form.

Beginning to address the issue of scale, presumes the starting point of conceptual categories such as uneven development, accumulation crisis and the rise of a powerful and simultaneously vulnerable financial circuits within the world economy that need securing, and utilizing this position enables us to pose the problem as the underlying dynamic of capital expansion and contraction. Questions concerning neoliberalism are thus vital to the logic of so-called globalization witnessed in the switching of scales in the application of transition from the national, to the urban, regional and supra-national. Thus then the transnational is not reducible to its component parts, but arises from the multiple dialectical relations of the production process. Consequently, the separate parts are implicated in the constitution of the 'thing', never outside the process of its making.

Instead of a nation-state driven process, these changes constitute an important break with the immediate past and signal in a crude interpretation the subordination of the interests of national social forces to the requirements of globally mobile capital (van Apeldoorn 2000; Shields 2004). It is this subordination that has configured neoliberal forms of state based on the now well-known blueprint of sound money and open markets. The ideas associated with this are transmitted through a range of formal and informal national, international, regional and transnational agencies. This historically novel form of predominantly economic constitutionalism is more than just a set of substantive rules. Alternatively, this transnational regulatory governance establishes social and economic procedural requirements in the form of systems of benchmarking, monitoring and auditing that now impinge throughout the global political economy (Jayasuriya 2005).

The challenge that this poses to more traditional scholars of transition in CEE is to unravel the political and institutional ways that capital has been (re)structured and consent (re)organized from the communist era. In relation to Poland more directly this encourages us to explore the historical embeddedness of the ongoing practical transformations as well as a normative appraisal of the dangers and opportunities that these changes represent for emancipatory alternatives to develop. In what follows, I explore these concerns in relation to the Polish transition and focus on three main questions. First, how might we begin to think through the implications of a transnational context for transition? Second, what has generated, sustained and legitimated neoliberal hegemony in Poland? And third, where are the elements of this process visible?

Thus it becomes essential to start to identify the agents of transnationally oriented capital: those individuals and groups that benefit from constructing and then maintaining a particular formulation of what counts as common sense (Augelli and Murphy 1988: 13–29; 35–41; Murphy and Tooze 1991). One step in this process to reveal how certain ideas about legitimate roads to transition have become accepted as common sense so as to be so naturalized that they are considered unquestionable, objective 'facts' of transition. In Poland, neoliberal policies of Shock Therapy and transitological theoretical approaches have been presented as an unproblematic formulation of both institutions and class relationships (Lipton and Sachs 1990; Sachs 1993b, 1990). However, MacLean maintains that the implications of this approach were that transition rapidly became formulated as a set of pragmatic problems, and even though opinion might differ on the minor details:

> A dominant view was quickly established. What variance and dispute
> there is has become located much more with views and speculation

about the likely consequences of, and possible future developments out of these events, than with evaluation about what the events signify.

(Maclean 1996: 184)

Thinking of transition in this way therefore casts transition as concerned with the construction of a dominant form of consciousness in CEE concerning underdevelopment as managed by western political and economic power, and disseminated by state agencies and IFIs. The universalization of a partial knowledge is a crucial factor in the construction of class hegemony to formulate an integral mode of accumulation, an international division of labour, and a legitimate political order. Additionally it is ideology conditioning historical consciousness to allow accumulation, and social order to occur in a specific historical form. As Augelli and Murphy continue, 'ideologies are always instruments of power, because it is only with a merging of thought and action that the historical role of humanity…can be regained' (1988: 21). The chapter now turns to the integral form of accumulation.

Transition and structural change in the global political economy

This section of the chapter briefly conceptualizes the different dimensions of structural change experienced in the global political economy since the decline of Keynesianism and the crisis of Fordism in the late 1960s and early 1970s. This set of changes has three principal components: first an ideological dimension, with the rise to hegemony of neoliberal ideas and philosophy expressing the interests of a particular class fraction of transnational capital; second, a material dimension, with the transformation in the bases of finance and production capital changing from an overarching national state scale to global orientation; and third, an institutional dimension, which has altered forms of state and world order through emerging transnational structures of governance and policy making that have in effect 'managed' change since the 1970s (Jayasuriya 2005). The problem, as Panitch has identified, lies in the danger of 'misrepresenting as cooperative understandings what were in reality structural manifestations of a hierarchically organized international political economy' (2000: 13). How are these more abstract changes associated with prevailing ideas in post-communist transition? I outline here three responses to this question.

The first point to reflect on is that certain fractions of transnational capital have emerged as a coherent class formation:

> The elite within this class fraction can be said to be at the zenith of an emerging transnational historical bloc, whose material interests and key ideas (within a broader political consciousness) are bound up with the progressive transnationalization and liberalization of the global political economy. Among its key members are top owners and key executives of [multinational corporations]; central and other bankers; many though not all, leading politicians and civil servants in most advanced capitalist countries, and in some developing countries.
>
> (Gill 1993b: 261)

Members of the Polish post-communist elite need to be considered as belonging to a wider transnational establishment, improved transportation and communications technology have doubtless facilitated the growth of such a class fraction. Private and public institutions have improved dialogue and interaction between elite groups advancing a common identity and a shared consciousness promoting a closer identification of interests. Thus, the class becomes, to paraphrase Marx, more a class for itself than merely a collection of disparate social and material forces (van der Pijl 2004; Robinson and Harris 2000; Shields 2003; Sklair 1997).

The second concern is that the linkages and networks established by this class fraction have come to fruition in association with the transnationalization of the state whereby state policy and institutional arrangements have increasingly been conditioned by the power of globally mobile capital (Robinson and Harris 2000). The transnational state is

> attempting to fulfil the functions for world capitalism that in earlier periods were fulfilled by ... a dominant capitalist power that has the resources and the structural position which allows it to organize world capitalism as a whole and impose the rules, regulatory environment, etc, that allows the system to function.
>
> (Robinson 2004: 44)

But the crucial point to underline is the 'continued existence of the national-state system ... a central condition for the power of transnational capital because transnational fractions among dominant groups are able to use these core states to mould transnational structures' (Robinson 2004: 47). What this begins to account for are the changing trajectories of political economy, and a nation-statecentric focus fails to take into account the changing form of political economy, thus missing out on the transnational context in which national economies function and the social purpose of the wider transformation in the global political economy.

Prioritizing the determination of national in this way does not accurately come to terms with the question of how capital has re-authored its behaviour since the 1970s to take advantage of the competitive process at a variety of different scales both above and below the traditional explanation of the embedded national scale. State form is fundamentally co-determined by transnational social forces extending and transcending different territorial 'levels'. What I want to suggest here is that rather than constituting an extra 'level', as opposed to say the global, the supra-national or the international, that we instead understand the transnational as a historical spatial and scalar relation that extends across, beyond and transcends different territorial 'levels of analysis'. This does not occlude the state from our analysis but enables an appreciation of the transnational that includes 'state, supra-state and sub-state in a multi-level conception which can also accommodate non-territorial phenomena' (Anderson 2002: 16). The transnational is therefore not merely a way of considering long-term cyclical patterns of development. As a more nuanced approach to restructuring I maintain this is a key strategy for the regulation and attempted resolution of Fordist crisis. In a more general sense, though we cannot understand a particular scale without analysing its relationships to other scales. The meaning and importance of each scale is unavoidably embedded in its inter-scalar relationships. Scale is therefore a relational concept. At its most prosaic, global restructuring is not just discovered in ostensibly 'global' governance of capital but a whole series of complimentary and/or competitive scales where capital in general attempts to valourize. IR/IPE, due to its philosophical and methodological roots in the neo–neo debate and rejection of Marxist perspectives, has worked with an overwhelmingly one-dimensional understanding of global restructuring, with few attempts to move beyond the global as an additional autonomous level of analysis added on to the international (van Apeldoorn 2004; Overbeek 2004).

As Overbeek and van der Pijl note, one of the crucial dimensions of change in the historical process of capitalist development progresses is capital's paradigmatic scale of operation, referring to the spatial dimensions of the process, in particular the widening scale of operation of productive capital, from local in the early capitalist period to national in the nineteenth century, to Atlantic in the mid-twentieth century, and to global in the early twenty-first century (Overbeek and van der Pijl 1993). There are different levels of 'where' capital can operate most efficiently and the transnational indicates the relationship between scales, not a zero-sum game but relational processes that can as easily be in contradiction and competition with one another, as complimentary.

It is not just state policies being redefined but regional and urban policies on the market, on labour-capital relations, and the socio-economic framework appropriate for a neoliberal conception of development to be installed in an incremental and cumulative course (van Apeldoorn 2004; Brenner 2004). The implication of this for CEE is the ceding of responsibilities to foreign capital. Foreign direct investment (FDI) was almost universally proclaimed as a fundamental component of the reconstruction of post-communist economies. Indeed the virtuous circle provided by FDI is still considered an essential strategy for economic recovery throughout CEE (Fischer 2000). Supposedly it would provide benefits like employment, access to Western markets, integration into MNC research and development networks and associated technology transfer, management quality control techniques, modernized production techniques and the burgeoning small- and medium-sized enterprises that were 'missing' under state-socialism (see contributions to Beyer 2002; Zloch-Christy 1995). However, FDI is also consolidating a general social system in CEE as it reproduces capitalist relations of production. As Panitch argues, 'when multinational capital penetrates a host social formation, it arrives not merely as abstract "direct foreign investment", but as a transformative social force within the country' (Panitch 2000: 8). In terms of an examination of the state this indicates the penetrative but consensual process that leave sufficient space to understand the *active authoring* role of states in globalization (Poulantzas 1975: 60–63).

Finance and economic ministries have come to prominence in government over this period. State agencies linked to industry, employment and welfare are downgraded as the competitive race for FDI intensifies (Bohle and Greskovits 2006). Corporatist agencies, at a global level those associated with Keynesianism or the developmental state, have been increasingly marginalized. The political role of organized labour has declined as small-scale 'national' manufacturing industry is pressurized by international competition and regional arrangements like the EU's Lisbon Strategy. One recent example of such transformative transnational social forces pertaining to CEE is the High Level Group report on the Lisbon Strategy that asserted:

> 'Competitiveness' is not just some dry economic indicator that is often unintelligible to the man on the street; rather, it provides a

diagnosis of the state of economic health of a country or region. In the present circumstances, the clear message must be: if we want to preserve and improve our social model we have to adapt: it is not too late to change. In any event the status quo is not an option.

(European Communities 2004: 44)[1]

A particular neoliberal model of what constitutes a normal economy rapidly came to dominate (Blejer and Coricelli 1994: 100) through agents that have a number of links to the obvious institutions of transnational capital like the IMF, World Bank and the WTO – which have assumed 'management' of the global economy. Inside these powerful supranational institutions, the objective needs of capital are replacing parochial national interests. This shift is evident elsewhere in less obvious but nonetheless active transnational private consultative and planning bodies 'beyond' the state, like Bilderberg, the Trilateral Commission, and the World Economic Forum (WEF) at Davos, where economics and politics are synthesized in a dialogue between the corporate elite and a managerial cadre class (van der Pijl 1998; Gill 1990).

The third aspect that needs noting when exploring changes in the global political economy in relation to CEE is that political and economic changes have occurred in a period when the prevailing ideological situation shifted. The corollary of this has been the reformulation of what is and what is not considered contestable in the realm of appropriate policy choice. Indeed the distinctiveness of the contemporary agenda lies in the fact that market reform and social policy are so intimately connected. Opinion has converged since the 1970s over the use of price and monetary stability to reduce inflationary pressures, and on an ever increasing market orientation to reduce the input of the government and the transfer of emphasis to private initiatives. Fundamental in this process is the installation of neoliberal ideas and practices that have reinforced the promotion of flexible exchange markets, control of inflation and public expenditure, reification of the private sector relative to the public sector, and labour market flexibility, all endorsed and enforced by an obliging collection of International Financial Institutions (IFIs).

As Barnett and Finnemore clarify, IFIs have assigned normative value to certain modes of behaviour as they participate in the construction of the social world in a particular neoliberal image (Barnett and Finnemore 2004). IFIs aid in fixing meaning, establishing rules and transmitting norms around the global system. In this way, they act as *disciplinary mechanisms* of the abstract application of neoliberalism, de-limiting that which is considered possible and constraining struggles for progressive political alternatives (van der Pijl 1998: 51) It is in the naturalization and normalization of these ideas that the restriction of possibilities for subordinate classes to engage with the global order prevails at an ideological level: hence the familiar neoliberal mantra that there is no alternative represents, in effect, the concrete manifestation of a particular class ideology as an incontestable structure of thought and its extension into the transition on the collapse of communism (Maclean 1996).

In an uneasy dystopian echo of Polanyi, the re-configuration of societies and the social relations of production has been based, since the 1970s, on a particular formulation that includes the reification of international competitiveness and the celebration of the market as the most, if not the only, efficient mechanism for organizing social life wealth, and anti-unionism, all translated into a powerful, self-evident, everyday discourse. This is particularly evident in transition Poland after the disintegration of Solidarity in the early 1990s as a result of its own confused and contradictory role in transition: dissident, anti-communist, pro-Western social democracy movement and pro-labour union (Ashwin 1998; Crowley 2004). Policies of marketization and privatization have been advanced through private business leaders and expert economists, and mediated through inter-governmental institutions. The 'triumph' of neoliberal economics since the 1970s has become so powerfully engrained as common sense that the states of CEE adopted the strategy of neoliberal transition regardless of whether or not such reforms have been appropriate or not. Transition states have been forced to change their foreign and domestic social and economic policies in a particular way to engage with a particular model of international trade and FDI that emphasizes the re-configuration of the 'national' economy to attract foreign capital (Biersteker 1992: 105).

The unfolding neoliberal order has effectively usurped the previous overriding regulation of the relationship between capital and labour at the nation-state level and replaced this with a far more fluid alternative where states are, in Cerny or Cox's view, acting to accommodate and favour capital. Hence Cerny's notion of the 'competition' state and Cox's analogy of a 'transmission belt' from the global into the national economic sphere (Cox 1992b; Cerny 1997). For both, the state is withdrawing from its embedded liberal compromise as arbitrator between capital and citizen unable to pursue growth as a 'domestic' problem any more. Instead with the global investment climate promulgating enhanced competitiveness the state is increasingly forced to act as a market player itself, shaping policy to promote returns from market forces in a global setting (Cerny 1997). The problem here though is that both Cerny and Cox argue that the dynamic between international relations and unequal development relies on an immanent problematizing of how globalization modifies the international-state system and the prospects for 'national' development.

This reification of the nation-state, particularly the nationally bounded correspondence between class process and national border is misplaced. Can it be that the contradictions of capitalism manifest themselves as contradictions between nation-states representing the interests of competing national capitals? I would assert that competition corresponds even less (if it ever did) to merely the nation-state scale given that capitalism has always been a global system; globally integrated production, the increasing internationalization of services, and the hyper-mobility of capital have transformed a system historically based on competing national capitals into one characterized by increasingly interpenetration of formerly 'national' capitals and the transnationalization of capital and of class relations (van der Pijl 1984; Robinson 1998: 12).

The particular characteristics of the transition state in its formerly state-socialist guise meant that domestic neoliberal social forces developed surreptitiously, in a capillary way (Shields 2006: 480), or as van der Pijl terms it 'molecularly' in the direction of the prevailing pattern in the west (van der Pijl 1995: 112) secured through a multitude of think tanks, public and private meetings, conferences, academic and popular publications and lobbying 'in which the bearers of ideas which have few powerful adherents work away until the material forces begin to change in their direction' (Sklair 1997: 516). Since then it has come to be sustained and reinforced by a much broader-based coalition of social forces (see Fourcade-Gourinchas and Babb 2002) so that at a certain point a class was constituted through integration into the circuits of global capital and links to networks of transnational elites. In Poland this occurred with increasing velocity from the 1970s through to the 1990s. While for the half century of communist rule Poland had been formally separated from the mainstream of international economics formal re-integration into the neoliberal mainstream was precipitated by the problems associated with the Gierek debt crisis (Shields 2006: 484–488). Having outlined the material and ideational contours of the transnational context of transition the chapter now turns to an examination of the representatives of the transnational capitalist class and their intervention in Poland's transition to a market economy.

The emergence of polish social forces for neoliberalization

Poland's neoliberal revolution was introduced on 1 January 1990 and has been designated the Balcerowicz Plan following the chief architect or Shock Therapy, with the deliberate aim of offering a comprehensive transformation as opposed to the more usual arbitrary, ad hoc, partial measures that had existed before to build capitalism. As Balcerowicz's accomplice Jeffrey Sachs regaled observers around the time:

> The economic reforms will set in motion a sustained process of economic restructuring...Once market forces are unleashed, there should be a strong pull of resources into the previously neglected [service] sector....Agriculture is another area where we should expect major restructuring....the third major trend that we should expect is a complete restructuring within the industrial sector, from energy-intensive heavy industry to more labor-intensive and skill-intensive industries that can compete on the world market...Western firms...are likely to set up operations...for the sake of export production, in the same way as European firms are investing in Spain.
>
> (Sachs 1993a: 209)

The Balcerowicz Plan required a reduction in the role of the state in the economy, therefore, and no longer provided production plans, investment or subsidies. Markets would instead determine supply, demand and price. Welfare and social spending was to be cut in areas such as unemployment benefit and consumer subsidies. As many state firms as possible were to be privatized as private firms respond to markets and discipline their workforces more efficiently than state firms. Private firms have the added advantage of disciplining non-privately owned firms to become more efficient and competitive. And of course unemployment would discipline labour by initiating competition. Western capital and products were given favourable conditions for entry into the Polish market through a mixture of low import duties, a weakened currency (the zloty) and low wages. Thus the path forwards was simple, the oft repeated mantra of stabilization, liberalization and privatization.

The key transformation in social relations came in the alteration from a political critique of communism to a primarily economic reform debate. The economic sphere became the overriding concern as 'the important problem became not who will rule and who he [sic] will rule, but whether the government will be limited...[allowing]...the economy to function freely' (Szacki 1995: 122). The activities of particular social forces engaged in these transformations can be decoded in the re-articulation of anti-communism as the emergence in Poland of van der Pijl's transnationally oriented Lockean social forces (van der Pijl 1995). The ideological shifts that occurred in the 1970s and the material-ization of a neoliberal discourse served to legitimate the self-constitution of an intellectual and cadre class, the abandonment of labour-related concerns, employee self-management schemes and other 'social demo-cratic' or socialist ideas tainted through their association with the men-dacious communist state and earlier incarnations of Solidarity.[2] Walicki (1988), for example, criticized Solidarity for being too socialist, too 'workerist'; and the response of workers to this criticism was ambivalent as they increasingly squabbled amongst themselves (Kramer 1995). As Gramsci detected in his discussion of Americanism and Fordism, there was a lag between contemporary ideologies of organized labour and the new kind of working class being constructed by Fordism (Gramsci 1971: 286). In the Polish context, trade unions were still fighting the strug-gles of the previous decade while neoliberalism was determining a new type of labour better suited to a post-communist productive regime. The implications of this for Balcerowicz and like-minded reformers would be to reinforce an elitist attitude to the transition, reluctant participation in democratic practices and a single-minded legislative construction of the parameters to a market society after 1989 devoid of consideration for wider social support other than the oft-repeated notion of a 'new middle class' who would support reforms. The prominence of the fun-damental role of individual freedom through economic activity echoes the social arrangements that Gramsci termed the 'implacable play of free competition' that purges the state of 'its noxious elements through the free clash of bourgeois social forces' (Gramsci 1977: 46). It is at this point that we begin to see clearly the emergence of Polish social forces for neoliberalism.

In 1978, Balcerowicz had convened an informal group of economists. Throughout the 1980s this group of economists together with other sympathetic economists scattered around Poland, and with the help of émigré economists, began to pursue the idea of transforming the scle-rotic Polish economy. Balcerowicz provides useful illustration of this in relation to Poland when discussing the role of a core group of 'excellent advisors' in the late 1980s:

And there were some other advisors, some of them of Polish ori-gin like Stanislaw Gomulka, who worked at the London School of Economics, and he came to Poland.... Jacek Rostowski, who was of

Polish origin who was born in Britain, but he spoke perfect Polish and was a very good economist. So I think that I had who a core group of excellent advisors who helped us on working out some legal strategies in the program.

(Interview with Leszek Balcerowicz 2000)

According to Lane studies of émigrés show a consistent pattern of changing support in the 1980s, the young were much more critical of state socialism; whereas the earlier post-war generation had been more supportive (Lane 2005; Zubek 1997: 185). This group not only included Balcerowicz but also others who would later form part of the Shock Therapy team at the Ministry of Finance (Balcerowicz 1996). A decade later he acknowledged the importance and extent of this network:

I think I was lucky in my first choice of my partners, my colleagues. I was sort of a leader of an economic team within the government, and ... created a group in the late seventies. And some members of the group worked with me as academics, but very practical-oriented academics, and in the eighties they entered the government.... Marek Dabrowski was one of the members of the original group ... and then he entered the government with me as my deputy in the Ministry of Finance, which was crucial. The minister of finance became very powerful in Poland, and rightly so, as a center of stabilization and structural reforms.

(Interview with Leszek Balcerowicz 2000)

The group put together included Marek Dabrowski, as noted above a personal friend of Balcerowicz, Rafal Krawczyk, a particularly enthusiastic proponent of one-off voucher privatization and vigorously opposed to non-private forms of ownership and Grzegorz Kolodko, one of Balcerowicz's successors as deputy premier and minister of finance from 1994 to 1997. The impact of this group should not be understated. Their role during the 1980s in a party-sponsored reform debate was crucial in engulfing the whole of Polish society and the emergence of virtual consensus that the economic system was bankrupt and needed the massive, immediate, wholesale dismantling of state socialism and the introduction of a market economy (Kuzinski 1987; Sadownik and Wawrzyniak 1985). By 1988, Walicki contended that this group of reforming economists directly involved in the debate had 'already been successful in changing the intellectual climate of Poland' (1988: 22).

During the political liberalization of the 1970s many young academics obtained various grants to participate in exchanges with Western universities. Subsequently in the 1980s a distinctive intellectual and entrepreneurial group conscientiously and openly championed neoliberalism (Zubek 1997: 184). From its inception, Polish neoliberalism has therefore been an intrinsically elitist movement, intimately connected to its transnational counterparts. Yet what distinguishes the Gramscian analysis proffered here from conventional elite sociological transformation models (Nee 1996; Róna-Tas 1994; Szelenyi and Kostello 1996) is the constancy of ideological cohesion between the various groups. Members of the Polish elite and intellectual neoliberals realigned the central problem facing society by articulating an argument that moved from the political critique of communism to the overt notion that economic freedom precedes all other liberties. This helped to constitute the claim that systemic transformation necessitated instituting a specific form of market economy. The Polish neoliberals participated in fundamentally re-configuring anti-communism so that the solution was no longer the collective self-liberation of a society, as per Solidarity, but a new future constructed in the domain of non-state economic activity.

By the late 1980s formal discussions between Solidarity and the Communist Party at the Round Table negotiations that followed the initial reform debate appeared on the surface to be addressing matters of deep ideological difference and consequence. However, the reality is that they focused more directly on procedural and systemic matters, because the two sides were already in agreement as to the future direction Poland should take. In the period leading up to the negotiations, the societal consensus on Poland's future as a market economy was so embedded and widespread on both sides that the Party negotiators appeared even more committed to a rapid and drastic transformation to a capitalist economy than their Solidarity counterparts (Dziewanowski 1989). Not only had communism been discredited and declared intellectually bankrupt, but it had been unable to demonstrate the ability to produce innovative reform. Moreover, not even reform elements within the party had proved able to launch their own model of 'reform socialism'. In short, the neoliberals had successfully constructed a position whereby the only viable option remaining was to change the entire system by introducing a market-driven economy.

It is worth accentuating at this juncture that the Polish neoliberals aimed to introduce their reforms without the direct participation of the general population preferring instead a Leninist vanguard approach to top-down reconstruction of the social order. For this group of insulated technocratic reformers, the involvement of civil society would only delay the necessary changes (Przeworski 1991: 187).[3] The practical result of this was Solidarity and the regime reformers having a series of acrimonious disagreements, organizational splintering and the inability to form coalitions in the face of genuine political opponents (Wierzbicki 1985). As Balcerowicz and others argued, existing social groups were part of the problem (Balcerowicz 1996; Greskovits 1998: 139). The fact that this particular group of people dominated the all-powerful Polish finance ministry was central to the success of neoliberal transition. They triumphed, not necessarily because of their policies but because they were well organized in tight, entrenched, secluded bureaucratic teams isolated from society and united by their personal ties and common backgrounds (Greskovits 1998: Chapter 3) and had already been working together for years on aspects of the transition to a market economy. In December 1989, *The Economist* noted:

> [Balcerowicz] hand-picked his group, mostly younger colleagues from Poland's economic academies...One Polish cabinet minister...said there were now 'two Polish governments; the Balcerowicz team and the rest of us...we just have to accept what they say'.
>
> (*The Economist* 1989)

The Balcerowicz Group had spent the end of 1989 developing the theoretical effort they had worked on through the 1970s and 1980s into an executable programme for reform, which, significantly, '[secured] the approval of the IMF and the World Bank' (Slay 1994: 91). The IMF and World Bank reciprocated by aiding the Ministry of Finance and in the case of privatization, the Ministry of Ownership Change (Meaney 1995). The World Bank assisted the privatization ministry during its creation and provided a steady stream of technical assistants (World Bank 1996: 110) The ministry was exempted from the usual ceiling on civil service pay scales thus enabling it to attract the most capable staff (Amsden et al. 1995: 119).

In September 1989, with the formal collapse of communism, the Balcerowicz Group officially gained power as part of the first non-Communist Party government led by Tadeusz Mazowiecki. Thus, there was a specific class fraction connected to the ideological and policy networks of transnational neoliberalism present at the outset of Polish reforms. By the end of the year, domestic representatives of neoliberalism had achieved a virtual monopoly on advice and policy application throughout CEE, not just Poland, due in part to their links to the external social forces of neoliberalism. With almost total dominance of the domestic reform debate, it is not altogether a surprise that transition had a neoliberal essence. These individuals had gained power and influence, materially and ideologically, through their links to the external social forces of transnational capital. The neoliberal technocrats took over the state in the 1990s in an attempt to manage the transition to a completely different economic model by deploying a rejection of the state socialist and clientalist mechanisms of the previous order, which in practice included Solidarity. They succeeded in the sense that they prevented (and continue to prevent) political opposition from blocking further neoliberal transition.

Conclusion

This chapter endeavoured to provide an analysis of the political role played by an emergent transnational capitalist class in a longer term analysis of transition in the CEE to a market economy. In this way it has shown how states that were considered semi-peripheral during the Cold War era, with the elitist characteristics of their respective political structures seen as being one of their features (Arrighi 1990), have adopted neoliberal regimes through a configuration in elite political strategies and changes in forms of everyday social life.

By focussing on Poland, this has provided a case study of how this process of elitist restructuring has taken place in the most watertight example of neoliberalization. From the case outlined above it is important to recognize that the rise of this class fraction committed to neoliberalism in Poland is not so much an imposition from outside but a reflection of an internal evolution in which a fraction of the 'national' elite has become integrated into transnational circuits of capital accumulation – as comfortable with their consumption of Big Macs and Mercedes as their foreign counterparts. What is now necessary is further investigation into the possibilities for, and actual operation of some kind of counter-hegemony, that is, the welding together of different strands of resistance into a potential coalition of forces capable of engaging in a strategy to gain power. What this also reminds us is that social change, emancipatory or regressive, does not automatically follow economic developments, but is instead produced by historically situated social agents whose actions are enabled and constrained by their social self-understandings (Gramsci 1971: 326).

Notes

1. I am particularly grateful to Greig Charnock for his suggestions on the issue of competitiveness.
2. Neoliberalism became increasingly fashionable in the 1980s with a proliferation of translations of Friedman and Hayek and publications by key 'reoriented' economists. This phenomenon known as politicization (*upolitycznienie*), had little concern with trade union issues, the lived experiences of communism or the day-to-day concerns of average citizens.
3. Balcerowicz would eventually concede the necessity for political engagement, leading *Unia Wolnosci* – the Freedom Union party – from 1995. However since 2000 he has again reinsulated himself from politics in his role as Chairman of the National Bank of Poland.

10
A Semi-Periphery to Global Capital: Global Governance and Lines of Flight for Caribbean Offshore Financial Centres

William Vlcek

A frequent and readily accessible indicator for globalisation are figures demonstrating the increase in cross-border capital flows, whether foreign exchange, portfolio investment or direct investment. The re-configuration of core-periphery relations brought about by globalisation is seen in the relocation of production facilities leading to the creation of global production chains. A parallel re-configuration has occurred in global finance with the end of the Bretton Woods system and a decline in the use of capital controls. These events served to release capital to find new and innovative investment vehicles that in turn opened avenues for increased global financialisation. Offshore financial centres (OFCs) evolved with this reconfiguration from simple tax havens for wealthy individuals to become pivotal nodal points in the expansion of global circuits of capital. They have emerged as a semi-periphery for global finance, operating between the leading financial centres in London and New York and the myriad of production sites throughout the periphery. One example for this situation is the fact that the British Virgin Islands is the second major source of foreign direct investment (FDI) capital to China, after Hong Kong. Advancing from the brute geography of physical location and size, these small islands have developed into virtual powerhouses in the vast electronic financial markets operating 24/7 from Tokyo to London to New York. This aspect is the crucial point, because beyond the figures and graphs financial globalisation does not have the same physical presence found, for example, with a new Intel chip foundry in Vietnam. One must look closely at the evidence of financial flows to discover the presence of the core/semi-periphery/periphery relationship in global finance.

Offshore financial centres represent the changing nature of the concept of the semi-periphery from its past emphasis on manufacturing capacity to an expanded recognition for the strategic importance of finance capital in globalisation. This chapter builds on the characterisation of the semi-periphery established in the theoretical chapters and applies it to global finance, situating the OFC and global financial networks in this framework. It is reflected here through listings aggregated from a number of sources that name the OFCs, and demonstrated using data from the Bank for International Settlements (BIS) to show the role and function of OFCs as the semi-periphery for global finance. Global financial governance is interrogated through the question of whether it serves to benefit the semi-periphery (and is thus truly global in its objectives), or if governance acts to benefit the interests of core states alone. The existence of a space for resistance by these small states is represented through the failure of one specific international initiative against harmful tax competition launched by the Organisation for Economic Co-operation and Development (OECD) that proposed to constrain OFC operations and re-affirm the dominance of financial centres located in core states. On balance, other global financial governance initiatives (including those to counter money laundering and terrorist financing) have been implemented with less difficulty as they serve more broadly acknowledged global collective benefits. Yet the uneven nature of the processes that produce these forms of global governance is a reflection of the unevenness of inter-state relations, and it reproduces existing power relations that limit the freedom for action by the semi-peripheral OFC.

Offshore finance is used by a number of small (mostly island) jurisdictions as a means for economic development, and to some extent it has proven a successful strategy.[1] At it's most basic, hosting an offshore financial services industry is a strategy to collect rents from the financial transactions intentionally attracted to this location through regulatory arbitrage (in taxation, information collection and exchange, or corporate governance). A further benefit to the host jurisdiction is the economic spillover effects for employment opportunities, tourism, and construction. This economic development method is increasing difficult to maintain under the pressure created by the global governance initiatives (Vlcek, 2007).

It is argued by a number of core state institutions (the OECD and IMF, for example) and the governments of core states themselves that the activities of the OFCs contain within them a variety of corrosive effects that reach beyond their sandy shores (tax avoidance/evasion, capital flight, money laundering). These views prompted several initiatives during the past two decades to eliminate both regulatory arbitrage and financial criminality in the offshore realm. A further consequence of these programmes would be the reduction, if not elimination, of those beneficial aspects sought by these small jurisdictions in their pursuit of development. They are trapped by a 'scissors effect' of rising regulatory compliance costs and declining revenue from licensing fees (Sharman, 2005: 312). The predicament afflicting the semi-peripheral and peripheral states as they struggle to participate in the world economy is that the range and quantity of these international financial regulations can exceed their capacity and capability to implement and enforce them (Vlcek, 2008b).

The following discussion considers one aspect of the implications that globalisation holds for governance in the semi-periphery, that of global financial governance and its impact on offshore finance as a development strategy. The case explored here involves offshore finance in the Caribbean and the chapter is structured in four main sections. First, offshore finance will be shown as a semi-periphery operating in the global political economy. The point from this discussion is to demonstrate that OFCs are crucial nodes for the global financial network. Second is a discussion of the dimensions of capital on deposit in offshore centres, with particular reference to Caribbean OFCs. Third is a review of three regulatory programmes in the global financial governance structure imposed by core states over the past 30 years in an attempt to re-assert control of global finance. The fourth section gathers these points together and takes up the question of whether these circumstances produce governance or neo-colonialism. The chapter concludes with thoughts on the consequences and future trajectory for regulatory arbitrage in the semi-peripheral Caribbean. The overall effect from these regulatory measures is to guarantee the operation and reproduction of the existing global financial system for the benefit of the core states, while disregarding the economic (and subsequently social) impact imposed on the supporting states of the semi-periphery.

A semi-periphery in global finance

Defining the semi-periphery tends to involve the status of the national economy and in particular its manufacturing and industrial capacity and prevailing wage levels (Shannon, 1989: 32; Önis and Aysan, 2000: 120). This approach reproduces a concept of the semi-periphery as a transitional space for economic activity in the world economy. The four characteristics of the semi-periphery identified by Christopher Chase-Dunn are more useful for an analysis of global finance.

1. A semi-peripheral region may be one which mixes within the same area both core and peripheral forms of organisation.
2. Also a semi-peripheral region may be spatially located in between core and peripheral regions.
3. Mediating activities between core and peripheral areas may be carried out there.
4. In addition, a semi-peripheral area may be one in which institutional features are in some sense intermediate between those of the relevant core and periphery.

(Chase-Dunn, 1988: 30)

Within the context of global finance these points are generally applicable, especially characteristic number three. To identify the OFC as semi-peripheral marks it out as operating within the larger structure of financial centres in the world economy as an intermediate node for transactions among core financial centres and between the periphery and the core. The accompanying table (Table 10.1) provides a listing of jurisdictions recognised at different times over the past several decades as possessing an OFC. Graphically, global finance in the world economy with offshore finance as the semi-periphery could be depicted as seen here (Figure 10.1).

For global finance within the world economy, the core states represent an onshore space in opposition to the offshore space encompassed by a variety of semi-peripheral and peripheral states. The offshore world is a legal and political structure created by the inter-state system and distinguished as different from the domestic (onshore) space (Palan, 1998). It is a legislative structure defined by the jurisdiction to regulate and supervise a regime distinct and independent from comparable domestic institutions. The focus in this chapter is on offshore finance, in particular banking services. The 'offshore world' itself, however, consists of regulatory arbitrage opportunities in a number of areas, including shipping registries, international business corporation registries, captive insurance and re-insurance firms, mutual/hedge funds, Internet domain name licensing (i.e. – [dot]TV from Tuvalu), and other Internet-related commerce, including on-line gambling (Palan, 2003). Many of these areas are the object of new or revived international regulation beyond the initiatives discussed below. An offshore regime

Table 10.1   Offshore financial centres over the past 4 decades

UK Government Working Group Report, 1973	McCarthy, 1979	Johns, 1983	Offshore Group of Banking Supervisors	Errico and Musalem, 1999		Financial Stability Forum, 2000	OECD, 2002[‡]
'Established British Dependent Tax Havens'			Members			Group I	
The Bahamas	Anguilla	Andorra	Aruba	Andorra	Monaco	Dublin (Ireland)	Andorra
Bermuda	The Bahamas	Anguilla	The Bahamas	Anguilla	Montserrat	Guernsey	Anguilla
British Virgin Islands	Bahrain	The Bahamas*	Bahrain	Antigua	Nauru	Hong Kong SAR	Antigua and Barbuda
Cayman Islands	Barbados	Bahrain	Barbados	Aruba	Netherlands Antilles	Isle of Man	Aruba
Gibraltar	Cayman Islands	Barbados*	Bermuda	Australia	Netherlands	Jersey	The Bahamas
Hong Kong	Costa Rica	Bermuda*	Cayman Islands	Austria	Nicaragua	Luxembourg	Bahrain
Montserrat	Guernsey	British Virgin Islands	Cyprus	The Bahamas	Niue	Singapore	Barbados
	Hong Kong	Campione	Gibraltar	Bahrain	Oman	Switzerland	Belize

Table 10.1   (Continued)

UK Government Working Group Report, 1973	McCarthy, 1979	Johns, 1983	Offshore Group of Banking Supervisors	Errico and Musalem, 1999		Financial Stability Forum, 2000	OECD, 2002‡
'Potential British Dependent Tax Havens'	Isle of Man	Cayman Islands*	Guernsey	Barbados	Panama	Group II	British Virgin Islands
British Solomon Islands	Jersey	Costa Rica	Hong Kong	Belize	Philippines	Andorra	Cook Islands
Gilbert and Ellice Islands	Lebanon	Cyprus	Isle of Man	Bermuda	Puerto Rico	Bahrain	Dominica
St. Helena	Luxembourg	Guernsey	Jersey	British Virgin Islands	Russia	Barbados	Gibraltar
Turks and Caicos Islands	Netherland Antilles	Hong Kong*	Labuan	Campione	Seychelles	Bermuda	Grenada
	New Hebrides	Isle of Man	Macau	Cayman Islands	Singapore	Gibraltar	Guernsey/Sark/Alderney
	Nicaragua	Jersey	Mauritius	Cook Islands	St. Kitts and Nevis	Labuan (Malaysia)	Isle of Man
	Panama	Lebanon*	Netherlands Antilles	Costa Rica	St. Lucia	Macau SAR	Jersey
	Philipinnes	Liberia*	Panama	Cyprus	St. Vincent	Malta	Liberia
	Seychelles	Liechtenstein	Singapore	Djibouti	Switzerland	Monaco	Liechtenstein
	Singapore	Luxembourg	Vanuatu	Dominica	Tangier	Group III	The Maldives

St. Vincent	Malta		Dubai	Thailand (International Banking Facility)	Anguilla	The Marshall Islands
United Arab Emirates	Monaco	Observers	Gibraltar	Turks and Caicos	Antigua and Barbuda	Monaco
	Nauru	British Virgin Islands	Grenada	United Arab Emirates	Aruba	Montserrat
	Netherland Antilles*	Eastern Caribbean Central Bank	Guam	United Kingdom (London)	The Bahamas	Nauru
	Nicaragua	Samoa	Guernsey	United States (International Banking Facilities)	Belize	Netherlands Antilles
	Panama*		Hong Kong	Uruguay	British Virgin Islands	Niue
	Philipinnes		Hungary	US Virgin Islands	Cayman Islands	Panama
	Seychelles		Ireland (Dublin)	Vanuatu (New Hebrides)	Cook Islands	Samoa
	Singapore		Israel	Western Samoa	Costa Rica	Seychelles
	St. Vincent		Isle of Man (& Sark)		Cyprus	St. Lucia

Table 10.1 (Continued)

UK Government Working Group Report, 1973	McCarthy, 1979	Johns, 1983	Offshore Group of Banking Supervisors	Errico and Musalem, 1999	Financial Stability Forum, 2000	OECD, 2002[‡]
		Switzerland		Japan (Japanese Offshore Market)	Lebanon	St. Christopher & Nevis
		Turks and Caicos		Jersey	Liechtenstein	St. Vincent and the Grenadines
		United Arab Emirates*		Kuwait	Marshall Islands	Tonga
		US Virgin Islands		Lebanon	Mauritius	Turks & Caicos
		Vanuatu (New Hebrides)*		Liberia	Nauru	US Virgin Islands
				Liechtenstein	Netherlands Antilles	Vanuatu
				Luxembourg	Niue	
				Macau	Panama	
				Madeira	Samoa	
				Malaysia (Labuan)	Seychelles	
				Malta	St. Kitts and Nevis	

Marianas	St. Lucia
Marshall Islands	St. Vincent and the Grenadines
Mauritius	Turks and Caicos
Micronesia	Vanuatu

Notes: * Identified by Johns as included in the Eurocurrency statistics of the BIS.

† The British West Indies includes Anguilla, Antigua and Barbuda, British Virgin Islands, St Kitts and Nevis, and Montserrat (*Financial Stability Review*, June 2001 (Issue 10): 107).

‡ Absent from this source document are the names of jurisdictions that had made an advance commitment to eliminate their 'harmful tax practices' in advance of the publication of the document, and even if they otherwise met the OECD criteria to determine a tax haven. Those jurisdictions were Bermuda, Cayman Islands, Cyprus, Malta, Mauritius, and San Marino.

Sources: (United Kingdom Public Record Office, 1973: Folio 1, page 4), 'British Dependent Territories and the Tax Haven Business', 15 July 1970.

(McCarthy, 1979)

(Johns, 1983: 21, Table V)

Offshore Group of Banking Supervisors <http://www.ogbs.net/members.htm> [accessed 24 January 2006]

(Errico and Musalem, 1999: 11, Table 2), 'Countries and Territories with Offshore Financial Centers'

(Financial Stability Forum, 2000: 2) The distribution of OFCs into three categories was based on a perception of their 'quality of supervision and perceived degree of co-operation. It is important to stress that the categorisation of OFCs into these three groupings is based on responses of OFC supervisors and the impressions of a wide range of onshore supervisors at a particular point in time.'

(Organisation for Economic Co-operation and Development, 2000: 17)

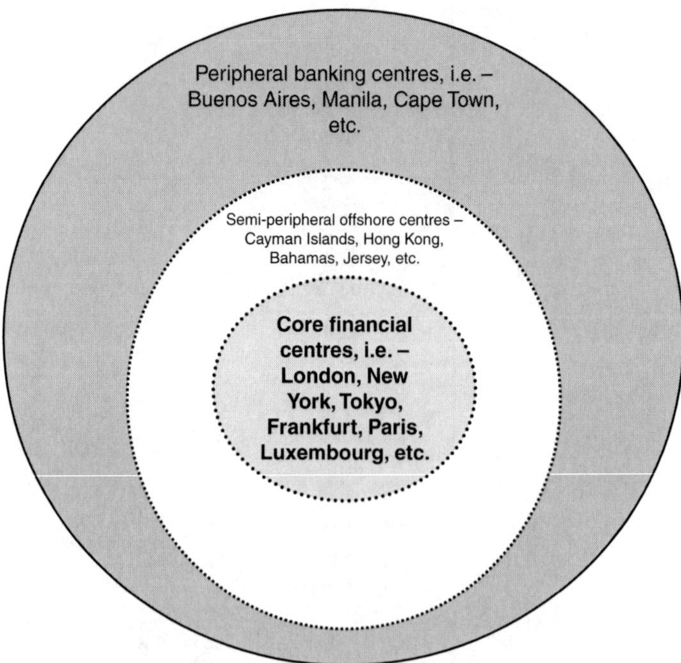

Figure 10.1   Core/periphery/semi-periphery in global finance

is an opportunity for regulatory difference that creates a comparative advantage for these small Caribbean jurisdictions to operate financial centres in co-operation with financial centres in the core and in this fashion achieve some level of economic development (Palan, 2002).

Offshore finance – global and Caribbean

This section moves from positioning offshore finance as the semi-periphery in global finance to a discussion of the specific nature of offshore financial flows. It begins by relating the historical emergence of the OFC as a form of economic development. Then the discussion introduces the data on banking assets used in this analysis. Data on financial flows has been used as evidence for the phenomenon of globalisation and to justify increased global governance. Here the data demonstrates that the vast majority of external banking assets reported globally are on deposit in the core, and not in this semi-periphery. Moreover, the assets recorded on deposit in semi-peripheral locations are not invested there, but rather pass through on the way to investments elsewhere.

Offshore financial services as a development strategy emerged in conjunction with formal decolonisation in the 1960s. Among the first jurisdictions was the current exemplar of an OFC, the Cayman Islands, while in late 1966 *The Sunday Times* (London) contained an article titled 'Bahamas: the tax-free haven' (United Kingdom Public Record Office, 1967–1969). One benefit from the development strategy is that the OFC offers employment opportunities for a wider skill base and educational background than are available from the tourism sector (Persaud, 2001: 209). At the same time, the impact upon the local environment from an OFC is less than it would be from a new (or expanded) tourism industry (Duffy, 2000: 556–562; Pattullo, 2005: 129–165). These phenomena from offshore finance as a development strategy were already recognised in the 1960s.

In subsequent decades the ebb and flow of financial regulation at both the international and state levels encouraged some observers to suggest the imminent stagnation, decline, demise and disappearance of the offshore industry. Observations included the suggestion in 1979 that there was 'little unsatisfied demand' for new OFCs, but another author in 1985 concluded the opposite and posited that as long as international banking grew the demand for offshore banking services also would grow (McCarthy, 1979: 48; Francis, 1985: 107). The perception that offshore finance could continue to provide a means for economic development motivated several Caribbean states to establish OFCs in the mid-1990s. They were impelled by the decline in the agricultural production resulting from the elimination of preferential trade quotas on bananas (Lewis, 2000; Armstrong and Read, 1998). More recent assessments reflect the emergence of the governance initiatives discussed below, for example, that 'cumulative pressures for reform will significantly re-configure the offshore finance industry. Offshore finance may return onshore to the large, functional financial centers such as London or New York' (Hampton and Christensen, 2002: 1667). These dire predictions for the imminent demise of the industry must be placed against the list of 'usual suspects' possessing an OFC collected in Table 10.1. Note that while there is variance in the membership of the different lists, a number of jurisdictions consistently are identified.

The overall picture of the offshore financial landscape developed here uses data collected by the BIS in Basel, Switzerland. The data set used comes from the sectoral and geographical breakdown of banking data the BIS first introduced in the early 1970s in an effort 'to provide

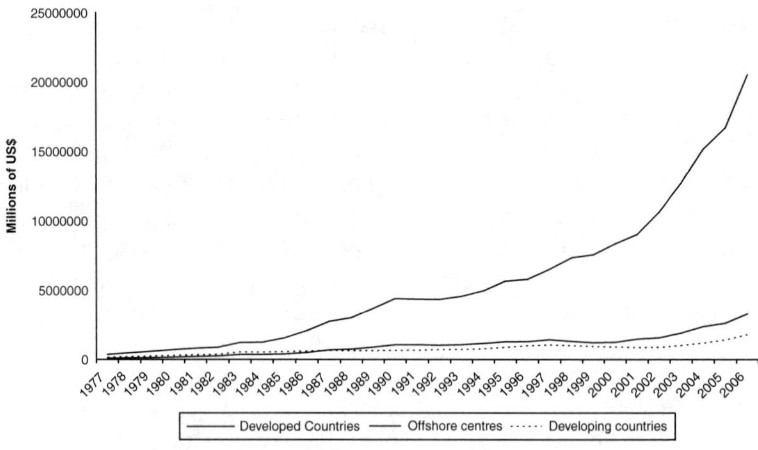

Figure 10.2   External position of reporting banks vis à vis individual countries (assets)

Source: BIS *Quarterly Review*, June 2007, Table 6a

information on the development and growth of the eurocurrency markets' (Monetary and Economic Department, 2003: 1).[2] Figure 10.2 provides the historical overview of this data from 1977 to 2006. It demonstrates not only the increase in foreign assets on deposit in offshore banks, but also highlights the much greater increase to be found in the quantity of foreign deposits held within the core.[3] The large dashed line for the 'developed countries' substantiates an observation made about economic globalisation, that most FDI (and international financial flows in general) involve financial transfers within the core, and not between the core and periphery.[4] This figure shows the trend among developed states, the BIS-designated offshore centres, and developing states. The list of jurisdictions that have been identified by the BIS as an offshore centre in their data set has evolved. The changes identified since 2000 are listed in Table 10.2, they depict the refinement of their criteria for selection as well as changes within the operation of individual OFCs.

The data represented here is limited to the figures for outstanding assets reported on deposit in these jurisdictions with respect to other specified jurisdictions. As already noted, there have been several different lists of OFCs designated by the BIS for use in its consolidated reporting and that list is substantially smaller than those created by other institutions (compare Table 10.2 to Table 10.1). The BIS is

Table 10.2   Bank for International Settlements (BIS) offshore centres*

Bank of England, Financial *Stability Review* (June 2001), p. 107	BIS Papers No. 16 – *Guide to the international banking statistics* (April 2003), p. 85	Table 6a – *BIS Quarterly Review*, March 2003 – **International banking and financial market developments, p. A21**	Table 6a – *BIS Quarterly Review*, June 2007 – **International banking and financial market developments, p. A21**
Aruba	Aruba	Aruba	Aruba
Bahamas	Bahamas	Bahamas	Bahamas
Bahrain	Bahrain	Bahrain	Bahrain
Barbados	Barbados	Barbados	Barbados
Bermuda	Bermuda	Bermuda	Bermuda
Cayman Islands	Cayman Islands	Cayman Islands	Cayman Islands
Lebanon	Hong Kong	Guernsey	Gibraltar
Liberia	Lebanon	Hong Kong SAR	Guernsey
Netherlands Antilles	Macau SAR	Isle of Man	Hong Kong SAR
Panama	Mauritius	Jersey	Isle of Man
Singapore	Netherlands Antilles	Lebanon	Jersey
Vanuatu	Panama	Liberia	Lebanon
West Indies UK†	Singapore	Netherlands Antilles	Macau SAR
	Vanuatu	Panama	Mauritius
		Singapore	Netherlands Antilles
		Vanuatu	Panama
		West Indies UK†	Samoa
			Singapore
			Vanuatu
			West Indies UK†

* Offshore centres – An expression used to describe countries with banking sectors dealing primarily with non-residents and/or in foreign currency on a scale out of proportion to the size of the host economy. (Monetary and Economic Department, 2006: 60)

† West Indies UK represents a synthetic jurisdiction used by the BIS to aggregate data from Anguilla, Antigua and Barbuda, British Virgin Islands, St Kitts and Nevis, and Montserrat; Guernsey, Jersey, and the Isle of Man were aggregated with the United Kingdom until the BIS began reporting data from these jurisdictions independently in the fourth quarter of 2001. See the 'Breaks in series' table at <http://www.bis.org/statistics/breakstables.pdf>.

Note: A grey highlighted entry indicates a change from the previous list.

concerned with assets and liabilities and their effects on the banking system, whereas other organisations are emphasising the existence of legal structures intended to attract foreign deposits when creating their lists of OFCs. The BIS classified a jurisdiction as an offshore centre when its banking sector deals 'primarily with non-residents and/or in foreign currency on a scale out of proportion to the size of the host economy' (Monetary and Economic Department, 2006: 70). The essential point to observe from Figure 10.2 is that offshore banking, as a component in global assets, is small (averaging around 15 per cent in this data set) when compared to total external assets reported. Thus, taken by itself, the quantity is large ($3.30 trillion in 2006 for OFCs), yet as part of the larger picture of global external banking assets it is not substantial ($26.09 trillion for all reporting jurisdictions).

The nature of capital flows through the Caribbean, and specifically of four jurisdictions in the Caribbean, were presented elsewhere (Vlcek, 2007). The significant conclusion noted was the marked decline in the number of financial institutions registered in these Caribbean OFCs since 1996. The continued growth of offshore financial flows, even though now they are utilising fewer institutions suggested that global finance has not been significantly influenced by global governance initiatives, at least as measured by capital flows. At the same time, the Caribbean economies themselves were impacted just as anticipated (Sanders, 2002; Simmons, 2002). Employment and licensing fee revenue from offshore banking within these specific small economies declined, again since 1996. Fewer institutions employ fewer citizens and pay less in licensing and other fees. Meanwhile mobile capital continued to flow to OFCs, in the Caribbean and elsewhere, before being recycled to return as other investments in the core states.

Financial governance – international standards and best practices for the offshore

The Bretton Woods' institutions formed the foundations for governance in international finance following the Second World War. Since the liberalisation of national economies and the reduction of financial regulation from the 1970s problems have emerged to encourage the return of some regulation within international finance. OFCs have been implicated in the 1997 Asian Financial Crisis, capital flight from the periphery to the core and with facilitating money laundering and tax evasion. A variety of measures have been crafted by international organisations that are dominated by core states to re-establish global financial regulation. Three specific initiatives will be highlighted here: the OECD and tax competition, the Financial Action Task Force (FATF) and money laundering/terrorist financing, and the IMF's Offshore Financial Assessment Program. Collectively, these three multilateral initiatives begin to create a structure of global financial governance. Each addresses some aspect of cross-border finance – reporting taxable income, interdicting money laundering and monitoring the compliance of OFCs in order to prevent some form of 'financial contagion' from infecting the global financial system (Eatwell and Taylor, 2000: 5).

The G7 requested in 1996 that the OECD Secretariat develop an approach to counter the 'distorting effects of harmful tax competition'. This activity led to the publication of *Harmful Tax Competition: An Emerging Global Issue*, and a campaign against the OFCs of non-member states (Organisation for Economic Co-operation and Development, 1998). A second OECD report, *Towards Global Tax Co-operation: Progress in Identifying and Eliminating Harmful Tax Practices*, identified harmful tax regimes (in the semi-periphery/periphery) and preferential tax regimes (located in the core) (Organisation for Economic Co-operation and Development, 2000). The dichotomy of this breakdown between core and periphery is a by-product of the evaluation criteria used by the OECD. This fact combined with the notable absence of jurisdictions identified by other organisations as tax havens (i.e. Singapore) and served to increase the intensity of the debate (Vlcek, 2008a: Chapter 4). In addition to several reports on the progress of the programme against tax competition, the OECD has formed a Global Forum on Taxation in an effort to be more inclusive and broaden its mandate to create global regulations. This global forum now includes non-OECD states in its deliberations, however, the meetings of this and other OECD forums remain dominated by the issues and concerns of the core states (Woodward, 2004: 120).

Another program directed by the G7 affecting OFCs is managed by the FATF, which first produced its *Forty Recommendations* in 1990 'as an initiative to combat the misuse of financial systems by persons laundering drug money' (Financial Action Task Force, 2003b: iii). The organisation has evolved and grown to assume global responsibility for developing standards and policies not only to counter money laundering but also, since 2001, to combat terrorist financing (Financial Action Task Force, 2001). The problem of money laundering requires consistent and comprehensive international regulation because of the integrated relationship of national banking systems with each other across borders. It does no good for a single state to establish comprehensive surveillance of its banking system to prevent the introduction of the 'profits of crime' if criminals simply deposit their profits in a foreign bank and retrieve the money via a wire transfer. As part of their effort to prevent the introduction of criminal money into the international financial system, the FATF identified a number of jurisdictions as non-co-operative with its standards in June 2000. The publication of this list formed part of the effort to eradicate money laundering from banking and finance (both domestically and internationally) by essentially banning transactions with the named jurisdictions. The effect was to implicate as 'potentially criminal' any transaction executed with a financial institution located in one of the listed territories. From the Caribbean the list contained the Bahamas, the Cayman Islands, Dominica, St. Kitts and Nevis, and St. Vincent and the Grenadines (Financial Action Task Force, 2000).[5] Most jurisdictions rapidly moved to comply with the anti-money laundering recommendations, including the additional eight jurisdictions reviewed by the FATF and added to a later edition of the blacklist (Sharman, 2007).

A more comprehensive approach to global financial governance is the Offshore Financial Center Assessment Program of the IMF. Initiated in 2000, by February 2005, it had conducted assessments on 41 out of a total of 44 identified jurisdictions (Monetary and Financial Systems Department, 2005). These assessments function as a companion to (and are interchangeable with) the IMF/World Bank Financial Sector Assessment Program (FSAP), which was established in May 1999 'in response to calls by the international community...to facilitate early detection of financial sector vulnerabilities and development needs...' (World Bank and International Monetary Fund, 2003: 8).[6] Both programs notably assess the jurisdiction against standards that were produced by a variety of international bodies. This collection of quasi-governmental and non-governmental organisations includes the Basel Committee on Banking Supervision (BCBS), International Organisation of Securities Commissions (IOSCO), International Association of Insurance Supervisors (IAIS) and the FATF (World Bank and International Monetary Fund, 2003: 23; Monetary and Financial Systems Department, 2005: 4). Co-operation with the IMF assessment procedure effectively leads to the imposition of these standards without recourse to legislation in order to implement them as part of the domestic regulatory structure. At the same time, *enforcement* in the event of non-compliance with a standard remains the responsibility of that jurisdiction's regulatory agencies. So the result is to create, de facto, a global regulatory structure with these 'global' standards, without the participation of all affected jurisdictions in the process of their formulation.[7]

Governance or neo-colonialism for the semi-periphery?

The situation confronting the small jurisdictions was characterised by Ronald Sanders in 2002 as 'fiscal colonialism'. In his view, the OECD harmful tax competition project was 'nothing less than a determined attempt by the world's wealthiest economies to bend powerless countries to their will' (Sanders, 2002: 326). Certainly, the emphasis on 'good governance' by core states is undoubtedly biased towards the needs of core-based global finance.

> Altogether these investigations, initiatives and reports [against money laundering] coincided with deliberate attempts by core countries to remove anti-competitive onshore financial distortions. The intent is to one: position onshore financial centres to attract flight capital escaping the poor economic policies of some Third World countries, and two: blunt the comparative advantage offshore service providers enjoy.
>
> (Marshall, 2003: 71)

Together with transfer pricing and weak domestic tax administrations, capital flight makes it very difficult for peripheral states to secure local capital for investment and development.

The noted economist Charles P. Kindleberger offered a liberal definition for capital flight in 1985. 'A narrow economic reading might regard the action as a speculative position based on the prospect of currency devaluation. A broader socio-political view would call it a middle-class strike' (Kindleberger, 1987: 58). Thus we have capital flight framed as a form of resistance to the state while it is running away to the detriment of the domestic society. From this viewpoint the actions of the OECD with its project to claw back taxes on the foreign accounts of residents may represent an effort to counter the transnational openness that globalisation offers even to the citizen of ordinary means (Vlcek, 2004). On this argument for 'capital strike' Gerald Epstein noted that 'capital flight raises large and important issues of political economy. When does the sovereignty of capital undermine the sovereignty of the state?' (Epstein, 2005: 6). In essence, when does the profit motive of those with liquid assets supersede the common good of society? The point behind this brief introduction to capital flight is to identify first, that the offshore finance phenomenon carries with it problems for the periphery, though onshore financial centres are just as complicit, if not more so, in supporting and encouraging these mobile deposits. Second, these forms of financial governance are promoted as 'global' in nature and substance, yet explicitly are not. Rather, they serve the needs and desires of the core states, their institutions and their firms.

'Lines of flight' – a conclusion

For Gilles Deleuze and Felix Guattari, a 'line of flight' is the term used to describe 'a movement of deterritorialisation and destratification' leading to transformation within an assemblage (Deleuze and Guattari, 2003: 3–4). This is admittedly a limited explanation for a concept that is fundamental to the analysis that is *A Thousand Plateaus*. For purposes of this discussion, capital mobility exists as one such line of flight, not in that it represents an escape from one economy, but rather that it is a deterritorialisation of capital, detaching it from the ground upon which capital was formerly fixed by labour (Bauman, 2000: 58). The image proposed here would be one of foot-loose capital gliding from one venue to the next seeking to reconfigure itself. Capital mobility is thus conceptualised not as simple avoidance of taxation, expropriation or devaluation, or even the pursuit of a higher return on investment, but rather as capital reconstituting itself elsewhere as part of a different investment or form of investment. This movement changes the possibilities of both the economy that it departs and the point (financial institution) at which it comes to rest, however briefly. The absence of the capital from one economy limits opportunities (for improvement as well as confiscation), while its presence affords potentialities for productive investment (development) in other locations (Epstein, 2005).

My concern here rests not with the efforts made by core states to interdict capital flight *from* the core, as represented by the OECD project on harmful tax competition. Rather it is with the essentially undemocratic way in which regulations are developed before emerging from these institutions to become global financial governance. This governance reproduces standards and procedures consistent with the domestic structures of core states, methods that challenge the capability and capacity of semi-peripheral and peripheral states (Vlcek, 2008b). These procedures are of far greater benefit to core states, and core-based global accounting firms, than they are to the periphery/semi-periphery. Global financial governance, as outlined in the preceding sections, is structured to deal with the political economy of the core, without regard to the material constraints afflicting the political economy of the periphery. Most proposals for reforming, re-invigorating or re-creating the international financial architecture are fundamentally concerned with core state financial systems and firms (Eatwell and Taylor, 2000).

There is a convergence of the global governance objectives implied by these various initiatives against money laundering, tax evasion, and the financing of terrorism. Some proponents have argued explicitly in support of convergence, perhaps in an effort to broaden the base of public support for their desired objectives. A former Special Advisor to the Secretary of the Treasury (1999–2001), for example, argued specifically in support of a '"top-down" approach' to the development of global regulation. In his view the 'nations committed to regulatory and law enforcement regimes' (i.e. core states) should develop the governance mechanisms that these nations know are best for the world and simply impose them on 'those who lacked the commitment' to implement them (by implication the semi-peripheral/peripheral states). William Wechsler's problem with a more inclusive multilateral approach for developing regulations was that 'if the debate were brought to the UN General Assembly, for example, nations with underregulated financial regimes would easily outvote those with a commitment to strong international standards' (Wechsler, 2001: 49).

The conclusion that emerges from the foregoing discussion of offshore finance and global financial governance is that governance has become synonymous with control (as a form of constraint or subjugation) of the semi-periphery by the core. In particular, given the dissent of the OFCs belonging to the OECD – Luxembourg and Switzerland (Organisation for Economic Co-operation and Development, 1998: 73–78) – and the glaring absence of a number of other 'tax havens' from the OECD list, the OECD project has all the appearances of 'fiscal colonialism' (Sanders, 2002). In a similar fashion, the FATF has been quite assertive in its actions against semi-peripheral and peripheral states, for example, in forcing the Philippines to change laws as part of its anti-money laundering campaign (Casayuran, 2003; Financial Action Task Force, 2003a). The success (or lack thereof) by core states and their financial institutions against money laundering, however, has not been confronted in the same aggressive manner. For example, there is this headline from *The Wall Street Journal Europe* – 'In Europe, Finance Lobby Sways Terror-Funding Law; Legislators with Close Ties to Industry Water Down Money-Laundering Rules' (Simpson, 2005). The line of flight for semi-peripheral OFCs appears to be resistant when possible and co-operation where necessary. Opportunities for transformation benefiting the semi-periphery/periphery are limited without effective participation in the formation of global governance. The uneven nature of the processes that form governance in the world economy reflects the inherent unevenness of core-periphery relations, in global finance just as much as in global trade. Consequently, the core is erecting a governance structure that operates as a form of 'financial colonialism' while it seeks to reassert control over its foot-loose capital, and to close the scissors on the peripheral jurisdiction using the OFC as a development path into the semi-peripheral offshore world.

Acknowledgements

I am grateful for the feedback I received from my colleagues Miriam Allam and Andreas Antoniades in their efforts to help me refine the initial version of this analysis and to the editors for their persistence with this book project and feedback on this contribution. Nonetheless, the usual disclaimer applies for my responsibility in the case of any errors of fact or logic.

Notes

1. The offshore financial centre is hosted by both sovereign states and non-self-governing territories (such as the Cayman Islands and Jersey), therefore the term 'jurisdiction' is used to include both territorial entities.
2. An alternative analysis of global finance looked at cross-border portfolio investment patterns as geographical networks, using the IMF's Coordinated Portfolio Investment Survey. The benefit from this network analysis approach rests in its pictorial representation of portfolio investment flows. The result is a clear demonstration of the crucial presence of the OFC as a node in the re-circulation of finance capital (Coates and Rafferty, 2007).
3. The BIS list of 'developed states' contains: Austria, Andorra, Australia, Belgium, Canada, Denmark, Finland, France, Germany, Greece, Iceland, Ireland, Italy, Japan, Liechtenstein, Luxembourg, Netherlands, New Zealand, Norway, Portugal, Spain, Sweden, Switzerland, United Kingdom, United States, and Vatican.
4. See, for example (Hirst and Thompson, 1996; Held et al., 1999).
5. The other jurisdictions identified on this first 'blacklist' were the Cook Islands, Israel, Lebanon, Liechtenstein, the Marshall Islands, Nauru, Niue, Panama, Philippines, and Russia. This list was based on the review of documents collected on 29 jurisdictions.
6. The IMF Executive Board agreed to integrate these two programmes on 30 May 2008 (IMF External Relations Department, 2008).
7. In addition to these initiatives the World Bank and the IMF have organised a more extensive financial surveillance programme. The Reports on the

Observances of Standards and Codes (ROSCs) consist of an extensive collection of standards and practices created and maintained by a variety of public and private international organisations. As with the components of global financial governance presented here, the peripheral states are largely excluded from the development of these standards while they are expected to implement and enforce them as part of a domestic regulatory structure (Soederberg, 2004).

11

Toward a Democratic and Collectively Rational Global Commonwealth: Semi-Peripheral Transformation in a Post-Peak World-System

Kirk Lawrence

Russian President Dmitry Medvedev's proclamation of the need for 'a just and democratic world order, based on collective action,' made as part of the country's new Foreign Policy Strategy, was a striking move in support of a framework for global governance. While still largely couched in nation-state terms, and of course providing Russia with a central role in its formation and operation, the call for a 'polarless world' with greater input from a larger number of people is noteworthy to say the least. A global democratic state, and more precisely, a democratic and collectively rational global commonwealth, is not just an attractive alternative to the current core-dominated interstate system and world economy, it is essential if humanity is to successfully navigate its way through imminent crises; for example, economic failure, resource shortages, environmental degradation, disease, and warfare (Chase-Dunn and Lerro 2008).

While the myriad perils that endanger the biosphere are all causes for grave concern, and also interrelated, the focus is on energy in this chapter. In doing so, the comparative world-systems perspective will be utilized, which offers an important framework for identifying the problems and evaluating proposed solutions to complex social systemic issues. The possibilities of global governance of the world-system will be explored, and the implications for that transition during a time when many have predicted that oil has reached or passed peak production and when the current costs and benefits of energy use are unequally distributed. Future energy options must also protect the environment;

we cannot accept the destruction of the environment from the burning of fossil fuels nor the millennia of potential contamination from nuclear waste. A shift to a new world-system structure – a global democratic and collectively rational commonwealth – fuelled by an equitable and sustainable energy regime is necessary. Moreover, it is the semi-periphery that is a likely source of innovation and leadership for that transition.

Global governance and the semi-periphery

Visions and calls for global governance are not new, of course. Sargon, who established the Akkadian empire in Mesopotamia, and more so his grandson, Naram-Sin, envisioned rule over the known universe (van de Mieroop 2007: 64–73). Alexander the Great is said to have wept upon sensing there were no more worlds to conquer and command. Immanuel Kant, Victor Hugo, Thorstein Veblen, J. A. Hobson, Karl Kautsky, H. G. Wells, and John Maynard Keynes all contemplated a form of world republic or state (Patomäki 2008). Anthropologists Leslie White, Bronislaw Malinowski, and even Franz Boas predicted its occurrence, the latter stating that 'the grand spectacle of the grouping of man in units of ever increasing size' is one of 'the inexorable laws of history'. Probabilities based on that trend have been calculated and predictions made; for example, Robert Carneiro projected the decline in autonomous political units from 600,000 in 1500 BCE to a single government in 2300 CE (Carneiro 2004: 176). Indeed, since the Stone Age the number of polities has decreased, while the population and territorial sizes have both increased in waves of globalisation.

The expansion of formal democracy in waves is another trend in the world-system (Markoff 1996). Yet, substantive global democracy cannot be assessed as just the sum of multiple democratic nation-states. A global democracy must have broad and just rights, decided upon by the majority, and ideally all, of the world's people. It must exist in local, regional, and global institutions. We need a global democratic and collectively rational commonwealth because we live in a world with global problems requiring global solutions. Simultaneously, communities must be strengthened so that they can solve local issues. In order for billions of *Homo sapiens sapiens* to survive in a just and sustainable way, we need to collectively establish mechanisms for – at minimum – preventing conflict, regulating the use of resources, and for dealing with myriad issues related to pervasive and persistent inequality (Boswell and Chase-Dunn 2000; Chase-Dunn and Lerro 2008; Patomäki 2008; Wagar 1999).

The comparative world-systems perspective provides a framework for understanding the dynamics of the global political economy, as well as pre-modern social systems. It attempts to understand relationships between societies by analyzing their networks of regular interaction or exchange (Chase-Dunn and Hall 1997). Additionally, inter-societal networks can be shaped by the different levels of complexity and population density of their constituent societies, called core/periphery differentiation, or by relations of economic, ideological, and/or political domination and subordination, called core/periphery hierarchy. The hierarchy can also be three tiered, with an intermediate level called the semi-periphery. This region may be identified by being spatially located between core and periphery regions or by its mediation of activities between those regions. Additionally, a semi-periphery may have both core and peripheral institutional features or forms of organization, but in an intermediate way. The semi-periphery is relational to the core and periphery. But the existence and characteristics of a semi-periphery in a particular world-system, and the type of relations that distinguish a differentiation or hierarchy of societies, are unknowable without empirical testing. All world-systems do not have core/periphery hierarchies; in those that do, the nature and presence of the semi-periphery depends on how the hierarchy is structured.

Innovation, both technological and structural, have most often come from the semi-periphery, and it is from that intermediate position that change in world-systems frequently emerges. Societies in the semi-periphery, relative to the core, have less of an investment in the current system and so they have more freedom to implement new technologies and forms of organization, possibly fostering the development of a new lead industry (Modelski and Thompson 1996) or otherwise leapfrogging over those stuck in the freedom-reducing friction of an older infrastructure. Additionally, societies in the semi-periphery, relative to the periphery, may have enough resources to make the move into the core and possibly compete for hegemony and the chance to rewrite the rules in their favour, and the resources may have come through exploitation of the periphery. Societies in the semi-periphery, then, are materially and structurally positioned to make the most radical changes in the system.

As Chase-Dunn and Hall detail, there are several different types of semi-peripheries, and some not only transform systems but they also often take over and become new core societies (Chase-Dunn and Hall 1992). The societies that conquered and unified a number of smaller chiefdoms into larger paramount chiefdoms were usually from semi-peripheral locations. Peripheral peoples did not usually have the institutional and material resources that would allow them to make important inventions and to implement these or to take over older core regions. It was in the semi-periphery that core and peripheral social characteristics could be recombined in new ways. Sometimes this meant that new techniques of power or political legitimacy were invented and implemented in semi-peripheral societies. Much better known than semi-peripheral marcher chiefdoms is the phenomenon of semi-peripheral marcher states. The largest empires have been assembled by conquerors who come from semi-peripheral societies. The following semi-peripheral marchers are well known: the Achaemenid Persians, the Macedonians led by Alexander the Great, the Romans, the Ottomans, the Manchus, and the Aztecs. Moreover, current research is revealing the existence of additional variants of semi-peripheral development that have occurred throughout history, specifically those causing dramatic increases in the scale of cities and empires – a phenomenon we call upward sweeps (Chase-Dunn and Lerro 2008).

Some semi-peripheries transform institutions but do not take over. The semi-peripheral capitalist city-states operated on the edges of the tributary empires where they bought and sold goods in widely separate locations, encouraging people to produce a surplus for trade. The Phoenician cities (e.g., Tyre, Carthage, etc.), as well as Malacca, Venice, and Genoa, spread commodification by producing manufactured goods and trading them across great regions. In this way the semi-peripheral capitalist city-states were agents of the development of markets and the expansion of trade networks, and so they helped to transform the world of the tributary empires without themselves becoming new core powers.

Changes in the logic of the world-system have historically emerged as 'globalisations from below' (della Porta 2006). For example, the direct democracy of the various workers' councils that have appeared, such as in the Paris Commune of 1871, the Russian Revolution of 1917, the Spanish Revolution of 1936–1939, the Chilean Revolution of 1970–1973, and the Seattle General Strike of 1919. It is still occurring in factory committees in Argentina and Venezuela and peasant councils in Brazil and the rise of Leftist regimes in Latin America that represent another challenge to the current capitalist hegemonic system (Chase-Dunn and Lerro 2008; Robinson 2008). The past decades have seen the rise of transnational social movements including the anti-corporate globalisation movements, as responses to the strength of transnational corporations (and, often related, environmental/environmental justice movements (Curran 2006; Pellow 2007; Roberts and Parks 2007).

Additionally, the World Social Forums (WSF), established as an alternative to the World Economic Forum meetings, were initially organized by the Brazilian labour movement and the landless peasant movement; the meetings have been held exclusively, with the exception of regional gatherings, in countries outside of the dominant western powers: Brazil, India, Kenya, Mali, and Pakistan. The WSF events are open spaces of dialogue, where members of the global justice movement, the 'movement of movements' and all who oppose neoliberal globalisation can meet, discuss, debate, and coordinate actions and are remarkable attempts to build the foundation for a just and democratic world (Mertes 2004; Patomäki and Ulvila 2008).

Energy in evolution

The evolutionary trend of semi-peripheral-led transformation is expected to continue; yet, if a global democratic state is to emerge, as a result of action in the semi-periphery or elsewhere, it will face a constraint that all previous increases in systemic complexity have encountered – managing energy flow. Energy can be defined as 'the ability to transform a system' (Smil 2008: 12–13). Since the origin of the Universe, approximately 14 billion years ago, energy dynamics have been essential to physical, biological, and sociocultural evolution (Chaisson 2005; Christian 2004). Taken together, effective energy capture, transformation, and waste disposal have been one of the primary means to expand a society or system of societies, or to out-compete them. Hebert Spencer (asserted that increases, and decreases, in the heterogeneity and complexity that formed the basis of his evolutionary laws were constrained by energy flows from the physical through the social world (Spencer 1882). Alfred Lotka developed a principal that sees a surplus of available energy as essential in evolution: the general trend of organic systems is for natural selection to result in an increase in their total mass, which is both dependent upon, and generative of, more energy. Lotka also noted an advantage for biological species able to more effectively utilize surplus energy to maximize power output than their competitors; they are *selected for* in evolution (Lotka 1925, 1945).

However, we know from ecology that organisms reach energy-based limits on their growth; for example, lions are only as big and as numerous as their niche allows, further growth would be energetically and thus evolutionarily disadvantageous. Moreover, the overall mass of species takes the shape of a pyramid (known as the Eltonian pyramid) with discrete steps as you move up the food chain. This is due to the net loss of energy that occurs during the process of capturing, consuming, and metabolizing prey (Colinvaux 1978). The same seems to be true for human societies. The scale of cities and empires – a phenomenon we call upward sweeps – shows discrete jumps in size (Chase-Dunn and Lerro 2008). White attributed the relative stagnation of 'the great civilizations of China, India, Egypt, the Near East, Central America and Peru,' to their failure to further extend the transformation of energy, whilst Kaplan explains the fates of both the Plains Indians in the United States at the hands of European agriculturalists and the northern Chinese from the invading pastoral steppe nomads as instances of societies succumbing to others more superior in energy management (Kaplan 1960; White 1943). In addition, Joseph Tainter, asserts that increasing energy flow is necessary for sociopolitical organization and complexity (evinced by large and heterogeneous societies, with more governmental control over population and provision of defence and distribution of surplus) (Tainter 1988). However, there are decreasing marginal returns for the cost of each additional unit of complexity. Energy shortages create less flexibility for complex societies to manoeuvre when faced with stress and can therefore lead to a decline in complexity (Smil 2008; Sahlins and Service 1960).

Podobnik takes energy flow analyses to the level of world-systems. Revealing the patterns in the production, transportation, and consumption of primary energy resources that have fuelled intra-societal growth and inter-societal competition, his unifying concept is an energy shift: 'the process whereby a new primary energy resource is harnessed for large-scale human consumption' (p. 4) (Podobnik 2006b). The resource becomes the basis of an energy regime that includes technology, infrastructure, and the social, economic, and political structures. He then traces geopolitical rivalry through attempts by city-states and states to obtain energy sources from outside their borders. For example, conquests for wood, one of the earliest primary energy resources, but also for construction, were conducted over the centuries from at least 3000 BCE in the Ancient Near East, Athens, and then by the Roman Empire, China, India, North Africa, and Western Europe at varying times in their histories. The U.S., then a semi-peripheral state, replaced Britain's coal-based dominance by an oil-based regime (Chew 2007; Perlin 1989).

Physics governing energy flows explain part of the relationship between complexity and inequality in world-systems. From the Second Law of Thermodynamics, which reveals time's arrow and irreversibility, we know that the amount of free energy, that which is *'available* to us for producing some mechanical work' dissipates over time (Georgescu-Roegen 1971: 5). As energy is used for work, a portion of the free energy is lost as heat as it is transformed from low entropy, or an ordered state that is far from equilibrium, to one that has high entropy, or disorder. The Eltonian pyramid of species mass in food chains, discussed earlier, is a result of this law. Because of this dissipative nature of structures not at equilibrium, increasing inputs of free energy are necessary to keep the process going – the consequence is increasing amounts of waste. Additionally, in complex adaptive systems, increases in energy can produce self-emergent transformations from one state to another, turning disorder into order, or negentropy. The process creates discrete jumps; for example, from ice to water to steam for H_2O (Ball 2004; LePoire 2007; Prigogine 2000; Prigogine and Stengers 1984).

Applied to social societies, Giampietro and Pimental (1991) calculated the energy expenditures and inputs necessary for a particular level of societal mass and density. Studying a chimpanzee troupe, hunters and gatherers, pastoralists, a village of horticulturalists, a village of those practising agriculture with chemicals, and (post)industrial, fossil-fuel based, Japan, they found orders of magnitude increases in energy inputs at each step up in complexity. This is consistent with the history of our species over the past 50,000 years. Nomadic hunting and gathering, which was the dominant mode of production until at least the last 12,000 years, relied almost exclusively on human power. According to David LePoire (2007), the average human intake of calories is 2,500 per day, which generates about 100 watts of power. The average current energy use per capita in the United States, in a post-industrial or knowledge-based economy, is 15 kilowatts, or 150 times a hunter and gatherer. This works out to about 3.5 factors of the Feigenbaum number, a mathematical constant that indicates the increase in the ordering parameter necessary for bifurcation, ~ 4.7. For increases in energy flow, this corresponds to the point at which phase transitions to higher ordered states take place (Prigogine 2000). LePoire's calculation of 3.5 Feigenbaum numbers from hunting and gathering to modern post-industrial society suggests that there may have been three to four energy transitions in the past. LePoire ties the three energy shifts that have previously taken place, from natural renewables (animal power, wind, and wood) to coal to oil, to leadership transitions. But LePoire points out an additional transition that has been taking place since the mid-1970s – the increase of conservation and efficiency.

But the increases in energy and material flows that generate greater complexity and systemic power also create environmental degradation.

Marx saw this as the 'metabolic rift' between town and country as he, and Engels, attempted to understand soil degradation stemming from urbanization and the resultant unequal energy flows between the producers and users of resources (Burkett and Foster 2006; Foster 1999, Foster and Burkett 2008; Moore 2000, 2003). Andre Gunder Frank contended that imbalances of trade and consequent development in the structure and functioning of the interstate system have, since at least the nineteenth century, allowed powerful states in the global North to import negative entropy and export or transfer entropy to the weaker states in the global South (Frank 1979). The North extracted and accumulated capital while the South became the North's social and environmental wasteland. The semi-periphery, and even more so the periphery, has often been exploited by the core, particularly for natural resources. For example, in Brazil's Amazon Basin, Bunker describes over three centuries of underdevelopment that have been the result of harboring an extractive economy. The value of its raw materials – particularly rubber, metals and lumber, as well as grazing land for cattle – have been exploited by colonial powers from within by the government and capitalists. This pattern of development-hindering exploitation has been revealed in numerous studies of unequal exchange – ecological, financial, and material – have confirmed the existence of inter-societal inequality that varies in degree by tier across the modern world-system (Bunker 2007).

A bifurcation point?

For some time now Wallerstein (e.g. 1998, 2004a, 2004b) has been drawing upon the chaos theory of system dynamics to make his argument that the modern world-system, while regularly cycling, has secular trends that can reach asymptotes, placing the system in crisis. Most of the crises are resolvable (at least temporarily) within the current system framework. But systems far from equilibrium, such as those with high-energy bases, can become highly unstable and reach a bifurcation point in which the crisis can only be resolved by the emergence of a new logic. And the resiliency of a complex system is lowered when the energy that fuels it declines (Gunderson and Holling 2002). Furthermore, the greater the complexity of the system the more vulnerable it is to various shocks. In his study of societies that have succeeded or collapsed during climate changes, Fagan calls this scalar effect the result of a society 'trading up on the scale of vulnerability' (Fagan 2004).

It seems clear that the system is in crisis. In fact, the world-system has been on a long decline in economic growth since the oil crises in the 1970s (Patomäki 2008: 101–104). There may now be a 'perfect storm' of crises. As we write, the 'Group of 20' economically powerful countries (19 plus the EU) are gathering to discuss the global financial crisis. There is an ongoing environmental meltdown, global pandemics, and persistent and pervasive poverty and malnourishment, to list just a few of the most pressing matters.

Part of the cause of systemic crisis is the instability and inequality of the current energy regime. The price of oil, at least partially reflecting and affecting the economy, skyrocketed in mid-2008, with crude oil futures reaching around $145/barrel in August, from around $95/barrel at the beginning of the year, which was followed by a late-year dramatic decline in price and then oscillation. Moreover, the fossil fuel age is coming to a close, as peak oil will be, or has already been, reached and natural gas, coal, and uranium are not far behind. In 2006, oil constituted 34.4 per cent of world total primary energy supply (TPES) (International Energy Agency 2008). Not only do we use oil in transportation, and so on, but it also is essential to our industrial agriculture system, a system already pressed to expand production by another 30 per cent to feed projected population by 2030 (Mann 2008: 88–90). Coal (26 per cent of world TPES) is relatively abundant but the environmental consequences of its use; for example, global warming, particulate emissions, stream fouling, are life threatening if not also increasingly socially unacceptable. Nuclear fission (6.2 per cent of world TPES), which produces waste that is radioactive for millennia and the material and technology used in weapons for annihilating life on a massive scale, has also met strong social opposition. Moreover, the current energy regime is highly unequal. The use of energy in the world is highly skewed toward the core countries, with a range of less than 1 gigajoule (GJ) per capita in sub-Saharan Africa to around 450 GJ for Canada. Within-country energy inequality is also dramatic; a pastoralist in Africa and an average Canadian may have over a 1,000-fold difference in their energy consumption (Smil 2008: 257–259. This inequality in resource consumption is dramatically illustrated by the range of ecological footprints of nations, which measures the amount of productive land necessary to produce resources and absorb wastes for an entity. The deleterious effects of climate change are also disproportionately borne by the less-powerful countries; that is, the periphery, the Global South (Jorgenson and Rice 2005, 2007; Roberts and Parks 2007).

From these estimates, it is clear that the current high-energy and highly unequal world-system is failing. Noting the regular occurrence of systemic transitions in the past – French Revolution of 1789, Russian Revolution of 1917, and more so in the world revolutions of 1848 and 1968 – Wallerstein goes too far to argue that the post-1989 capitalist world-system is at or near a bifurcation point, and is expecting a collapse by 2050 (Wallerstein 2004a). Equally, through observing the social movements taking place around the globe, Chase-Dunn believes that we are already experiencing another world revolution, calling it the 'world-revolution 20 dos equis' (20xx) due to the indeterminacy of its symbolic start date. And as we reach the possibility of a bifurcation point, the struggle is over who gets to decide what direction the system goes (Chase-Dunn 2007).

The future

In their synopsis on the conviction in the inevitable fallibility of the collapse of the contemporary system, Wallerstein and Chase-Dunn are proponents of the belief in the possibility for the creation of a new system logic out of the ashes of the old. But for this advance in system complexity – a vertical and horizontal increase in interconnection – to come to fruition, it will be imperative for its base to be built on a new energy regime. It is possible, however, that the current systemic clashes over securing diminishing petroleum supplies, what Foster calls 'energy imperialism,' and Brown calls the 'geopolitics of scarcity' will result in interstate war (Brown 2008; Foster 2008a). Indeed, as its economic and political power wanes, the U.S. can no longer obtain cheap energy; instead, it has resorted to military might, an imperial overreach that is a further sign of weakness (Harvey 2005; Mann 2003). While the historical trend is of war preceding changes in hegemony, it is an obviously undesirable scenario, particularly in nuclear age.

Considering the options we face in a post-peak world, one result would see conflict over resources as a possible path. Another is the techno-fix, in which we rely upon innovation to rescue us, as Boserup once envisaged for food supply when facing population pressures (Boserup 1965). While technology has clearly allowed for greater food production and also energy efficiencies, research has demonstrated the failed hope of ecological modernization theory's 'environmental Kuznet's curve,' in which development reduces environmental impact (York and Rosa 2003). This is consistent with 'Jevons Paradox' in which William Stanley Jevons observed that gains expected from the increased energy efficiency of the Watt coal-fired steam engine failed to materialize; in fact, more coal was consumed than before (Jevons 1965). Recently, Jevons Paradox appears in a study by the World Bank revealing that increased carbon dioxide emissions of nations that offset reductions from efficiency or other sources (World Bank 2008). We might instead at least hope in the better choices 'are cooperation, conservation, and sharing' and 'community solidarity and preservation' that Heinberg has prescribed. He believes that current decision-making elites, the movements in opposition to the elites, and everyone else will need to choose from those options as we proceed (Heinberg 2004: 14–15).

A new energy regime is necessary from a perspective championing the long-term sustainability of our biosphere and geosphere. Moreover, I believe that the global collectivity should decide the direction forward and the best way to accomplish this is via a low-energy global state. There are three reasons for the need of low-energy solutions. One is the impending or existence of a post-peak oil system. It will be very difficult, with known technology, to produce enough energy from sustainable sources. Smil rules out the feasibility of the 'currently fashionable scenarios' given current technology, time and cost considerations, and social values: carbon sequestration (costly, scaling challenge); hydrogen (costly, too far into future); nuclear fission (social protest over radiation danger, weapons); nuclear fusion (too expensive and unproven, e.g., the U.S. has spent $250 million a year for the past 50 years without any measurable progress); solar (requires massive land appropriation, stochasticity of energy flows); biomass (low power density, diversion of net primary productivity (NPP) of earth away from ecosystems/agriculture); wind, waves, hydroelectricity, geothermal, tides, and currents (low maximum potential power) (Smil 2008: 381–384). Alternatively, others suggest that a combination of renewables and nuclear fission is the likely source for the next energy regime, but that assumes a social change in tolerance of the dangers of nuclear (Devezas et al. 2008).

The second need for low-energy global governance is that increases in complexity can only come from increases in the energy process. A jump from the current level of global development to one that is at or greater than the current core level is increasingly unlikely in a post-peak world. Barring a technological miracle, finding energy sources that can produce a factor of 4.7 increase in output, Feigenbaum's number, does not seem possible. In fact, it is not at all certain that the current levels of energy use can be maintained. A re-organization and even a reduction in the overall complexity of the world-system is therefore needed. We already have the framework of a proto-global state, with world-level institutions, such as the United Nations, World Health Organization, and the International Criminal Court. The global-level of governance must be strengthened. This can be accomplished by eliminating redundancies. For example, transferring security responsibility to a global institution could reduce the extensive military industrial complexes maintained not only by nation-states but also by other NATO groups. (We are hopeful that a global democratic and rational commonwealth would also need a much smaller military than extant throughout the world today.) The legitimacy of world institutions has also been undermined; for example, the United Nations Security Council or the World Trade Organization, are nowhere close to fully representative. A global democratic government must have the support of – at least – the majority of the world's people. Legitimate and substantive democracy is difficult to develop, sustain, and has often been reversed (Tilly 2007). But it is what we must strive for. Ulrich Beck notably claims that globalization has increased cosmopolitanism, a recognition and appreciation of differences, and this is important if nationalistic and xenophobic divisiveness is to be eliminated (Beck 2005). The national governments need not disappear; in fact, some hierarchy will need to exist between the global and the local in order to administer global decisions and to represent local interests at the global level, but even this may wither as the global–local nexus becomes more efficient and effective.

Strengthening the local level of governance will also be important. A number of people have advocated self-governing local communities, with Lester Brown suggesting that we are already moving toward local energy and food production (Brown 2008). Here, I prefer the line with taken by Wagar, who supports the idea of local communities but also a global-level community of communities and a world political party (Wagar 1999). Similarly, there are those that have called for a global peoples parliament and that inventions such as the Internet has made it easier to come together on multiple scales and imagine such a scenario (Hopkins 2008). Global meetings such as those held by the WSF involve intercontinental travel by large numbers of individuals who attend small meetings and large gatherings. These meetings are expensive in both money and carbon terms. A much cheaper and cleaner alternative to flying humans from continent to continent so that they may communicate face-to-face is emerging in 3D interactive digital worlds such as in 'Second Life.' The world computer system still gobbles electricity; in 2005, world consumption for servers was 123 billion kilowatt hours (kWh), up from just 58 in 2000, but this still represents less than 1 per cent of the world total in 2005 (15,021 billion kWh, International Energy Agency 2008).

The new governance structure must also ensure a more equitable share in the costs and benefits of energy use and other resources. Smil observes this when he notes that the range of TPES for a society with a high quality of life at the beginning of the twentieth century was 50–70 GJ per capita, he recommends targeting that range for the future (Smith 2008: 257–259). The *mean* TPES for all countries in 2000 was 58 GJ per capita, which had increased to 70 by 2003, and again to 75 by 2006. But the range, in 2006, was from 6.3 GJ per capita in Eritrea, to 346.5 in Canada, to 924.7 in Qatar. For electricity consumption, in 2006, the world per capita rate was 2659 kWh, but the range was from 37 in Haiti, to 16,766 in Canada, to 31,306 in Iceland (International Energy Agency 2008). Moreover, nearly a third of the world's population did not have residential electricity at all (Smil 2008: 258–259).

The third reason for a low-energy global state is the waste produced by core-like development. It is estimated that we need five earths for everyone in the world to live like the average person in the United States (Global Footprint Network 2008), which would require a five-fold increase in global energy use (Smil 2008). There are limits to growth and one of them is the unassimilatable pollution produced during the energy process. Of course, finding ways to dispose of waste generated from energy flow in ways that does not foul the sustainability of the environment is one of the challenges of the new millennium. We have already had such an impact in the last 200 years that scientists are saying we have left the Holocene and are now in the Anthropocene (Chase-Dunn and Hall 1997; Ponting 2007). We believe it is important to link the growth of global democracy with ecological sustainability and justice; they are inseperable. Like Vandana Shiva exhorts, we need an 'Earth democracy.' And for all of these reasons, it must be an eco-socialist political economy (cf. Catton 1980; Shiva 2006; Wallis 2008).

The semi-periphery is structurally advantaged to take the lead in this endeavour. From an energy/ecology standpoint, there are already impressive innovations. For example, Cuba has developed a massive organic farming and urban garden food system, and found ways to reduce its fuel use, particularly following the 'Special Period' after the fall of the Soviet Union. Kenya's Green Belt Movement plants trees to improve the environment and empower women. Venezuela has used its oil wealth to implement 'petro-socialism.' Bolivia is attempting to return control over resources to the indigenous population. The cities of Curitiba and Porto Alegre in Brazil, and the state of Kerala in India offer 'islands of hope' for a sustainable and community-based political economy. But the pathways taken by countries in the semi-periphery are uneven. Brazil leads the world in sugarcane-based ethanol production, followed by India, while Malaysia and Indonesia are major producers of palm oil, but the production of biofuels, including switchgrass, has potentially crippling impacts on the food system and the net energy/ecological gain is low or possibly negative in some cases (Brown 2008; Magdoff 2008). Countries such as Nicaragua and Russia have implemented structural adjustment programs as part of the increasing capitalist penetration that have increased inequality and devastated small farmers, while Cuba and China have taken a more measured approach with lower negative impacts (Enriquez, 2009/2010). But China is now the world's largest polluter, although behind the U.S. on a per capita basis. Chase-Dunn (1998) found a rise in consumption of energy in the semi-periphery, as a percentage of the world's share but without a corresponding rise in GDP, suggesting that the industrialization of many semi-peripheral countries does not necessarily translate into efficient and profitable economic growth.

Conclusion

Energy flow has been an essential component of biological, physical, and social evolution. The rise of complexity, the rise and demise of societies, and success or failure in intersystem competition are all impacted by energy capture, transformation, and waste management. We are now on the verge of a new energy regime as the fossil fuel era wanes. 'What is next' should be a world-system with an energy base utilizing sustainable resources and with equally shared costs and benefits. Given current and projected technology, it is likely to have lower total energy use and higher costs per unit. Given the myriad crises we immediately face, and the energy constraints on increasing complexity, we cannot wait until after disorder reigns; the time to act is running now.

The world-system has been marked by waves of increasing democracy and global state formation. This should continue. The form that will best suited for the future, as envisioned in this chapter, is a global democratic and rational commonwealth. The source of that sweeping change is already emerging in the semi-periphery, and also the periphery, of the interstate hierarchy. Indeed, it is the semi-periphery that should be scrutinized for leadership in this transition to a new world-system. The most powerful challenges to capitalism in the twentieth century came from semi-peripheral Russia and China, and the strongest supporters of the contemporary global justice movement are semi-peripheral countries such as Brazil, Mexico, and Venezuela. And waves of democracy have sprung from the semi-periphery. It is typically an unusually fertile location for the invention and implementation of new institutional structures. And semi-peripheral societies are not constrained to the same degree as older core societies from having invested huge resources in doing things in the old way. So they are freer to implement new institutions, and many of those institutions have expanded and transformed many small systems into the particular kind of global system that we have today. This observation would not be possible without the conceptual apparatus of the comparative world-systems perspective.

The historically transformative role of the semi-periphery is expected to continue. The core way is not sustainable. The semi-peripheral way may not be either, but it is closer to where we need to go and provides a window into what a post peak system may look like. But regardless of the source of change, it is certain that the future world-system will look much different than it does today. While a particular structure has been discussed in this chapter, it is not assumed to be the only or the best solution. It is only put forth in hope that it be considered in planning for a world-system that will be peaceful, equitable and just, while sustaining, and even improving our biosphere.

Note

1. Special thanks to Christopher Chase-Dunn, Director of the Institute for Research on World-Systems at the University of California Riverside, for his comments, encouragement, and insight that made this chapter possible.

12
Semi-Peripheral Development and Global Democracy

Christopher Chase-Dunn and Terry Boswell

The previous chapters have all looked at ways in which the semi-periphery has re-embedded itself within the global economy or as we favor, the world-system. This final chapter is geared toward illustrating how the semi-periphery remains the most likely to produce resistance to the character of the current world-system.[1] As we have seen in recent years, the backlash against globalization is promoting transnational social movements that are seeking to reform and restructure both national societies and global governance. Some of these movements are reactionary, while others are progressive. We will distinguish between:

- **antisystemic movements** that seek to democratize global governance by means of globalization from below and
- **antiglobalization movements** that attack the powers that be in order to revitalize traditional non-democratic civilizational values.

Ironically, many of the antisystemic movements have been labelled 'anti-globalization.' As they constantly point out, this is a misnomer. Their goal is to transform globalization to make it more equal and more just. The real antiglobalization movements are not called by that name. They are called terrorists.

The argument presented here is that the progressive antisystemic movements will find their greatest support in the semi-periphery. Democratic socialist parties and regimes that are coming to power in the semi-peripheral countries will be the forereachers that show how the progressive transnational movements (feminism, environmentalism, labor, indigenism) can work together to democratize global governance. The semi-peripheral development idea is an important tool for understanding the real possibilities for global social change because semi-peripheral countries are the weakest link in the global capitalist system – the zone where the most powerful antisystemic movements have emerged in the past and where vital and transformative developments are likely to occur in the future.

One implication of the comparative world-systems perspective (Chase-Dunn and Hall 1997) is that all hierarchical and complex world-systems exhibit a 'power cycle' in which political/military power becomes more centralized followed by a phase of decentralization. This is likely to be true of the future of the world-system as well, though the form of the power cycle may change. Our species needs to invent political and cultural institutions that allow adjustments in the global political and economic structures to take place without resort to warfare. This is analogous to the problem of succession within single states, and the solution is obvious – a global government that represents the interests of the majority of the peoples of the Earth and allows for political restructuring to occur by democratic processes.

Capitalist accumulation usually favors a multicentric interstate system because it provides greater opportunities for the maneuverability of capital than would exist in a world state. Big capitals can play national states off against one another and can escape movements that try to regulate investment or redistribute profits by abandoning the national states in which such movements attain political power. The modern world-system has experienced long waves of economic and political integration over recent centuries. We use the term 'structural globalisation' to denote intercontinental economic and political integration. These waves of global integration are the contemporary incarnations of the pulsations of widening and deepening of interaction networks that have been important characteristics of all world-systems for millennia. But since the nineteenth century these have occurred in a single global system. Figure 12.1 shows the waves of global trade integration in the nineteenth and twentieth centuries (Chase-Dunn, Kawano and Brewer 2000). The crucial comparison is between the late nineteenth century (1890–1914) and recent decades (1980–). These are the periods when the cycle of globalization makes a qualitative shift upwards. The shift is so steep that it changes the culture and people become terribly aware of their global interdependence.

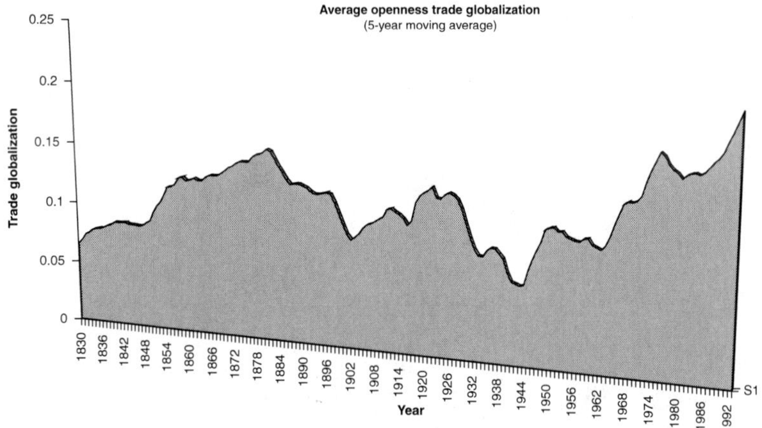

Figure 12.1   International trade relative to the size of the global economy, 1830–1994 (from Chase-Dunn, Kawano and Brewer 2000)

Capitalist globalization

We understand the historical development of the modern world-system in terms of the evolution of institutions. These key institutions: commodity production, technology and techniques of power, have been shaped by tremendous struggles. These include conflict among contending powers and between the core and the periphery over the past six centuries as Europe rose to hegemony and capitalist globalization expanded in waves of commodification and integration.

The story of how global orders have been restructured in order to facilitate capitalist accumulation must be told in deep temporal perspective in order for us to understand how the most recent wave of corporate globalization is similar to, or different from, earlier waves of globalization. Of particular interest here is the phenomenon of world revolutions and increasingly transnational antisystemic movements. In order to comprehend the possibilities for the emergence of global democracy we need to understand the history of popular movements that have tried to democratize the world-system in the past. The most relevant for comprehending our own era is the story of the nineteenth century and its *tsunami* (tidal wave) of capitalist globalization under the auspices of British hegemony. Transnational antisystemic movements, especially the trade union movement and the feminist movement, emerged to contend with global capitalism. Workers and women consciously took the role of world citizens, organizing international movements to contend with the increasingly transnational organization of an emergent global capitalist class. Political and economic elites, especially finance capitalists, had already been consciously operating on an intercontinental scale for centuries, but the degree of international integration of these elites reached a very high level in the late nineteenth century.[2]

The British created the Concert of Europe after defeating Napoleon. This was an alliance of conservative dynasties and politicians who were dedicated to the prevention of any future French revolutions. The British Royal Navy suppressed the slave trade and encouraged decolonization of the Spanish colonies in the Americas. The English *Anti-Corn Law League's* advocacy of international free trade (carried abroad by British diplomats and businessmen) was adopted by most European and American states in the middle of the century. The gold standard was an important support of a huge increase in international trade and investment (O'Rourke and Williamson 1999; Chase-Dunn, Kawano and Brewer 2000). The expanding Atlantic economy, already firmly attached to the Indian Ocean, was accompanied by an expanding Pacific economy as Japan and China were more completely and directly brought into the trade and investment networks of Europe and North America. American Ginseng was harvested in Pennsylvania as an important commodity export that could be used in lieu of silver in the trade for Chinese silk and 'china.'

The nineteenth-century wave of capitalist globalization was massively contested in a great globalization backlash. The decolonization of Latin America extended the formal aspects of state sovereignty to a large chunk of the periphery. Slave revolts, abolitionism and the further incorporation of Africa into the capitalist world-system eventually led to the abolition of slavery almost everywhere. Within Europe socialist and democratic demands for political and economic rights of the nonpropertied classes strongly emerged in the world revolution of 1848. An important aspect of our model of world-systems evolution is the idea of *semi-peripheral development* (Chase-Dunn and Hall 1997: chapter 5). Institutional development in premodern world-systems occurred because innovations and implementations of new techniques and organizational forms have tended to occur in societies that have semi-peripheral positions within larger core/periphery hierarchies. Semi-peripheral marcher chiefdoms conquered adjacent core polities to create larger paramount chiefdoms. And semi-peripheral marcher states conquered adjacent core states to create larger and larger core-wide empires (e.g. Chin, Akkad, Assyrian, Achaemenid Persians, Alexander, Rome, Abbasid Caliphate, etc.) and semi-peripheral capitalist city-states (Dilmun, Phoenician Tyre, Sidon, and Carthage; Venice, Genoa, Malacca, etc.) expanded commercialized trade networks and encouraged commodity production within and between the tributary empires and peripheral regions, linking larger and larger regions together to eventually become the single global economy of today.

The modern hegemons (the Dutch Republic of the seventeenth century, the United Kingdom of Great Britain in the nineteenth century, and the United States of America in the twentieth century) were all formerly semi-peripheral nation-states that rose to the position of hegemony by transforming the institutional bases of economic and political/military power in response to challenges from contenders for hegemony and challenges from popular movements contesting the injustices of capitalism and modern colonial imperialism. The modern world-system has experienced system-wide waves of democracy rather than separate and disconnected sequences of democratization within individual countries (Markoff 1996). These waves have tended to start in semi-peripheral countries and the institutional inventions that have diffused from country to country have disproportionately been invented and implemented in semi-peripheral countries first (Markoff 1999). Both the Russian and Chinese Communist challenges to capitalism emerged from the semi-periphery.

The worker's movement became increasingly organized on an international basis during the nineteenth century. Mass production made working conditions increasingly similar for industrial workers around the world. Labor organizers were able to make good use of cheap and rapid transportation as well as new modes of communication (the telegraph) in order to link struggles in distant locations. And the huge migration of workers from Europe to the New World spread the ideas and the strategies of the labor movement. Socialists, anarchists and communists challenged the rule of capital while they competed with each other for leadership of an increasingly global antisystemic movement that sought to democratize the world-system.

The decline of British hegemony, and the failure of efforts after World War I to erect an effective structure of global governance, led to the collapse of capitalist globalization during the depression of the 1930s, culminating in World War II. In our perspective, capitalist globalization is a cycle as well as a trend. The great wave of the nineteenth century was followed by a collapse in the early twentieth century and then a re-emergence in the period after World War II. The global institutions of the post–World War II order, now under the sponsorship of the hegemonic United States, were intended to resolve the problems that were perceived to have caused the military conflagrations and economic disasters of the early twentieth century. The United Nations was a stronger version of a global proto-state than the League of Nations had been, though still a long way from the 'monopoly of legitimate violence' that is the effective centre of a real state.

The Bretton Woods institutions – the World Bank and the International Monetary Fund (IMF) – were originally intended to promote Keynesian national development rather than a globalized market of investment flows. Free trade was encouraged, but important efforts were made to track international investments and to encourage the efforts of national states to use fiscal policy as a tool of national development. The architects of the Bretton Woods institutions were chary (suspicious) about the effects of volatile waves of international capital flows on economic development and political stability because of what they perceived to have been the lessons of the 1920s. The restarting of the world economy after World War II under the aegis of the Bretton Woods institutions and U.S. support for relatively autonomous capitalism in Europe and Japan succeeded tremendously. But the growing power of unions within the core, and the perceived constraints on U.S. fiscal and financial interests imposed by the Bretton Woods currency regime, along with the oil crisis of the early 1970s, led the United States to abandon Bretton Woods in favor of a free world market of capital mobility. The 'Washington Consensus' was basically Reaganism–Thatcherism on a global scale – deregulation, privatization and reneging on the 'social contract' with core labor unions and the welfare state. The IMF was turned into a tool for imposing these policies on countries all over the world.

This U.S./British-led neo-liberal regime of global capitalism (Reaganism–Thatcherism) was a reaction to the successes of the Third World and the core labor movements, not in achieving true global democracy, but in getting a somewhat larger share of the profits of global capitalism. The attack on the institutions of Keynesian national development (labor unions and the welfare state), was also a delayed response to the world revolution of 1968 in which students, women, environmentalists, Third Worldists, indigenous peoples, democracy movements, and radical parts of the labor movement had critiqued and resisted the inadequacies of welfare capitalism and business unionism from the Left. The New Right appropriated some of the ideology and many of the tactics of the '68ers,' – demonstrations, civil disobedience, guerrilla armies, drug financing, mobilization of sub-nations, and so on. These tactics have come back to haunt the powers that be. In the recent wave of 'blowback' organizations and ideologies formerly supported by the U.S. Central Intelligence Agency (CIA) as instruments against the Soviet Union (e.g. *Al Qaeda*) have turned against their former sponsors, employing dirty tricks to besmirch symbols of global power and to murder innocent bystanders in the heart of the core (Johnson 2000).

We contend that the current historical moment is similar to the end of the nineteenth century. Like the British hegemony, the U.S. hegemony is declining. Contenders for global economic power have been emerging in German-led Europe and in Japan-led Asia. Popular movements and institutions have been under attack, especially since the rise to ideological hegemony of the neo-liberal 'globalisation project.' Antisystemic movements are struggling to find new paths for dealing with capitalist globalization. New communications technologies such as the Internet provide possibilities for creating coordinated and integrated movements in favor of global democracy. The liberating potential of decentred and democratized communications is great. But cheap interactive and mass communications also facilitate increasing differentiation and specialization of political mobilization, which can undercut efforts to promote inter-movement coordination. We hold that the Internet will be, on balance, a liberating force, but the big gains in movement integration will probably come as a response to the economic, political and ecological disasters that globalized capitalism is producing.

We expect that the current resistance to global capitalism will, in large part, take the form of local self-reliance, the revitalization of diverse cultural forms and the rejection of the cultural and technological totems of corporate capitalism. Thus the characterization of the global justice movements as 'anti-globalisation' is partially correct, but it is misleading. Self-reliance may take forms that are progressive or forms that promote divisions among the people based on ethnicity, nation or race. And self-reliance by itself is not an adequate strategy for transforming capitalism into a more humane and sustainable social system. Rather the building of self-reliant communities needs also to organize with and participate in a coordinated movement of 'globalisation from below' that will seek to reform, or create *de novo*, global institutions that will promote social justice and environmental sustainability.

The theorists who have delineated a recent stage of 'global capitalism' contend that the latest wave of integration has created a single integrated global bourgeoisie that has overthrown the dynamics of the hegemonic sequence (hegemonic rise and fall and interstate rivalry) (e.g. Sassen 1991; Robinson 1996; Robinson and Harris 2000). While most world-systems theorists hold that the U.S. hegemony continues the decline that began in the 1970s, many other observers interpret the demise of the Soviet Union and the relatively greater U.S. economic growth in the 1990s as ushering in a renewal of U.S. hegemony. While some interpret this U.S. upturn in the 1990s as the beginning of another wave of U.S. 'leadership' in the global economy based on comparative advantages in information technology and biotechnology, Giovanni's Arrighi sees the 1990s as another wave of financialization comparable to the *'belle epoque'* or 'Edwardian Indian summer' that occurred in the last decades of the nineteenth century. Much of the economic expansion in the U.S. economy was due to huge inflows of investment capital from Europe and East Asia during the 1990s. The theorists of global capitalism contend that the U.S. state (and other core states) are now instruments of the integrated global capitalist class rather than of separate and competing groups of national capitalists.

We agree with Walter Goldfrank (personal communication) that both models (global capitalism and the hegemonic sequence) continue to operate simultaneously and to interact with one another in complicated ways. Despite the rather high degree of international integration among economic and political elites, there is quite likely to be another round of rivalry among core states. Global elites achieved a rather high degree of international integration during the late nineteenth-century wave of globalization, but this did not prevent the World Wars of the twentieth century.

Admitting to some aspects of the 'global capitalism' thesis does not require buying the whole cake. Some claim that information technology has changed everything and that we have entered a new age of global history in which comparisons with what happened before 1960 are completely inappropriate. The most important slice of the cake is the part about global class formation, and this needs to be analyzed for workers and farmers as well as for elites (Goldfrank 1977). Research is currently under way to compare the nineteenth- and twentieth-century global elites as to their degree of international integration, as well as changes in the patterns of alliances and connections among the wealthiest and most powerful people on Earth. Meanwhile, the hegemonic sequence (the rise and fall of hegemonic core powers) is not usefully understood as a cycle that takes the same form each time around. Rather, as Giovanni Arrighi (1994) has so convincingly shown, each 'systemic cycle of accumulation' involves a reorganization of the relationships among big capitals and states. And the evolutionary aspects of hegemony not only adapt to changes in scale, geography and technology, but they must also solve problems created by resistance from below (Arrighi and Silver 1999; Boswell and Chase-Dunn 2000). Workers and farmers in the world-system are not inert objects of exploitation and domination. Rather, they develop new organizational and institutional instruments of protection and resistance. So the interaction between the powerful and less powerful is a spiral of domination and resistance that is one of the most important driving forces of the developmental history of modern capitalism.

The discourse produced by world-systems scholars about 'the family of antisystemic movements' has been an important contribution to our understanding of how different social movements act *vis a vis* each other on the terrain of the whole system (Arrighi, Hopkins and Wallerstein 1989). It is unfortunate that public discourse about globalization has characterized recent protest movements in terms of 'antiglobalisation.' This has occurred because, in the popular mind, globalization has been associated primarily with what Phil McMichael (2000) has termed the 'globalisation project' – the neoliberal policies of the 'Washington Consensus' and the hegemony of corporate capitalism. This is the political ideology of Reaganism–Thatcherism – market magic, deregulation, privatization, and allegedly no alternative to submitting to the 'realities' of global capitalist competition.[3] The terminology of 'antiglobalisation' is a disaster because it conflates two different meanings of 'globalisation' and it implies that the only sensible form of resistance to globalization involves the construction of local institutions to defend against the forces of global capitalism. Structural globalization means economic, political and cultural, international and transnational integration. This should be analytically separated from the political ideology of the 'globalisation project' (Chase-Dunn 1999).

Local protectionism will undoubtedly be an important component of the emerging resistance to corporate globalization and neo-liberal policies. But one lesson we can derive from earlier efforts to confront and transform capitalism is that local resistance cannot, by itself, overcome the strong forces of modern capitalism. What is needed is globalization from below. Global politics has mainly been the politics of the powerful because they have had the resources to establish long-distance connections and to structure global institutions. But waves of elite transnational integration have been accompanied by upsurges of transnational linkages, strategies and institutions formed by workers, farmers and popular challenges to the logic of capitalist accumulation. Globalization from below means the transnationalization of antisystemic movements and the active participation of popular movements in global politics and global citizenship.

An analysis of earlier waves of the spiral of domination and resistance demonstrates that 'socialism in one country' and other strategies of local protection have not been capable of overcoming the negative aspects of capitalist development in the past, and they are even less likely to succeed in the more densely integrated global system of the future. Strategies that mobilize people to organize themselves locally must be complimented and coordinated with transnational strategies to democratize or replace existing global institutions and to create new organizational structures that facilitate collective rationality for all the peoples of the world.

The major transnational antisystemic movements are the labor movement, the women's movement, the environmental movement and the indigenous movement. Of these, the environmental movement and the women's movement have had the most recent successes in forming transnational linkages and confronting the difficult issues posed by regional, national and core/periphery differences. But the labor and indigenous movements have made important efforts to catch up. Cross-border organizing efforts and support for demonstrations against corporate globalization show that the AFL–CIO is interested in new directions. One important task for world-systems scholars is to study these movements and to help devise initiatives that can produce tactical and strategic transnational alliances. Bruce Podobnik's (2002) careful and systematic study of globalization protests shows how these have emerged over the last decade in the core and noncore countries. There was an important wave of anti-IMF struggles in the 1980s researched by John Walton and David Seddon (1994). Podobnik's research shows that between 1900 and June 2002 about 44 per cent of the globalization protests occurred in core (developed) countries and 56 per cent occurred in noncore (less-developed) countries. The percentage of protestors injured, arrested and killed was far higher in the noncore than in the core countries. Podobnik also shows that these protests were temporarily dampened by the events of 11 September 2001 but that they rebounded to in the months following. Contrary to popular opinion, the globalization protests were not stopped by the events of September 11.

Growing inequalities

Growing inequalities (both within and among countries) were an important source of globalization backlash in the late nineteenth century

(O'Rourke and Williamson 1999) and are already shaping up to be an important driving force in the coming world revolution. Mike Davis's (2001) analysis of late Victorian drought–famine disasters in Brazil, India and China shows how these were partly caused by newly expanded market forces impinging upon regions that were subject to international political/military coercion. He also documents how starving peasants created millenarian movements that promised to end the domination of the foreign devils or restore the rule of the good king. Islamic fundamentalism is a contemporary functional equivalent.

Huge and visible injustices provoke people to resist, and in the absence of true histories and theories, they utilize whatever ideological apparatus is at hand. The world-systems perspective offers a useful systematic understanding of history that cannot be found elsewhere. The phenomenon of semi-peripheral development suggests that social organizational innovations that can transform the predominant logic of accumulation will continue to emerge from the semi-periphery. The Russian and Chinese revolutions of the twentieth century were efforts to restructure capitalist institutions and developmental logic that succeeded mainly in spurring the U.S. hegemony and the post–World War II expansion of capitalism. The Soviet and Chinese efforts were compromised from the start by their inability to rely on participatory democracy. In order to survive in a world still strongly dominated by capitalist states they were forced to construct authoritarian socialism, a contradiction in terms.

We can expect that democratic socialist regimes will come to state power in the semi-periphery by electoral means, as already happened in Allende's Chile. Brazil, Mexico, and Korea are strong candidates, and India, Argentina, Indonesia and China are possibilities. Democratic socialism in the semi-periphery is a good strategy for fending off many of the worst aspects of corporate globalization. The transnational anti-systemic movements will want to support and will be supported by these new socialist democracies. This has already begun to happen in Brazil, where the new labour party (PT) government supports the global social justice movement. President Lula's current support for fiscal austerity in order to woo global finance capital is likely to fade once it becomes clear that not enough finance capital will flow in to make much difference. If Lula is not willing to confront global capital some other leader from his party or from a new party is likely to do it. The Brazilian working class does not need foreign capital to construct a national economy that can provide a good living for all Brazilians. And a Brazilian democratic socialism will support and will be supported by friendly regimes in other

Latin American countries. Friends of socialism in the United States may need to prevent the bond traders from mobilizing an intervention.

The ability of capitalist core states to destabilize democratic socialist regimes in the semi-periphery is great, and this is why support movements within the core are so important. Information technology can certainly be a great aid to transborder organizing. Issues such as sweatshop exploitation can help to make students aware of core/periphery inequalities and to link them with activists far away. The emergence of democratically elected challengers to global corporate capitalism will strain the ideologues of 'polyarchy' and will facilitate the contestation of narrow definitions of democracy. The emergence of a World Party to educate activists about the world historical dimensions of capitalism and the lessons of earlier world revolutions will add the leaven that may move the coming backlash against corporate globalization in a progressive direction. A world historical perspective will help political campaigns and organizing efforts make tactical and strategic decisions and will provide a structurally informed basis for the building of a democratic and collectively rational global commonwealth.

The 'New' imperialism

The theorists of a global stage of capitalism organized by an integrated global capitalist class have elaborated their distinction between national and international capital in order to deal with what seems to be a renewed round of inter-imperial rivalry among the core states. Those who have been saying all along that neo-liberalism is mainly an Anglo-American thing rather than the permanent emergence of a global 'new economy' based on finance capital seem to be vindicated. And the assumption that military power has been permanently transcended by economic power is also now debated.

Giovanni Arrighi (2004) contends that the U.S. superpower is trying to morph its hegemony into a world state in which the U.S. balance of payments surplus becomes a tribute paid by foreigners in exchange for the provision of global security. A version of this hypothesis was discussed after the first Gulf War, ironically in terms of the U.S. serving the function of Global 911 (an emergency phone number in the United States). Critics of the world-systems perspective as well as apologists for global capitalism have long downplayed the importance of the core/periphery hierarchy. Some claimed that core/periphery inequality ended with decolonization. Dependency theory was declared a dead letter by 'post-structuralists' just at the time that many Third World countries were being subjected to the structural adjustment programs of the IMF. Others claimed that the categories of core and periphery, or First World and Third World were no longer valid because countries in Africa, Asia and Latin America have different histories. But no one ever claimed that all peripheral countries were the same. Core and periphery are relational concepts and the nature of the power-dependence relations changes over time, but the core/periphery hierarchy has not evaporated. The industrialization of some noncore countries and the nearly complete marginalization of many other countries (in what some have called the Fourth World) did not eliminate the core/periphery hierarchy. Neither did the formal decolonization of the Third World eliminate neo-colonial forms of domination by which core countries and international financial institutions came to exercise power over Third World countries. Imperialism in the sense of unequal power among countries has not been eliminated by the organizational changes in the world division of labor that have taken place since World War II. So the discovery of a 'new imperialism' needs to be clear as to how what is allegedly new differs from what went before.

David Harvey (2003) contends that U.S. unilateralism constitutes a renewal of capitalist primitive accumulation based on military geopolitical power. The world-systems perspective on capitalism (Chase-Dunn 1998) has long argued that primitive accumulation was not a stage in the creation of capitalist world economy, but has rather been a constant and necessary feature of capitalism all along. Peripheral capitalism has used political coercion in mobilizing labor since the expansion of slavery in the New World and the development of 'capitalist serfdom' in the peripheralized economies of Eastern Europe. After the abolition of capitalist slavery and serfdom Third World working conditions have continued to be conditioned by political coercion in the form of state-organized and core-supported suppression of labor unions and peasant movements. So primitive accumulation has been an important component of the capitalist world economy all along. The ideology of democracy and free markets was used as a smokescreen to cover the political coercion of labor and subjection of the periphery to politically organized domination. The fact that the IMF imposed structural adjustment on Third World countries while ignoring the massive fiscal deficits and balance of trade deficits of the United States is only one of the most flagrant instances of core/periphery domination in recent decades.

The rediscovery of the importance of military power in the structuring of the capitalist world economy is another instance in which even the critics of global capitalism have been bamboozled by the rhetoric of the free market. Military Keynesianism in which the U.S. federal government has spent over half of its total discretionary budget on 'defence' began in earnest during the Korean War, and these huge expenditures have continued despite the demise of the 'Soviet threat' that was the main justification for this massive use of public monies to pump up the U.S. economy. The U.S. has been a welfare state for the military-corporate complex since the early 1950s. But is there not something new in the willingness of the Bush administration to ignore the will of French, German and Russian allies in the conquest of Iraq? What is new and frightening is what appears to be the beginning of a breach in the core-wide multilateral foreign policies of the post–World War II period. Certainly the Bush administration pursued a more open and pronounced unilateralism and disdain for multilateral solutions than previous U.S. administrations. But did the Bush regime do this? We contend that this is similar in many respects to the British use of its comparative advantage in military power during its decline of economic comparative advantage. The United States has a massive advantage in military technology because of the huge investments that military Keynesianism provided. The development and production of military technology is not an ideal industry from the point of view of profit-making in the world market, because selling the technologies puts destructive weaponry in the hands of potential future rivals and may fuel regional conflicts. But direct conquest can provide important geopolitical returns, especially where the control of significant scarce raw materials (oil) is concerned. So the declining hegemon plays one of the only cards it has left – the military card. Dick Cheney says, 'give war a chance.'

The problem with this strategy is that it is likely to be counterproductive, especially if it is overused. Unilateral conquest provokes opposition and resistance. It does little to overcome the more basic problems of the loss of comparative advantage in new lead industries that can produce significant profits by selling products to buyers abroad (or at home). The other U.S. advantage has been its centrality in global financial transactions and the importance of the U.S. dollar in international financial and trade transactions. The world market for oil is denominated in U.S. dollars. And the U.S. trade imbalance has been counteracted by a huge inflow of foreign lending for the last decade. Moneys from Europe and East Asia has flown into U.S. stock and bond markets, making the United States extremely dependent on these inflows of foreign moneys to finance its growing trade imbalance.

The recent decline of the U.S. dollar relative to the Euro could fore-shadow a new kind of structural adjustment. Foreign investors believed in U.S. superiority in information technology and biotechnology, but the dot.com collapse and the Enron scandal have shaken the confidence of these foreign investors to some extent. The very size of the U.S. market and its ability to generate prodigious new forms of financial 'security' (e.g. derivatives) mean that the alternatives for receiving some return on the huge amounts of 'fictitious capital' that are now flowing in the world financial markets are few. At the new exchange rate the GDP of the European Union (EU) is now larger than the U.S. GDP. But the EU does not have the capacity to absorb the vast financial capital that is now invested in the United States What this means is that there will probably not be a rapid exodus of finance capital from the United States unless the whole system collapses. If crisis management continues to work for a few more years the air will go out of the U.S. balloon slowly.

Imagining global democracy

What might global democracy look like? And how could we get from here to there? A consideration of global democracy must confront two main issues: huge and growing inequalities within and between countries; and the grave problems of environmental sustainability that capitalist (and Communist) industrialization has produced. Rather than drawing the blueprint of a global utopia and then arguing the fine points it makes more sense to learn from the heritages of earlier efforts. Utopias may be useful for those who are unable to imagine any possible improvement over existing institutions. But they also function to delegitimize efforts to make social change because they often appear to be unattainable. A more useful approach is to imagine an historically apt next step, one that the relevant constituencies can agree is a significant improvement and one that is plausibly attainable.

Global democracy means real economic, political and cultural rights and influence for the majority of the world's people over the local and global institutions that affect their lives. Local and national democracy is part of the problem, but not the whole problem. Global democracy requires that local institutions and national states be democratic and the building of democratic institutions of global governance. We support the proposals for radically reforming the United Nations and for establishing an institutional framework for global finance proposed by Camilleri, Malhotra and Tehranian (2000). Their principles and thoughtful step-by-step proposals for democratizing global governance address most of the issues quite well. The *principle of subsidiarity*, proposes the decentralization of control over all issues that can be effectively resolved at that level (2000: 46). This principle is similarly applied to the national and international regional levels, so that global-level institutions deal with problems that can only find effective solutions at the global level. We agree with this important principle. They also abjure the term 'global government' and prefer terms such as 'interlocking institutions' and 'international regimes' for describing global governance. Alberto Martinelli's (2005) insightful discussion of democratizing global governance also categorically rejects the notion of global government. We understand the political sensitivities involved in this choice of terms, and we agree that it is important to use language wisely. There is a lot of resistance to the idea of an emerging world state because people understandably fear that such an institution might become an instrument of repression or exploitation. But we are concerned that careful rhetoric might obscure or paper over issues that need to be confronted explicitly. The main reason that the United Nations has been largely ineffective at stopping interstate warfare is that it is not a state in the Weberian sense – a **monopoly of legitimate violence**. International law is not truly law according to Weber because it is not backed up by institutionalized sanctions.

Our position is that the human species needs to establish a real global government that is legitimate, effective and democratic. This does not require the centralization of everything. As stated above, we agree with the principle of subsidiarity in which everything that can effectively be left to local, national and regional bodies should be. But inequality, environmental problems, population pressure and peace are all global problems that can only be effectively solved by a democratic global government with the power to enforce the law. Thus, reforming the United Nations must move in the direction of the establishment of a democratic global government. This is in the interest of all the people of the Earth, but, especially the dispossessed. The Westphalian interstate system has allowed powerful capitalists to repeatedly escape the institutional controls that have emerged from antisystemic movements that have sought to protect workers and communities from exploitation. Only a democratic world state can produce institutions that can guarantee social justice.

We also support the establishment of new institutions to provide a framework for global financial relations that can support local and national development, and increased oversight of these by the United

Nations (Patomaki, Teivainen and Ronkko 2002). And we see a need to go beyond polyarchy at both the national and the global levels. Bill Robinson (1996) examines the struggle over the concept of democracy. He redefines the meaning of the term 'polyarchy' which was coined by Robert Dahl to signify pluralism. In Robinson's usage polyarchy means a system in which a small group actually rules and mass participation in decision-making is confined to leadership choice in elections carefully managed by competing elites. Institutionalized polyarchy prevents the emergence of more egalitarian popular democracy that would threaten the rule of those who hold power and property. The notion of popular democracy stresses human equality, participatory forms of decision-making, and a holistic integration of political, social and economic realms that are artificially kept separate in the polyarchic definition of democracy.

We are not satisfied with polyarchy (parliamentary democracy) at the national level. We contend that real democracy must address the issue of wealth and property, rather than defining these as beyond the bounds of political discourse. This said, we can also learn much from those failed experiments with collective property that were carried out in the socialist and Communist states in the twentieth century. State ownership works well for major infrastructure, such as utilities, health and education. But for the production of most goods and services, even when the state is itself truly democratic, state ownership creates grave economic problems because of the problem of 'soft budget constraints.' This is because state-owned firms are usually bailed out by the state for their economic mistakes, and they mainly respond to political exigencies rather than to consumer demand. In order to achieve a reasonable level of efficiency large firms need to compete with one another in markets, and they should also compete for financing by showing that they can make a profit.

We support John Roemer's (1994) advocacy of a kind of market socialism in which ownership shares of large firms are distributed to all adult citizens, who then invest their shares in a stock market that is the main source of capital for large firms. All citizens receive a set number shares at the age of majority and when they die their shares revert to the public weal. So there is no inheritance of corporate property, though personal property can be inherited. Firms, large and small, produce for markets and labor is rewarded in competitive labor markets. Small firms can be privately owned. This kind of market socialism equalizes income, though some inequalities due to skill differences will still exist. The economy will still be a market economy, but the democratic state will provide security, due process, and will oversee the redistribution of corporate shares across generations.

This model of public market socialism incentivizes technological change and efficiency without producing increasing inequalities. It will probably work well, especially in the core countries for which Roemer has intended it. But when we think about the global economy there are certain problems that are not addressed in Roemer's model. One of the main problems in the global economy is the huge difference in productivity between core and peripheral labor. This is why labor standards in international economic agreements are anathema to workers and unions in peripheral countries. A single worldwide minimum wage standard sounds good, but it would tend to function as a protectionist agreement for core workers, and undercut the ability of peripheral firms and workers to sell their products in core markets. Wage and other standards have to take into account local conditions, but their enforcement is the key to preventing the race to the bottom pursued by many transnational corporations. The real solution to this is to raise the level of productivity of peripheral labor. So global democracy needs to create institutions that can do this. Banning child labor worldwide while supporting the children's families to speed the demographic transition would be a giant first step in this direction.

This is why we need effective institutions of global governance. Anti-systemic movements cannot simply dismantle such institutions as the World Bank and the IMF. These must either be reformed (democratized and empowered) or they must be replaced. Market socialism in the core will not be enough. A movement for economic democracy in the core needs also to mobilize for economic democracy at the global level. Support for both more democratic national regimes and global socialist institutions is likely to come from the semi-periphery. We expect that some of the most potent efforts to democratize global capitalism will come out of movements and democratic socialist regimes that emerge in semi-peripheral countries. As in earlier epochs, semi-peripheral countries have the 'advantages of backwardness' – they are not already heavily invested in the existing organizational and political institutions and technologies – and so they have both the maneuverability and the resources to invest in new institutions.

Peripheral countries could also do this, but they are more completely dependent on the core and they are not able to mobilize sufficient resources to overcome this dependency. The large semi-peripheral countries such as Mexico, Brazil, Argentina, India, Indonesia and China, have opportunities that neither core nor peripheral countries have. If a democratic socialist regime is able to come to state power by legal means, and if this regime has the political will to mobilize the popular sectors in favor of democratic socialism, an experiment in Roemerian market socialism could be carried out. We expect that regimes of this type will in fact emerge in the near future as the options of kowtowing to the megacorps or demagoging the popular sectors (Chavez in Venezuela) become more obviously bankrupt. The smaller semi-peripheral countries (South Korea, Taiwan, South Africa, Israel) may also opt for democratic socialism, but we expect that these will only be able to do so after earlier efforts have been made in the large semi-peripheral countries. Much also depends on what happens in the contest for hegemony. Continued U.S. primacy will likely strengthen the resistance to democratizing global governance, while the rise of the EU, which has stronger social democratic traditions, will likely provide greater core support for democratizing global institutions and for emerging democratic socialist movements in the semi-periphery.

The semi-peripheral democratic socialist regimes will be the strongest organizational entities that can forge the links among the global anti-systemic movements and produce a network for bringing forth the institutions of global socialism. Globalization from below and the formation of global socialist institutions will need to be facilitated by an organized network of world citizens.

The postmodern prince and the World Party

In conclusion we would like to point to the vision of Stephen Gill (2000), who has had the courage to formulate the idea of a World Party, a peoples' international, which could help to coordinate the several antisystemic movements emerging in resistance to global corporate capitalist and neo-liberal policies. Gill invokes Gramci's characterization of the Italian Communist Party as the 'modern prince,' a network of organic intellectuals and workers who would challenge the hegemony of capital. Gill is careful to distance his idea from the putative errors of the Left parties of old – hierarchy, dogmatism, etc. He says, '. . . the multiple and diverse political forces that form the postmodern Prince combine both defensive and forward-looking strategies.' This is an appropriate stance, especially in light of what happened to the New Left in the 1970s. A period of broad encompassing social movement activism morphed into a bevy of small sectarian parties yelling slogans at potential organizees and at each other. The sectarian model is obviously not one to emulate and Gill is careful in this regard.

Warren Wagar (1996) proposed that an organized group of political actors making use of and further developing the world-systems perspective might come together in what he calls the World Party (1999). The angle here would be the use of a world historical and comparative perspective on the development of capitalism to help the family of antisystemic movements see the big picture and to cooperate with one another on feasible projects. The risks of Napoleonic hubris and accusations of Stalinism are probably worth taking because of the strategic and tactical importance of theoretical perspective for constructing a democratic and collectively ration global commonwealth. We have adopted the name given to such a confederation by Warren Wagar (1996) – the World Party. But this is not a party in the old sense of the Third International – a vanguard party of the world proletariat Rather the World Party we propose would be a network of individuals and representatives of popular organizations from all over the world who agree to help create a democratic and collectively rational global commonwealth. The World Party[4] will actively recruit people of all nations and religions and will seek to create the institutional bases for a culturally pluralistic, socially just and ecologically sustainable world society. This is what we mean by global democracy.

Notes

1. An Earlier version of this paper can be found on http://www.irows.ucr.edu/papers/csa02/csa02htm
2. The Institute for Research on World-Systems (IROWS) at the University of California, Riverside has completed a research project sponsored by the U.S. National Science Foundation that studies transnational elite integration in the nineteenth century (Chase-Dunn, Reifer and Barr, 2009).
3. Giovanni Arrighi has recently argued that the globalisation project that emerged in the 1970s was importantly a reaction to the world revolution of 1968 that appropriated the anti-state ideology and many of the tactics of the New Left. In the latest installment of ideological history the *Wall Street Journal* has declared that the Washington Consensus is dead.
4. http://csf.colorado.edu/wsystems/archive/praxis/wp/index.htm Research on the long emergence of world parties in the nineteenth and twentieth centuries is reviewed and new proposals for the future are discussed in Sehm-Patomaki and Ulvila (2007).

Bibliography

Abbott, J. (2003) *Developmentalism and Dependency in South East Asia: The Case of the Automobile Industry* (London: Routledge).

Abbott, J. P. and Worth, O. (2002) *Critical Perspectives on International Political Economy* (Basingstoke: Palgrave Macmillan).

Adam, A. and Moutos, T. (2008) 'The Trade Effects of the EU-Turkey V Customs Union', *The World Economy*, 31 (5), pp. 685–699.

Adapa, S. (2007) 'Development Remittances in India: A Micro Perspective', Paper presented at the FAU conference on financing and Development Aarhus & Copenhagen, 7–11 May.

Abdulsomad, K. (2001) 'Government Policy, Liberalisation and Globalization of the Automotive Industry in Thailand', *Business and Society*, 2 (1), pp. 57–76.

Alejandro, D. (1970) *Essays on the Economic History of the Argentine Republic* (New Haven, Yale).

Altimir, O., Beccaria, L. and Rozada Gonzalez, M. (2002) 'Income Distribution in Argentina, 1974–2000', *CEPAL Review*, 78, pp. 53–82.

Amin, S. (1976) *Unequal Development* (New York: Monthly Review Press, 1976).

Amin, S. (1980) 'The Class Structure of the Contemporary Imperialist System', *Monthly Review*, 31 (8), pp. 9–26.

Amin, S. (1997) *Capitalism in an Age of Globalization* (London: Zed Books).

Amin, S. (2006) *Beyond US Hegemony? Assessing the Prospects for a Multipolar World* (London: Zed).

Amsden, A. (1989) *Asia's Next Giant: South Korea and Late Industrialization* (Oxford: Oxford University Press).

Amsden, A. (1994) 'Why Isn't the Whole Experiment with the East Asian Model to Develop? *Review of the East Asian Miracle*', *World Development*, 22 (4), pp. 627–633.

Amsden, A. (1995) 'The Textile's Industry in Asian Industrialisation: A leading sector institutionally?', *Journal of Asian Economics* 5 (4), pp. 573–584.

Amsden, A. (2001) 'Like the Rest: Southeast Asia's "Late Industrialization"', *Journal of International Development*, 7 (5), pp. 791–800.

Amsden, A., Kochanowicz, J. and Taylor, L. (1995) *The Market Meets Its Match Restructuring the Economies of Eastern Europe* (Cambridge, Mass.: Harvard University Press).

Anderson, J. (2002) 'Questions of Democracy, Territoriality and Globalisation', in Anderson, J. (ed.) *Transnational Democracy: Political Spaces and Border Crossings* (London: Routledge), pp. 6–39.

Arestis, P. and Sawyer, M. (eds) (2007) *Political Economy of Latin America* (New York: Palgrave Macmillan).

Armstrong, H. W. and Read, R. (1998) 'Trade and Growth in Small States: The Impact of Global Trade Liberalisation', *World Economy*, 21 (4), pp. 563–585.

Arrighi, G. (ed.) (1985) *Semiperipheral Development* (London: Sage).

Arrighi, G. (1990) 'The Developmentalist Illusion: A Reconceptualization of the Semiperiphery', in Martin, W. (ed.) *Semiperipheral States in the World-Economy* (New York: Greenwood).

Arrighi, G. (1994/2002) *The Long Twentieth Century: Money, Power and the Origins of Our Times* (London: Verso).

Arrighi, G. (2004) 'Hegemony and Antisystemic Movements', in I. Wallerstein (ed.), *The Modern World-System in the Longue Duree* (Boulder, Co: Paradigm Publishers).

Arrighi, G. (2007) *Adam Smith in Beijing: Lineages of the Twenty-first Century* (London: Verso).

Arrighi, G. and Drangel, J. (1986) 'The Stratification of the World-Economy: An Exploration of the Semiperipheral Zone', *Review*, 10 (1), pp. 9–74.

Arrighi, G. and Silver, B. J. (1999) *Chaos and Governance in the Modern World System* (Minneapolis: University of Minnesota Press).

Arrighi, G. and Silver, B. J. (2003) 'Polanyi's Double Movement: The Belle Epoques of British and US hegemony compared', *Politics & Society*, 31 (2), pp. 325–355.

Arrighi, G., Hopkins, T. and Wallerstein, I. (1989) *Antisystemic Movements* (London and New York: Verso).

Ashley, R. K. (1983) 'Three Modes of Economism', *International Studies Quarterly*, 27 (4), pp. 463–496.

Ashwin, S. (1998) 'Endless Patience: Explaining Soviet and Post-Soviet Social Stability', *Communist and Post-Communist Studies*, 31 (2), pp. 187–198.

Asiaweek (2000) 'Skill Deficit: Thailand's Poorly Trained Workforce Costs the Country Business', 1 December.

Augelli, E. and Murphy, C. (1988) *America's Quest for Supremacy and the Third World* (London: Pinter).

Aydin, Z. (2005) *The Political Economy of Turkey* (London: Pluto).

Azpiazu, D., Basualdo, E. and Khavisse, M. (1989) *El nuevo poder económico en la Argentina de los años 80* (Buenos Aires: Legasa).

BBC (2008) 'Global Hunger Index', http://news.bbc.co.uk/2/low/in_depth/7670229.stm

Babones, S. J. (2005) 'The Country-Level Income Structure of the World-Economy', *Journal of World-Systems Research*, XI (I), pp. 29–55.

Bandeira, L. (2003) *Brazil, Argentina e Estados Unidos: Da Triplice Alianca ao Mercosul, 1870–2003* (Rio de Janeiro: Revan).

Bangkok Post (2000) 'Bank of Thailand Report', 15 April.

Bangkok Post (2002) 25 January.

Bank of Thailand (1999) *Annual Report.*

Bank for International Settlements (2005) *BIS Quarterly Review: International Banking and Financial Market Developments* (Basel: Bank for International Settlements).

Balasubramanyam, V. N. and Balasubramanyam, A. (1997) 'International Trade in Services: The Case of India's Computer Software', *The World Economy*, 20 (6), pp. 829–843.

Balcerowicz, L. (1996) *Socialism, Capitalism, Transformation* (Budapest: Central European University Press).

Ball, P. (2004) *Critical Mass: How One Thing Leads to Another* (New York: Farrar, Straus and Giroux).

Baran, P. A. (1957) *The Political Economy of Growth* (New York: Monthly Review Press).

Baran, P. and Sweezy, P. (1966) *Monopoly Capital* (New York: Monthly Review Press).

Barnett, M. and Finnemore, M. (2004) *Rules for the World: International Organizations in Global Politics* (Ithaca: Cornell University Press).

Basualdo, E. (2001) *Modelo de Acumulación y Sistema Político en Argentina: Notas sobre el Transformismo Argentine durante la Valorización Financiera (1976–2001)* (Buenos Aires: Universidad Nacional de Quilmes).

Bauman, Z. (2000) *Liquid Modernity* (Cambridge: Polity Press).

Beck, U. (2005) *Power in the Global Age* (Malden, MA: Polity Press).

Bedirhanoglu, P. (2004) 'The Nomenklatura's Passive Revolution in Russia', in McCann, L. (ed.) *Russian Transformations: Challenging the Global Narrative* (London: Routledge).

Bello, W. (2001) *The Future in the Balance: Essays on Globalization and Resistance* (Oakland, CA: Food First Books).

Bello, W. (2007) 'The Capitalist Conjuncture: over-accumulation, financial crises, and the retreat from globalization', *Third World Quarterly*, 27 (8), pp. 1345–1367.

Bernard, M. and Ravenhill, J. (1995) 'Beyond Product Cycles and Flying Geese: Regionalization, Hierarchy and Industrialization of East Asia', *World Politics*, 47, pp. 171–209.

Beyer, J. (2002) ' "Please Invest in Our Country" How Successful Were the Tax Incentives for Foreign Investment in Transition Countries?', *Communist and Post-Communist Studies*, 35 (2), pp. 191–211.

Bieler, A. and Morton, A. (2001) 'The Gordian Knot of Agency-Structure in International Relations: A neo-Gramscian Perspective', *European Journal of International Relations*, 7 (1), pp. 5–35.

Biersteker, T. J. (1992) 'The "Triumph" of Neoclassical Economics in the Developing World: Policy Convergence and Bases of Governance in the International Economic Order', in Rosenau, J. N. and Czempiel, E.-O. (eds) *Governance without Government: Order and Change in World Politics* (Cambridge: Cambridge University Press), pp. 174–196.

Blejer, M. I. and Coricelli, F. (1994) *The Making of Economic Reform in Eastern Europe: Conversations with Leading Reformers in Poland, Hungary, and the Czech Republic* (Aldershot: Elgar).

Boatca, M. (2006) 'Semiperipheries in the World system: Reflecting Eastern European and Latin American Experiences', *Journal of World Systems Research*, XII (II), pp. 321–346.

Bohle, D. and Greskovits, B. (2006) 'Capitalism without Compromise: Strong Businesses and Weak Labor in Eastern Europe's New Transnational Industries', *Studies in Comparative International Development*, 41 (1), pp. 3–25.

Bolkestein, F. and Derk Jan Eppink (2004) *The Limits of Europe* (Lannoo Uitgeverij).

Bornschier, V. and Chase-Dunn, C. (eds) (2000) *The Future of Global Conflict* (London: Sage).

Boserup, E. (1965) *The Conditions of Agricultural Growth: The Economics of Agrarian Change under Population Pressure* (Chicago, IL: Aldine).

Boswell, T. (ed.) (1989) *Revolution in the World-System* (New York: Greenwood).

Boswell, T. and Chase-Dunn, C. (2000) *The Spiral of Capitalism and Socialism: Toward Global Democracy* (Boulder, CO: Lynne Rienner).

Brenner, R. (1977) 'The Origins of Capitalist Development: A Critique of Neo-Smithian Marxism', *New Left Review*, 104, pp. 25–92.

Brenner, N. (2004) *New State Spaces: Urban Governance and the Rescaling of Statehood* (Oxford: Oxford University Press).

Brewer, A. (1990) *Marxist Theories of Imperialism* (London: Routledge).

Brown, L. (2008) *Plan B 3.0: Mobilizing to Save Civilization* (New York: W. W. Norton & Co).

Buchowski, M. (2006) 'The Specter of Orientalism in Europe: From Exotic Other to Stigmatized Brother', *Anthropological Quarterly*, 79 (3), pp. 463–482.

Bukharin, N. (1917/1929) *Imperialism and World Economy* (New York: Monthly Review Press).

Bulmer-Thomas, V. (2003) *The Economic History of Latin America since Independence* (New York: Cambridge University Press).

Bunker, S. (2007) 'Natural Values and the Physical Inevitability of Uneven Development under Capitalism', in Hornburg, A., McNeill, J. R. and Martinez-Alier, J. (eds) *Rethinking Environmental History: World-System History and Global Environmental Change* (Walnut Creek, CA: AltaMira), pp. 239–258.

Burkett, P. and Foster, J. B. (2006) 'Metabolism, Energy, and Entropy in Marx's Critique of Political Economy: Beyond the Podolinsky Myth', *Theory and Society*, 35 (1), pp. 109–156.

CIA (2008) *Fact book* (Washington DC: CIA).

Camilleri, Joseph A., Malhotra, K. and Tehranian, M. (2000) *Reimagining the Future: Towards Democratic Governance* (Melbourne: La Trobe University, Department of Politics).

Cammack, P. (2006) 'The Politics of Global Competitiveness', *Papers in the Politics of Global Competitiveness*, No. 1, Institute for Global Studies, Manchester Metropolitan University.

Cammack, P. (2007) 'Forget the Transnational State', *Papers in the Politics of Global Competitiveness*, No. 3, Manchester Metropolitan University.

Cardoso, F. H. (1973) 'Associated-dependent Development: Theoretical and Practical Implications', in Stepan, A. (ed.) *Authoritarian Brazil: Origins, Policies and Future* (New Haven: Yale University Press), pp. 142–178.

Cardoso, H. (2001) *Charting a New Course: The Politics of Globalisation and Social Transformation* (Lanham: Rowman & Littleman).

Cardoso, H. and Faletto, E. (1979) *Dependency and Development in Latin America* (Berkeley: University of California Press).

Carneiro, R. (2004) 'The Political Unification of the World: Whether, How—Some Speculations', *Cross-Cultural Research*, 38 (2), pp. 162–177.

Casayuran, M. B. (2003) *Senators Decry FATF 'unfairness, bias' vs Philippines. The Manila Bulletin*, http://www.mb.com.ph/news.php?art=27761§=1&fname=MN030215277761o.txt

Castells, M. (1996) *The Rise of the Network Society* (Oxford: Blackwell).

Castro, F. (2000) *Capitalism in Crisis: Globalisation and World Politics Today* (Melbourne: Ocean Press).

Catton, W. (1980) *Overshoot: The Ecological Basis of Revolutionary Change* (Urbana, IL: University of Illinois Press).

Çelik, Z. (1992) *Displaying the Orient: Architecture of Islam at Nineteenth-Century World's Fairs* (Berkeley: University of California Press).

Cerny, P. (1995) 'Globalization and the Changing Logic of Collective Action', *International Organization*, 49 (4), pp. 595–625.

Cerny, P. (1997) 'Paradoxes of the Competition State: The Dynamics of Political Globalization', *Government and Opposition*, 32 (1), pp. 251–274.

Cerny, P. (2000) 'Restructuring the Political Arena: Globalisation and the Paradoxes of the Competition State', in Germain, R. (ed.) *Globalisation and Its Critics* (Basingstoke: Palgrave Macmillan).

Chaisson, E. (2005) *Epic of Evolution: Seven Ages of the Cosmos* (New York: Columbia University Press).

Chase-Dunn, C. (1988) 'Comparing World-Systems: Toward a Theory of Semiperipheral Development', *Comparative Civilizations Review*, XIX, pp. 29–66.

Chase-Dunn, C. (1989) *Global Formation: Structures of the World Economy* (Oxford: Blackwells).

Chase-Dunn, C. (1990) 'Resistance to Imperialism: Semiperipheral Actors', *Review*, 13 (1), pp. 1–31.

Chase-Dunn, C. (1998) *Global Formations Structures of the World Economy*, 2nd edn (Lanham, MD: Rowan & Littlefield).

Chase-Dunn, C. (1999) 'Globalization: A World-Systems Perspective', in Chase-Dunn, C. and Babones, S. (eds) *Global Social Change* (Baltimore, MD: Johns Hopkins University Press), pp. 79–108.

Chase-Dunn, C. (2002) 'Globalization from Below: Toward a Collectively Rational and Democratic Global Commonwealth', *Annals of the American Academy of Political and Social Sciences*, 581, pp. 48–61.

Chase-Dunn, C. (2005) 'Social Evolution and the Future of World Society', *Journal of World-Systems Research*, 11 (2), pp. 171–192.

Chase-Dunn, C. (2007) 'The World Revolution of 20xx*', *Institute for Research on World Systems Working Papers*, 35, http://irows.ucr.edu/papers/irows35/irows35.htm.

Chase-Dunn, C. and Hall, T. D. (1992) 'World-systems and Modes of Production: Toward the Comparative Study of Transformations'. *Humboldt Journal of Social Relations*, 18 (1), pp. 81–117.

Chase-Dunn, C. and Hall, T. (1997) *Rise and Demise: Comparing World Systems* (Boulder, CO: Westview).

Chase-Dunn, C. and Lerro, B. (2008) 'Democratizing Global Governance: Strategy and Tactics in Evolutionary Perspective', *Institute for Research on World Systems Working Papers*, 40, http://irows.ucr.edu/papers/irows40/irows40.htm.

Chase-Dunn, C. and Podobnik, B. (1995) 'The Next World War: World-System Cycles and Trends', *Journal of World-Systems Research*, 1, 6, http://jwsr.ucr.edu/index.php

Chase-Dunn, C., Kawano, Y. and Brewer, B. (2000) 'Trade Globalization since 1795: Waves of Integration in the World-System', *American Sociological Review*, 65, pp. 77–95.

Chase-Dunn, C., Reifer, T. and Barr, K. (eds) (Forthcoming 2009) *The Global Nineteenth Century* (Boulder, CO: Paradigm).

Chew, S. (2007) *World Ecological Degradation: Accumulation, Urbanization, and Deforestation, 3000 B.C.–A.D. 2000* (Walnut Creek, CA: AltaMira Press).

Chirot, D. (ed.) (1989) *The Origins of Backwardness in Eastern Europe: Economics and Politics from the Middle Ages until the Early Twentieth Century* (Berkeley: University of California Press).

Chowdhury, A. and Islam, I. (1993) *The Newly Industrialising Economies of East Asia* (London: Routledge).

Christian, D. (2004) *Maps of Time: An Introduction to Big History* (Berkeley, CA: University of California Press).

Coates, D. (2000) *Models of Capitalism: Growth and Stagnation in the Modern Era* (Cambridge: Polity).

Coates, N. and Rafferty, M. (2007) 'Offshore Financial Centres, Hot Money and Hedge Funds: A Network Analysis of International Capital Flows', in Assassi, L., Nesvetailova, A. and Wigan, D. (eds) *Global Finance in the New Century: Beyond Deregulation* (Basingstoke: Palgrave Macmillan).

Cody, E. (2004) 'In China, Workers Turn Tough', in *Washington Post*, 27 November.

Cody, E. (2005) 'For Chinese, Peasant Revolt Is a Rare Victory', in *Washington Post*, 13 June.

Cohen, G. M. and Clarkson, S. (eds) (2004) *Governing Under Stress: Middle Powers and the Challenge of Globalization* (London: Zed Books).

Commission (2008) *Turkey 2008 Progress Report* SEC 2699, Brussels.

Colinvaux, P. (1978) *Why Big Fierce Animals Are Rare: An Ecologist's Perspective* (Princeton, NJ: Princeton University Press).

Collins, R. (1981) 'Long Term Social Change and the Territorial Power of States', in Collins, R. (ed.) *Sociology since Midcentury* (New York: Academic Press), pp. 71–106.

Cooper, J. (2007) *Mendelssohn, Goethe, and the Walpurgis Night* (Rochester: University of Rochester Press).

Cox, R. W. (1981) 'Social Forces, States and World Orders: Beyond International Relations Theory', *Millennium: Journal of International Studies*, 10 (2), pp. 126–155.

Cox, R. W. (1983) 'Gramsci, Hegemony, and International Relations: An Essay on Method', *Millennium: Journal of International Studies*, 12 (2), pp. 162–175.

Cox, R. W. (1987) *Production, Power, and World Order* (New York: Columbia University Press).

Cox, R. W. (1992a) 'Multilateralism and World Order', *Review of International Studies*, 18 (2), pp. 161–180.

Cox, R. W. (1992b) 'Global Perestroika', in Miliband, R. and Panitch, L. (eds) *New World Order? The Socialist Register* (London: The Merlin Press), pp. 26–43.

Cox, R. W. (with Sinclair, T. J.) (1996) *Approaches to World Order* (Cambridge: Cambridge University Press).

Cox, R. W. (2002) *Political Economy of a Plural World: Critical Reflections on Power, Morals and Civilizations* (London: Routledge).

Cox, R. W. (2004) 'Beyond Empire and Terror: Critical Reflections on the Political Economy of Order', *New Political Economy*, 9 (3), pp. 307–323.

Crowley, S. (2004) 'Explaining Labor Weakness in Post-Communist Europe: Historical Legacies and Comparative Perspective', *East European Politics and Societies*, 18 (3), pp. 394–429.

Cumings, B. (1987) 'The Origins and Development of the Northeast Asian Political Economy: Industrial Sectors, Product Cycles and Political Consequences', in Deyo, F. (ed.) *The Political Economy of the New Industrialism* (Ithaca and London: Cornell University Press).

Curran, G. (2006) *21st Century Dissent: Anarchism, Anti-Globalization and Environmentalism* (New York: Palgrave Macmillan).

Damill, M. and Frenkel, R. (2007) 'A Case of Disruptive International Financial Integration: Argentina and the Late Twentieth and Early Twenty-First Centuries', in Arestis, P. and Sawyer, M. (eds) *Political Economy of Latin America* (New York: Palgrave Macmillan).

Dannreuther, C. and Petit, P. (2008) 'Contemporary Capitalism and Internationalization: From One Diversity to Another', in Elsner, W. and Hanappi, H. (eds) *Varieties of Capitalisms and New Institutional Deals – Regulation, Welfare and the New Economy* (London: Edward Elgar).

Davatoglu, Ahmet Stratefik Derinlik (2001) *Turkiye'nin Uluslaroarasi Konumu* (Istanbul: Kure Yayinlari).

Davila, J. (2003) *Diploma of Whiteness: Race and Social Policy in Brazil, 1917–1945* (Durham, NC: Duke University Press).

Davis, S. (1996) *A Brotherhood of Arms: Brazil-United States Military Relations, 1945–1977* (Colorado: Niwot).

Davis, M. (2001) *Late Victorian Holocausts* (London: Verso).

Deleuze, G. and Guattari, F. (2003) *A Thousand Plateaus: Capitalism and Schizophrenia* (London: Continuum).

della Porta, D., Peterson, A. and Reiter, H. (eds.) (2006) *The Policing of Transnational Protest* (Aldershot: Ashgate).

della Porta, D., Andretta, M., Mosca, L. and Reiter, H. (2006) *Globalization from Below: Transnational Activists and Protest Network* (Minneapolis, MN: University of Minnesota Press).

Deringil, S. (1998) *The Well-Protected Domains: Ideology and the Legitimation of Power in the Ottoman Empire 1876–1909* (London: I.B. Tauris).

De Soto, H. (2001) *The Mystery of Capital: Why Capitalism Triumphs in the West and Fails Everywhere Else* (London: Black Swan).

De Sousa Santos, B. (2006) *The Rise of the Global Left: The World Social Forum and Beyond* (London: Zed Press).

Devezas, T., LePoire, D., Matias, J. and Silva, A. (2008) 'Energy Scenarios: Toward a New Energy Paradigm', *Futures*, 40, pp. 1–16.

Diez, T. (2007) 'The Ethical Implications of Turkey-EU Relations', *Ethics and International Affairs*, 21 (4), pp. 615–622.

Di Tella, G. and Dornbush, R. (eds) (1989) *The Political Economy of Argentina, 1946–83* (London: Macmillan and Saint Antony's College, Oxford).

Dornbusch, R. and Edwards, S. (1991) *The Macroeconomic of Populism in Latin America* (Chicago: Chicago University Press).

Dos Santos, T. (1970) 'The Structure of Dependence', *American Economic Review*, LX, May, pp. 231–236.

Duffy, R. (2000) 'Shadow Players: Ecotourism Development, Corruption and State Politics in Belize', *Third World Quarterly*, 21 (3), pp. 549–565.

Dziewanowski, K. (1989) 'Notatki spod stolika i na marginesie', *Tygodnik Powszechny*.

Eatwell, J. and Taylor, L. (2000) *Global Finance at Risk: The Case for International Regulation* (Cambridge: Polity Press).

The Economist (2006) 'Proton of Malaysia', November 30.

Economist Intelligence Unit (2005) *Russia: Country Profile* (London: Economist Intelligence Unit).

Emmanuel, A. (1972) *Unequal Exchange* (New York: Monthly Review).

Enriquez, L. (2009/2010). *Reacting to the Market: Small Farmers in the Economic Reshaping of Nicaragua, Cuba, Russia, and China* (University Park, PA: Pennsylvania State University Press).

Escude, C. and Cisneros, A. (2000) *Historia de las Relaciones Exteriores Argentinas* (Buenos Aires: Consejo Argentino para las Relaciones Exteriores, Centro de Estudios de Política Exterior).

Esping-Andersen, C. (1990) *The Three Worlds of Welfare Capitalism* (Cambridge: Polity).

Epstein, G. A. (2005) 'Capital Flight and Capital Controls in Developing Countries: An Introduction', in Epstein, G. A. (ed.) *Capital Flight and Capital Controls in Developing Countries* (Cheltenham: Edward Elgar).

Euractive (2004) 'EU-Turkey Relations', http://www.euractiv.com/en/enlargement/eu-turkey-relations/article-129678

EUROBAROMETER 5 (2008) *The European Union TODAY and Tomorrow* (Fieldwork: March–May 2008).

European Communities (2004) 'Facing the Challenges: The Lisbon Strategy for Growth and Employment'. Report from the High Level Group chaired by Wim Kok. Luxembourg, Office for Official Publications of the European Communities.

European Parliament (2008) 'European Parliament Resolution on Turkey's Progress Report 2008', B6-0000/2008 PE414.936v 01-00.

Errico, L. and Musalem, A. (1999) 'Offshore Banking: An Analysis of Micro- and Macro Prudential Issues', *Working Paper of the International Monetary Fund*, WP/99/5 (Washington, DC: International Monetary Fund).

Fabian, J. (1983) *Time and the Other: How Anthropology Makes Its Object* (Columbia University Press).

Fausto, B. (2006) *A Concise History of Brazil* (Cambridge: Cambridge University Press).

Fagan, B. (2004) *The Long Summer: How Climate Changed Civilization* (New York: Basic Books).

Financial Action Task Force (2000) 'Review to Identify Non-Cooperative Countries or Territories: Increasing the World-Wide Effectiveness of Anti-Money Laundering Measures', http://www.fatf-gafi.org/pdf/NCCT2000_en.pdf

Financial Action Task Force (2001) *Special Recommendations on Terrorist Financing*, English ed., Paris, 2002, last revised 31 October, available at http://www1.oecd.org/fatf/pdf/SRecTF_en.pdf.

Financial Action Task Force (2003a) 'Press Release – FATF Decides Not to Impose Counter Measures on the Philippines', http://www1.oecd.org/fatf/pdf/PR-20030313_en.pdf.

Financial Action Task Force (2003b) 'The Forty Recommendations', http://www.fatf gafi.org/dataoecd/38/47/34030579.pdf.

Financial Stability Forum (2000) 'Financial Stability Forum Releases Grouping of Offshore Financial Centres (OFCs) to Assist in Setting Priorities for Assessment', http://www.fsforum.org/publications/publication_23_41.html.

Fischer, P. (2000) *Foreign Direct Investment in Russia: A Strategy for Industrial Recovery* (London: Macmillan).

Fleming, K. E. (1999) *The Muslim Bonaparte: Diplomacy and Orientalism in Ali Pasha's Greece* (Princeton: Princeton University Press).

Foster, J. (1999) 'Marx's Theory of Metabolic Rift: Classical Foundations for Environmental Sociology', *American Journal of Sociology*, 105 (2), pp. 366–405.

Foster, J. (2002) *Ecology Against Capitalism* (New York: Monthly Review Press).

Foster, J. (2008a) 'Peak Oil and Energy Imperialism', *Monthly Review*, July–August, pp. 1–20.

Foster, J. (2008b) 'Ecology and the Transition from Capitalism to Socialism', *Monthly Review*, November, pp. 1–12.

Foster, J. and Burkett, P. (2008) 'Classical Marxism and the Second Law of Thermodynamics', *Organization & Environment*, 21 (1), pp. 3–37.

Fourcade-Gourinchas, M. and Babb, S. L. (2002) 'The Rebirth of the Liberal Creed: Paths to Neoliberalism in Four Countries', *American Journal of Sociology*, 108 (3), pp. 533–579.

Francis, C. Y. (1985) 'The Offshore Banking Sector in the Bahamas', *Social and Economic Studies*, 34 (4), pp. 91–110.

Franco, M. (2002) *Fases y Momento Actual de la Estructura Social Argentina* (Mendoza: Universidad Nacional de Cuyo).

Frank, A. G. (1966) 'The Development of Underdevelopment', *Monthly Review*, 18 (4), pp. 17–31.

Frank, A. G. (1967) *Capitalism and Underdevelopment in Latin America* (London: Monthly Review).

Frank, A. G. (1979) *Dependent Accumulation and Underdevelopment* (New York: Monthly Review Press).

Frank, A. G. (1984) *Critique and Anti-Critique* (London: Palgrave).

Frank, A. G. (1998) *Re-Orient: Global Economy in the Asian Age* (Berkeley: University of California Press).

Frank, A. G. and Gills, B. (eds) (1993) *The World System: Five Hundred Years or Five Thousand?* (London: Routledge).

Freeman, C. (ed.) (1986) *Design Innovation and Long Cycles in Economic Development* (London: Pinter).

Freidman (1982) *Capitalism and Freedom* (Chicago: Chicago University Press).

Friedman, M. and Friedman, R. (1980) *Free to Choose: A Personal Statement* (New York: Harcourt).

Friedman, J. and Chase-Dunn, C. (eds) (2004) *Hegemonic Declines: Past and Present* (Boulder CO: Paradigm).

Friedman, J and Chase-Dunn, C. (2005) *Hegemonic Declines: Past and Present* (Boulder CO: Paradigm).

Fukuyama, F. (1992) *The End of History and the Last Man* (London: Hamish Hamilton).

Furtado, C. (1959) *Furtado, The Economic Growth of Brazil*, Berkeley, University of California Press.

Furtado, C. (1970) *Economic Development of Latin American* (Cambridge: Cambridge University Press).

Gabriel, S. J. (2006) *Chinese Capitalism and the Modernist Vision* (London: Routledge).

Gaddy, C. G. and Ickes, B. W. (1998) 'Russia's Virtual Economy', *Foreign Affairs*, 77 (5), pp. 53–67.

Gamble, A. and Payne, A. (ed.) (1996) *Regionalism and World Order* (New York: St. Martins).

Georgescu-Roegen, N. (1971) *The Entropy Law and the Economic Process* (Cambridge, MA: Harvard University Press).

Germain, R. and Kenny, M. (1998) 'Engaging Gramsci: International Relations Theory and the New Gramscians', *Review of International Studies*, 24 (1), pp. 3–21.

Germani, G. (1956) 'La integración de las masas a la vida política y el totalitarismo', *Cursos y Conferencias*, 48 (273).

Gereffi, G. and Evans, P. B. (1981) 'Transnational Corporations, Dependent Development, and State Policy in the Semiperiphery', *Latin American Research Review*, 16 (3), pp. 31–64.

Giampietro, M. and Pimentel, D. (1991) Energy Efficiency: Assessing the Interaction between Humans and their Environment. *Ecological Economics*, 4, pp. 117–144.

Gill, S. (1990) *American Hegemony and the Trilateral Commission* (Cambridge: Cambridge University Press).

Gill, S. (ed.) (1993a) *Gramsci, Historical Materialism and International Relations* (Cambridge: Cambridge University Press).

Gill, S. (1993b) 'Neo-Liberalism and the Shift towards a US-Centred Transnational Hegemony', in Overbeek, H. (ed.) *Restructuring Hegemony in the Global Political Economy: The Rise of Transnational Neo-Liberalism in the 1980s* (London: Routledge), pp. 246–282.

Gill, S. (1995) 'Globalisation, Market Civilisation and Disciplinary Neoliberalism', *Millennium: Journal of International Studies*, 24 (3), pp. 399–423.

Gill, S. (1998) 'New Constitutionalism, Democratisation and Global Political Economy', *Pacifica Review*, 10 (1), pp. 23–38.

Gill, S. (2000) 'Toward a Postmodern Prince? The Battle in Seattle as a Moment in the New Politics of Globalisation', *Millennium*, 29 (1), pp. 131–141.

Gill, S. (2008) *Power and Resistance in the New World Order*, 2nd edn (Basingstoke: Palgrave Macmillan).

Gills, B. (ed.) (2000) *Globalisation and the Politics of Resistance* (Basingstoke: Palgrave Macmillan).

Glenday, D. (1989) 'Rich but Semiperipheral: Canada's Ambiguous Position in the World Economy', *Review*, 12 (2), pp. 209–261.

Global Business Policy Council (2007) 'New Concerns in an Uncertain World: The 2007 A.T. Kearney Foreign Direct Investment Confidence Index' (Vienna, Virginia: Global Business Policy Council).

Global Footprint Network (2008) 'Global Footprint Network: Advancing the Science of Sustainability', http://www.footprintnetwork.org/en/index.php/GFN/.

Goldfrank, W. (1977) 'Who Rules the World: Class Formation at the International Level', *Quarterly Journal of Ideology*, 1 (2), pp. 32–37.

Goldman, M. I. (2008) *Oilopoly: Putin, Power and the Rise of the New Russia* (Oxford: Oneworld Publications).

Goldstein, J. (1988) *Long Cycles: War and Prosperity in the Modern Age* (New Haven, CT: Yale University Press).

Göçek, F. (1996) *Rise of the Bourgeoisie, Demise of the Empire: Ottoman Westernization and Social Change* (Oxford: Oxford University Press).

Gore, C. (1996) 'Methodological Nationalism and the Misunderstanding of East Asian Industrialisation', *European Journal of Development Research*, 8 (1), pp. 77–122.

Gramsci, A. (1971) *Selections from the Prison Notebooks* (London: Lawrence and Wishart).

Gramsci, A. (1977) *Selections from Political Writings 1910–1920* (London: Lawrence and Wishart).

Greskovits, B. (1998) *The Political Economy of Protest and Patience: East European and Latin American Transformations Compared* (Budapest: Central European University Press).

Griffith-Jones, S. (1984) *International Finance and Latin America* (New York: St. Martin's Press).

Guha, R. (2007) *India after Gandhi: The History of the World's Largest Democracy* (New York: Harper Collins).

Gunderson, L. and Holling, C. (2002) *Panarchy: Understanding Transformations in Human and Natural Systems* (Washington, DC: Island Press).

GU-VShE (Gosudarstvennyi Universitet – Vysshaya Shkola Ekonomiki) (2007) 'Rossiiskaya Promyshlennost' Na Pereput'e: Chto Meshaet Nashim Firmam Stat' Konkurentosposobnymi', *Voprosy Ekonomiki*, 3, pp. 4–34.

Halperin Donghi, T. (1993) *The Contemporary History of Latin America*, 3rd edn (Durham: Duke University Press).

Hampton, M. P. and Christensen, J. (2002) 'Offshore Pariahs? Small Island Economies, Tax Havens, and the Re-Configuration of Global Finance', *World Development*, 30 (9), pp. 1657–1673.

Hanson, P. (2007) 'The Russian Economic Puzzle: Going Forwards, Backwards or Sideways?' *International Affairs*, 83 (5), pp. 869–889.

Harvey, D. (1992) *The Condition of Postmodernity: An Enquiry into the Origins of Cultural Change* (London: Wiley-Blackwell).

Harvey, D. (2003) *The New Imperialism* (Oxford: Oxford University Press).

Harvey, D. (2004) 'The New Imperialism: Accumulation by Dispossession', *Socialist Register* (London: The Merlin Press), pp. 63–87.

Harvey, D. (2005) *A Brief History of Neoliberalism* (Oxford: Oxford University Press).

Hayden, T. (ed.) (2002) *The Zapatista Reader* (New York: Thunder's Mouth Press).

Heinberg, R. (2004) *Power Down: Options and Actions for a Post-Carbon World* (Gabriola Island, BC, Canada: New Society Publishers).

Held, D., McGrew, A., Goldblatt, D. and Perraton, J. (1999) *Global Transformations: Politics, Economics and Culture* (Stanford, CA: Stanford University Press).

Heller, P. (1999) *The Labor of Development: Workers and the Transformation of Capitalism in Kerala, India* (Ithaca, NY: Cornell University Publishers).

Hilferding, R. (1910/2005) *Finance Capital* (London: Routledge).

Hill, F. and Gaddy, C. G. (2003) *The Siberian Curse: How Communist Planners Left Russia Out in the Cold* (Washington, DC: Brookings Institution).

Hill, H. (ed.) (1994) *Indonesia's New Order: The Dynamics of Socio-Economic Transformation* (Sydney: Allen and Unwin).

The Hindu (2001) 'The Human Development Race', 21 July, Source: http://www.hinduonnet.com/2001/07/21/stories/05212524.htm, Accessed: 11 November 2008.

Hinkalammert, F. (1972) *Dialectica del Desarrollo Desigual* (Valparaiso Ediciones: Universitarias de Valparaiso).

Hirst, P. and Thompson, G. (1996) *Globalization in Question: The International Economy and the Possibilities of Governance* (Cambridge: Polity Press).

Hobden, S. and Wyn Jones, R. (2008) 'Marxist Theories of International Relations', in Baylis, J., Smith, S. and Owens, P. (eds) *The Globalization of World Politics: An Introduction to International Relations*, 4th edn (Oxford: Oxford University Press) pp. 142–159.

Hobsbawn, E. (1994) *Age of Extremes* (London: Michael Joseph).

Hoffman, C. (2008) 'The Balkanization of Ottoman Rule: Premodern Origins of the Modern International System in Southeastern Europe', *Cooperation and Conflict*, 43, pp. 373–396.

Holman, O. (1993) 'Internationalisation and Democratistion: Southern Europe, Latin America and the World Economic Crisis', in Gill, S. (ed.) *Gramsci, Historical Materialism and International Relations* (Cambridge: Cambridge University Press).

Holtham, G. (2008) 'Workers of the World Compete', *Prospect Magazine*, December, http://www.prospect-magazine.co.uk/list.php?subject=119.

Hoogvelt, A. (1997) *Globalization and the Post-Colonial World* (Basingstoke: Macmillan).

Hopkins, R. (2008) *Transition Handbook: From Oil Dependency to Local Resilience* (Totnes: Green Books).

House of Commons Foreign Affairs Committee (2007) 'Visit to Turkey and Cyprus', Fifth Report of Session, *HC* 473 (The Stationery Office Limited 2006–2007).

Hunter Wade, R. (2008) 'Globalization, Growth, Poverty, Inequality, Resentment, and Imperialism', in Ravenhill, J. (ed.) *Global Political Economy* (Oxford: Oxford University Press), pp. 373–409.

Hutton, W. (2007) *The Writing on the Wall: China and the West in the 21st century* (London: Little Brown).

IMF External Relations Department (2008) 'IMF Executive Board Integrates the Offshore Financial Center Assessment Program with the FSAP' (Public Information Notice [PIN] No. 08/82)', *International Monetary Fund*, http://www.imf.org/external/np/sec/pn/2008/pn0882.htm

Inalcik, H. (1995) *From Empire to Republic: Essays on Ottoman and Turkish Social History* (Istanbul: The Isis Press).

The International Organization of Motor Vehicle Manufacturers (OIAC), *Annual Report*, 2007.

International Energy Agency (2008) *World Energy Outlook, 2008* (Paris: OECD).

International Monetary Fund (2004) 'Turkey: From Crisis to Recovery', *IMF Survey*, 33 (17), http://vlex.com/vid/turkey-from-crisis-to-recovery-51252801

International Monetary Fund (2008) 'Statement by the IMF Mission to Turkey', *Press Release*, 08/265.

Interview with Leszek Balcerowicz (2000) *Commanding Heights: The Battle for the World Economy*, PBS online http://www.pbs.org/wgbh/commandingheights/shared/minitext/int_leszekbalcerowicz.h ml#6

Islamoglu, H. and Keyder, C. (1987) 'Agenda for Ottoman History', in Huri Islamoglu-Inan (ed.), *The Ottoman Empire and the World-Economy* (Cambridge University Press) pp. 42–62.

Jayasuriya, K. (2005) *Reconstituting the Global Liberal Order: Legitimacy and Regulation* (London: Routledge).

Jevons, W. (1965) *The Coal Question: An Inquiry Concerning the Progress of the Nation, and the Probable Exhaustion of Our Coal-Mines*, 3rd edn (New York: A. M. Kelly).

Johns, R. A. (1983) *Tax Havens and Offshore Finance: A Study of Transnational Economic Development* (London: Frances Pinter).

Johnson, C. (2000) *Blowback* (London: Little, Brown and Company).

Jomo, K. S. (1993) *Industrializing Malaysia: Performance and Prospects* (London: Routledge).

Jomo, K. S. (1994) *Japan and Malaysian Development: In the Shadow of the Rising Sun* (London: Routledge).

Jomo, K. S., Felker, G. and Rashiah, R. (1999a) *Industrial Technology Development in Malaysia: Technology Competitiveness and the State* (London: Routledge).

Jomo, K. S., Felker, G. and Rashiah, R. (1999b) *Technology Competitiveness and the State: Malaysia's Industrial Policies* (London: Routledge).

Jorgenson, A. and Rice, J. (2005) 'Structural Dynamics of International Trade and Material Consumption: A Cross-National Study of the Ecological Footprint of Less-Developed Countries', *Journal of World-Systems Research*, XI (I), pp. 57–77.

Jorgenson, A. and Rice, J. (2007) 'Unequal Ecological Exchange and Consumption-Based Environmental Impacts: A Cross-National Comparison', in Hornburg, A., McNeil, J. R. and Martinez-Alier, J. (eds) *Rethinking Environmental History: World-System History and Global Environmental Change* (New York: AltaMira), pp. 273–288.

Kagarlitsky, B. (2008) *Empire of the Periphery: Russia and the World System* (London: Pluto Press).

Kaplan, D. (1960) 'The Law of Cultural Dominance', in Sahlins, M. and Service, E. (eds) *Evolution and Culture* (Ann Arbor, MI: University of Michigan Press), pp. 69–92.

Karpat, K. (2001) *The Politicization of Islam: Reconstructing Identity, State, Faith, and Community in the Late Ottoman State* (Oxford: Oxford University Press).

Kautsky, K. (1970) 'Ultraimperialism', *New Left Review*, 59, January–February, pp. 41–46.

Keohane, R. (1984) *After Hegemony: Cooperation and Discord in the World Political Economy* (Princeton: Princeton University Press).

Keyder, C. (1987) *State and Class in Turkey a Study in Capitalist Development* (London: Verso).

Kindleberger, C. P. (1987) *International Capital Movements* (Cambridge: Cambridge University Press).

Kirby, P. (2002) *The Celtic Tiger in Distress* (London: Palgrave Macmillan).

Klein, N. (2001) *No Logo, No Space, No Choice* (London: Flamingo).

Klein, N. (2007) *The Shock Doctrine: The Rise of Disaster Capitalism* (Basingstoke: Palgrave Macmillan).

Kowalewski, D. (1997) *Global Establishment: The Political Economy of North/Asian Networks* (New York: Macmillan Press).

Korzeniewicz, R. P. (1990) 'The Limits to Semiperipheral Development: Argentina in the Twentieth Century', in Martin, W. (ed.) *Semiperipheral States in the World-Economy* (New York: Greenwood).

Kramer, M. (1995) 'Polish Workers and the Post-Communist Transition, 1989–1993', *Communist and Post-Communist Studies*, 28 (1), pp. 71–114.

Kuzinski, S. (1987) *Polityka gospodarcza: realia, dylematy, propozycje* (Warsaw: Pwe).

Kynge, J. (2006) *China Shakes the World: The Rise of a Hungry Nation* (London: Phoenix).

Laclau, E. (1977) *Politics and Ideology in Marxist Theory* (London: Verso).

Laclau, E. (2005) *On Populist Reason* (London: Verso).

Lall, S. (1998) 'Malaysia: Industrial Success and the Role of Government', *Journal of International Development*, 7 (5), pp. 741–744.

Lane, D. (2005) 'Revolution, Class and Globalisation in the Transition from State Socialism', *European Societies*, 7 (1), pp. 131–155.

Larrain, J. (1989) *Theories of Development: Capitalism, Colonialism and Dependency* (Cambridge: Polity Press).

LePoire, D. (2007) 'Exploration of Connections Between Energy Use and Leadership Transitions', Presented at the Systemic Transitions Conference, 11–13 May (Indiana University, Bloomington, IN).

Lewis, P. (2000) 'A Future for Windward Islands' Bananas? Challenge and Prospect', *Commonwealth & Comparative Politics*, 38 (2), pp. 51–72.

Li, M. (2005) 'The Rise of China and the Demise of the Capitalist World Economy: Exploring Historical Possibilities in the 21st century', *Science & Society*, 69 (3), pp. 420–448.

Linklater, A. (1990) *Beyond Realism and Marxism* (London: Palgrave Macmillan).

Lipietz, A. (1982a) 'Towards Global Fordism?', *New Left Review*, 132, pp. 33–47.

Lipietz, A. (1982b) 'Marx or Rostow?', *New Left Review*, 132, pp. 48–58.

Lipietz, A. (1984a) 'Imperialism or the Beast of the Apocalypse', *Capital and Class*, 22, pp. 81–109.

Lipietz, A. (1984b) 'How Monetarism Has Choked Third World Industrialization', *New left Review*, pp. 71–87.

Lipietz, A. (1989) 'The Debt Problem, European Integration and the New Phase of World Crisis', *New Left Review*, 173, pp. 37–50.

Lipton, D. and Sachs, J. (1990) 'Creating a Market Economy in Eastern Europe: The Case of Poland', *Brookings Papers on Economic Activity 1*, pp. 75–147.

Little, R. (1995) 'The Triumph of Capitalism', in Booth, K. and Smith, S. (eds) *International Relations Theory Today* (Cambridge: Polity).

Lenin, V. I. (1916/1993) *Imperialism: The Highest Form of Capitalism* (London: Lawrence and Wishart).

Lester, J. (1995) *Modern Tsars and Princes* (London: Verso).

Lotka, A. (1925) *Elements of Physical Biology* (Baltimore, MD: Williams and Wilkins).

Lotka, A. (1945) 'The Law of Evolution as a Maximal Principal', *Proceedings of the National Academy of Sciences*, 8, pp. 147–151.

Luxemburg, R. (1915/2005) *The Accumulation of Capital* (London: Routledge Classics edition).

Lushin, A. and Oppenheimer, P. (2001) 'External Trade and Payments', in Granville, B. and Oppenheimer, P. (eds) *Russia's Post-Communist Economy* (Oxford: Oxford University Press).

MacDonald, C. (1985) 'The US, the Cold War and Peron', in Abel, C. and Lewis, C. (eds) *Latin America, Economic Imperialism and the State: The Political Economy of the External Connection from Independence to the Present* (London: Institute for Latin American Studies).

MacDonald, N. (2008) 'A Silver Lining for Russia', *Maclean's*, 121 (44), pp. 24–55.

Maclean, J. (1996) 'The Ideology of the End of Marxism/End of Socialism Thesis: A Critical, Global Perspective', in Einhorn, B., Kaldor, M. and Kavan, Z. (eds) *Citizenship and Democratic Control in Contemporary Europe* (Cheltenham: Edward Elgar).

Maddison, A. (2007) *Chinese Economic Performance in the Long Run: 960-2030AD* (Paris: OECD Publishing).

Magdoff, F. (2008) 'The Political Economy and Ecology of Biofuels', *Monthly Review*, 60 (3), pp. 34–50.

Makdisi, U. (2002) 'Ottoman Orientalism', *American Historical Review*, 107 (3), pp. 768–796.

Mandel, E. (1968) *Marxist Economic Theory* (New York: Monthly Review Press).

Mann, C. (2008) 'Our Good Earth: The Future Rests on Soil. Can We Protect It?', *National Geographic* (September), pp. 80–107.

Mann, M. (2003) *Incoherent Empire* (New York: Verso).

Marini, R. M. (1972) 'Brazilian Sub-Imperialism', *Monthly Review*, 23 (9), pp. 14–24.

Markoff, J. (1996) *Waves of Democracy: Social Movements and Political Change* (Thousand Oaks, CA: Pine Forge Press).

Marshall, D. D. (2003) 'Governance and Re-Regulation of Offshore Financial Centres: (Re)Framing the Confines of Legitimate Debate and Protest', in Barrow-Giles, C. and Marshall, D. D. (eds) *Living at the Borderlines: Issues in Caribbean Sovereignty and Development* (Kingston, Jamaica: Ian Randle Publishers).

Martin, W. (ed.) (1990) *Semiperipheral States in the World-Economy* (New York: Greenwood).

Martinelli, A. (2003) 'Markets, Governments, Communities and Global Governance', *International Sociology*, 18 (2), pp. 291–323.

Martinelli, A. (2005) *Global Modernization. Rethinking the Project of Modernity* (London: Sage).

Marx, K. (1967) *The Eighteenth Brumaire of Louis Bonaparte* (Moscow: Progress).

Marx, K. (1990) *Capital Volume One* (London: Penguin).

Maurseth, P. B. (2003) 'Divergence and Dispersion in the Russian Economy', *Europe-Asia Studies*, 55 (8), pp. 1165–1185.

McCarthy, I. (1979) 'Offshore Banking Centers: Benefits and Costs', *Finance and Development*, 16 (4), pp. 45–48.

McMichael, P. (2000) *Development and Social Change*, 2nd edn (Thousand Oaks, CA: Pine Forge).

Meaney, C. S. (1995) 'Foreign Experts, Capitalists, and Competing Agendas: Privatization in Poland, the Czech Republic, and Hungary', *Comparative Political Studies*, 28 (2), pp. 275–305.

Meier, G. M. and Seers, D. (eds) (1984) *Pioneers in Development* (Washington, DC: World Bank).

Mertes, T. (ed.) (2004) *Movement of Movements: Is Another World Really Possible?* (New York: Verso).

Mesa-Lago, C. (2000) 'Desarrollo social, reforma del estado y de la seguridad social, al umbral del siglo XXI', in *Serie Política Social* CEPAL.

Millar, P. (1995) *Thailand Automotive Market Review* (Bangkok: British Embassy Commercial Section).

Modelski, G. and Thompson, W. (1996) *Leading Sectors and World Powers: The Coevolution of Global Economics and Politics* (Columbia, SC: University of South Carolina Press).

Monetary and Economic Department (2003) *Guide to the International Banking Statistics*. BIS Papers, 16 (Basel: Bank for International Settlements).

Monetary and Economic Department (2006) *Guidelines to the International Locational Banking Statistics* (Basel: Bank for International Settlements).

Monetary and Financial Systems Department (2005) *Offshore Financial Centers: The Assessment Program—A Progress Report* (Washington, DC: International Monetary Fund).

Moore, J. (2000) 'Environmental Crises and the Metabolic Rift in World Historical Perspective', *Organization & Environment*, 13 (2), pp. 123–157.

Moore, J. (2003) 'The Modern World-System as Environmental History? Ecology and the Rise of Capitalism', *Theory and Society*, 32 (3), pp. 307–377.

Moore, J. (2007a) *Ecology and the Rise of Capitalism*. Ph.D. Dissertation. Department of Geography (Berkeley: University of California).

Moore, P. (2007b) *Globalisation and Labour Struggle in Asia: A Neo-Gramscian Critique of South Korea's Political Economy* (London: I. B. Tauris).

Moore, P. and Taylor, P. (2009) 'Exploitation of the Self in Community-Based Software Production – Workers' Freedoms or Firm Foundations?', *Capital and Class*, 97, pp. 99–121.

Moran, T. (2002) *Beyond Sweatshops: Foreign Direct Investment and Globalization in Developing Countries* (Washington DC: Brookings Institution Press).

Morton, A. (2003) 'Social Forces in the Struggle over Hegemony: Neo-Gramscian Perspectives in International Political Economy', *Rethinking Marxism*, 15 (2), pp. 153–179.

Morton, A. (2007) *Unravelling Gramsci* (London: Pluto).

Murmis, M. and Portantiero, J. (1971) *Estudios sobre los orígenes del Peronismo* (Buenos Aires: Siglo XXI).

Murphy, C. (1994) *International Organization and Industrial Change: Global Governance since 1850* (New York: Oxford).

Murphy, C. and Tooze, R. (eds) (1991) *The New Political Economy* (Boulder, CO: Lynne Rienner).

Naughton, B. (1996) *Growing Out of the Plan: Chinese Economic Reform, 1978–1993* (Cambridge: Cambridge University Press).

Nawadhinsukh, S. (1984) 'Ancillary Firm Development in the Thai Auto Industry', in Okada, K. (ed.) *The Motor Vehicle Industry in Asia: Ancillary Firm Development* (Singapore: The Singapore University Press).

Nealon, J. (1998) *Alterity Politics: Ethics and Performative Subjectivity* (Durham: Duke University Press).

Nederveen Pieterse, J. (2000) 'Globalization North and South: Representations of Uneven Development and the Interaction of Modernities', *Theory, Culture and Society*, 17 (1), pp. 129–137.

Nee, V. (1996) 'The Emergence of a Market Society: Changing Mechanisms of Stratification in China', *American Journal of Sociology*, 101 (4), pp. 908–949.

Nef, L. (1994) 'The Political Economy of Inter-American Relations: A Structural and Historical Overview', in Stubbs, R. and Underhill, G. (eds) *Political Economy and the Changing Global Order* (Oxford: Oxford University Press).

Nema, P. and Pokhariyal, P. (2008) 'SEZs as Growth Engines – India vs China', http://ssrn.com/abstract=1279023

OECD Economic Outlook 83, http://www.oecd.org/dataoecd/5/51/20213268.pdf.

O'Brien, R. and Williams, M. (2004) *Global Political Economy: Evolution and Dynamics* (Basingstoke: Palgrave Macmillan).

Ocampo, J. (2000) 'Recasting the International Agenda', *CEPA Working Paper Series III. 19*.

O'Donnell, G. (1973) *Modernization and Bureaucratic-Authoritarianism: Studies in South America Politics* (Berkeley: Institute for International Studies).

O'Rourke, K. and Williamson, J. (1999) *Globalization and History: The Evolution of a 19th Century Atlantic Economy* (Cambridge, MA: MIT Press).

Office of Industrial Economics (2006) 'The Automotive Industry in Thailand', *Ministry of Industry*, Thailand.

Offshore Groups of Banking Supervisors (2006) 'Members and Observers', http://www.ogbs.net/members.htm.

Oszlak, O. (1981) 'The Historical Formation of the State in Latin America: Some Theoretical and Methodological Guidelines for Its Study', *Latin American Research Review*, 16 (2), pp. 3–32.

Önis, Z. and Aysan, A. F. (2000) 'Neoliberal Globalisation, the Nation-State and Financial Crises in the Semi-Periphery: A Comparative Analysis', *Third World Quarterly*, 21 (1), pp. 119–139.

Organisation for Economic Co-Operation and Development (1998) *Harmful Tax Competition: An Emerging Global Issue* (Paris: OECD Publications).

Organisation for Economic Co-Operation and Development (2000) *Towards Global Tax Co Operation: Progress in Identifying and Eliminating Harmful Tax Practices* (Paris: OECD Publication).

Overbeek, H. (2004) 'Transnational Class Formation and Concepts of Control: Towards a Genealogy of the Amsterdam Project in International Political Economy', *Journal of International Relations & Development*, 7 (2), pp. 113–141.

Overbeek, H. and Van Der Pijl, K. (1993) 'Restructuring Capital and Restructuring Hegemony: Neo-Liberalism and the Unmaking of the Post-War Order', in Overbeek, H. (ed.) *Restructuring Hegemony in the Global Political Economy: The Rise of Transnational Neo-Liberalism in the 1980s* (London: Routledge), pp. 1–27.

Palan, R. (1998) 'Trying to Have Your Cake and Eating It: How and Why the State System has Created Offshore', *International Studies Quarterly*, 42, pp. 625–644.

Palan, R. (2002) 'Tax Havens and the Commercialization of State Sovereignty', *International Organization*, 56 (1), pp. 151–176.

Palan, R. (2003) *The Offshore World: Sovereign Markets, Virtual Places, and Nomad Millionaires* (Ithaca and London: Cornell University Press).

Palan, R. and Abbott, J. P. (1996/2000) *State Strategies in the Global Political Economy* (London: Pinter).

Palma, G. (1978) 'Dependency: A Formal Theory of Underdevelopment or a Methodology for the Analysis of Concrete Situations of Underdevelopment', *World Development*, 6, pp. 881–924.

Panitch, L. (2000) 'The New Imperial State', *New Left Review*, II (2), pp. 6–18.

Parfitt, T. (2006) 'Russia Turns Off Supplies to Ukraine in Payment Row and EU Feels Chill', *The Guardian*, 2 January.

Patomäki, H. (2008) *The Political Economy of Global Security: War, Future Crises and Changes in Global Governance* (London: Routledge).

Patomäki, K. S. and Ulvila, M. (eds) (2008) *Global Political Parties* (New York: Zed Books).

Patomäki, H., Teivainen, T. and Ronkko, M. (2002) Global Democracy Initiatives: The Art of Possible. NIGD Working Paper 2/2002. Helsinki, Finland: Network Institute for Global Democratization (NIGD) and Nottingham Trent University.

Pattullo, P. (2005) *Last Resorts: The Cost of Tourism in the Caribbean* (London: Latin American Bureau).

Payne, A. (1996) 'The United States and Its Enterprise for the Americas', in Payne, A. and Gamble, A. (eds) *Regionalism and World Order* (London: Macmillan), pp. 93–129.

Payne, A. (2005) *The Global Politics of Unequal Development* (Basingstoke: Palgrave Macmillan).

People's Daily Online (2008) http://english.peopledaily.com.cn/index.html.

Pellow, D. (2007) *Resisting Global Toxics: Transnational Movements for Environmental Justice* (Cambridge, MA: MIT Press).

Perkovich, G. (2003) 'Is India a major power?', *The Washington Quarterly*, 27 (1), pp. 129–144.

Perlin, J. (1989) *A Forest Journey: The Role of Wood in the Development of Civilization* (New York: W. W. Norton & Co).

Perraton, J., Goldblatt, D., Held, D. and McGrew, A. (1997) 'The Globalization of Economic Activity', *New Political Economy*, 2 (2), pp. 257–277.

Persaud, B. (2001) 'OECD Curbs on Offshore Financial Centres: A Major Issue for Small States', *The Round Table: The Commonwealth Journal of International Affairs*, 359, pp. 199–212.

Peschard, K. (2005) *Rethinking the Semi-Periphery: Some Conceptual Issues*, http://www.ualberta.ca/GLOBALISM/pdf/semi-periphery.lnk.pdf.

Phillips, N. (ed.) (2005) *Globalizing International Political Economy* (Basingstoke: Palgrave Macmillan).

Piñera, J. (2003) 'Latin America: A Way Out', *Cato Journal*, 22 (3), pp. 409–416.

Poapongsakorn, N. (2000) 'The Thai Automotive Industry', Report for ASEAN auto database, available at http://www.asean-org/thai/report.htm.

Podobnik, B. (2002) 'The Globalization Protest Movement: An Analysis of Broad Trends and the Impact of Sept. 11', Paper given at the American Sociological Meeting, Chicago, IL.

Podobnik, B. (2006a) 'Global Energy Inequalities: Exploring the Long-Term Implications', in Chase-Dunn, C. and Babones, S. (eds) *Global Social Change: Historical and Comparative Perspectives* (Baltimore, MD: Johns Hopkins University Press), pp. 135–158.

Podobnik, B. (2006b) *Global Energy Shifts: Fostering Sustainability in a Turbulent Age* (Philadelphia, PA: Temple University Press).

Podobnik, B. and Reifer, T. (2005) *Transforming Globalization: Challenges and Opportunities in the Post 9/11 Era* (Leiden: Brill).

Ponting, C. (2007) *A New Green History of the World: The Environment and the Collapse of Great Civilizations* (New York: Penguin Books)

Poulantzas, N. (1973) *Political Power and Social Classes* (London: Verso).

Poulantzas, N. (1975) *Classes in Contemporary Capitalism* (London: NLB).

Prasad, E. (2008) 'Economic Strategy: Chinese Road to Nowhere' in FT.com. Source: http://us.ft.com/ftgateway/superpage.ft?news_id=fto0124200807353 81906, Accessed 24 January 2008.

Preobrazhensky, E. (1973) *From New Economic Policy to Socialism: A Glance into the Future of Russia and Europe* (London: New Park Press).

Prestowitz, C. (2005) *Three Billion New Capitalists: The Great Shift of Wealth and Power to the East* (New York: Basic Books).

Prebisch, R. (1950) *The Economic Development of Latin American and Some of Its Principle Problems* (New York: United Nations).

Prebisch, R. (1959) 'Commercial Policy in the Underdeveloped Countries', *American Economic Review*, 49, pp. 251–273.

Prigogine, I. (2000) 'The Networked Society', *Journal of World-Systems Research*, 6 (1), pp. 892–898.

Prigogine, I. and Stengers, I. (1984) *Order out of Chaos: Man's New Dialogue with Nature* (New York: Bantam Books).

Przeworski, A. (1991) *Democracy and the Market: Political and Economic Reforms in Eastern Europe and Latin America* (Cambridge: Cambridge University Press).

Radice, H. (1984) 'The National Economy: A Keynesian Myth?', *Capital and Class*, 22, pp. 111–140.

Radice, H. (ed.) (1975) *International Firm and Modern Imperialism* (Harmondsworth: Penguin Books).

Radice, H. (1999) 'Taking Globalization Seriously', *The Socialist Register* (London: Merlin).

Radice, H. (2006) 'The Developmental State Under Global Neoliberalism: Who Is Doing What to Whom?', Paper presented for the conference *Globalization and the Semi-Periphery*, University of Limerick, 4 March.

Radice, H. (2008) 'The Developmental State Under Global Neoliberalism', *Third World Quarterly*, 29 (6), pp. 1153–1174.

Rapoport, M. and Cervo, A. (eds) (2002) *El Cono Sur: Una historia común* (Buenos Aires: Fondo de Cultura Económica).

Rapoport, M. (1988) 'El modelo agroexportador argentino', in Rapoport, M. (ed.) *Economía e historia: Contribuciones a la historia económica argentina* (Buenos Aires: Tesis).

Reddaway, P. and Glinski, D. (2001) *The Tragedy of Russia's Reforms: Market Bolshevism Against Democracy* (Washington DC: United States Institute of Peace Press).

Rehn, O. (2008) 'EU Commissioner for Enlargement 45 Years from the Signing of the Ankara Agreement: EU-Turkey – Cooperation Continues Conference on EC Turkey Association Agreement', SPEECH/08/581.

Rennstich, J. (2001) 'The Future of Great Power Rivalries', in Dunaway, W. (ed.) *New Theoretical Directions for the 21st Century World-System* (New York: Greenwood Press).

Reifer, T. (ed.) (2004) *Globalisation, Hegemony and Power* (Boulder CO: Paradigm).

Repetto, F. and Alonso, G. (2004) 'La economía política de la política social argentina: una mirada desde la desregulación y la descentralización', *Series Políticas Sociales*, 97, CEPAL.

Rittenberg, L. (1998) *The Political Economy of Turkey in the Post-Soviet Era: Going West and Looking East?* (Santa Barbara: Praeger Publishers).

Roberts, J. and Parks, B. (2007) *A Climate of Injustice: Global Inequality, North-South Politics, and Climate Policy* (Cambridge, MA: MIT Press).

Robinson, N. (2004) 'Global Economy, the USSR and Post-Soviet Change', in Robinson, N. (ed.) *Reforging the Weakest Link: Global Political Economy and Post-Soviet Change in Russia, Ukraine and Belarus* (Aldershot: Ashgate).

Robinson, W. (1996) *Promoting Polyarchy* (Cambridge: Cambridge University Press).

Robinson, W. (1998) 'Beyond Nation-State Paradigms: Globalization, Sociology, and the Challenge of Transnational Studies', *Sociological Forum*, 13 (4), pp. 561–594.

Robinson, W. (2003) *Transnational Conflicts: Central America, Social Change and Globlisation* (London: Verso).

Robinson, W. (2004) *A Theory of Global Capitalism: Production, Class and State in a Transnational World* (Baltimore; London: Johns Hopkins University Press).

Robinson, W. (2008) *Latin American and Global Capitalism: A Critical Globalization Perspective* (Baltimore, MD: Johns Hopkins University Press).

Robinson, W. and Harris, J. (2000) 'Towards a Global Ruling Class? Globalization and the Transnational Capitalist Class', *Science and Society*, 64 (1), pp. 11–54.

Rock, D. (1987) *Argentina, 1516–1987: From Spanish Colonization to the Falklands War and Alfonsin* (London: I.B. Tauris).

Rock, M. T. (1995) 'Thai Industrial Policy: How Relevant Was It to Export Success?', *Journal of International Development*, 7 (5), pp. 745–758.

Roemer, J. (1994) *A Future for Socialism* (New York: Harvard).

Róna-Tas, Á. (1994) 'The First Shall Be Last? Entrepreneurship and Communist Cadres in the Transition from Socialism', *American Journal of Sociology*, 100 (1), pp. 40–69.

Rostow, W. (1960) *The Stages of Economic Growth* (Cambridge: Cambridge University Press).

Rostow, W. (1984) 'Development: The Political Economy of the Marshallian Long Period', in Meier, G. M. and Seers, D. (eds) *Pioneers in Development* (Washington, DC: World Bank).

Ruccio, D. and Simon, L. (1992) 'Perspectives on Underdevelopment: Frank, the Modes of Production School and Amin', in Jameson, K. and Wilber, C. (eds) *The Political Economy of Development and Underdevelopment* (New York: Random House).

Ruggie, J. G. (1982) 'International Regimes: Transactions and Change: Embedded Liberalism in the Post-War Economic Order', *International Organizations*, 36 (2), pp. 379–415.

Rupert, M. (1993) 'Alienated, Capitalism and the Inter-State System', in Gill, S. (ed.) *Gramsci, Historical Materialism and International Materialism* (Cambridge: Cambridge University Press).

Saad-Filho, A., Iannini, F. and Molinari, E. (2007) 'Neoliberalism, Democracy and Economic Policy in Latin America', in Arestis, P. and Sawyer, M. (eds) *Political Economy of Latin America* (Basingstoke: Palgrave Macmillan).

Sachs, J. (1990) 'What Is to Be Done?', *The Economist*, 13 January.

Sachs, J. (1993a) 'The Economic Transformation of Eastern Europe: The Case of Poland', in Poznanski, K. (ed.) *Stabilization and Privatization in Poland* (Boston: Kluwer Academic Publishers).

Sachs, J. (1993b) *Poland's Jump to the Market Economy* (Cambridge, MA, London: MIT Press).

Sachs, J. (2005) *The End of Poverty: How We Can Make It Happen in Our Lifetime* (London: Penguin).

Sadownik, H. and Wawrzyniak, B. (eds) (1985) *Reforma gospodarcza: doswiadczenia I problemy* (Warsaw: PWE).

Sahlins, M. and Service, E. (eds) (1960) *Evolution and Culture* (AnnArbor, MI: University of Michigan Press).

Said, E. (1978) *Orientalism* (London: Routledge).

Sakwa, R. (2008a) *Putin: Russia's Choice*, 2nd edn (London: Routledge).

Sakwa, R. (2008b) *Russian Politics and Society*, 4th edn (London: Routledge).

Sanders, R. M. (2002) 'The Fight Against Fiscal Colonialism: The OECD and Small Jurisdictions', *The Round Table: The Commonwealth Journal of International Affairs*, 365, pp. 325–348.

Sasuga, K. (2008) 'The Globalizing Chinese Automotive Industry and Cross-Border Production Networks: Regionalization and Globalization in East Asia', Paper presented to 3rd Annual Meeting of the GARNET network (Network of Excellence on *Global Governance, Regionalisation and Regulation*) Bordeaux, France, 17–19 September.

Sassen, S. (1991) *The Global City* (New York: Princeton University Press).

Sayan, S. (1998) 'The Black Sea Economic Cooperation Project: Substite for or a Complement to Globalization Efforts in the Middle East and The Balkans?' *Working Paper*, No. 9806 (Cairo, Egypt: Economic Research Forum).

Sehm-Patomaki, K. and Ulvila, M. (2007) *Global Political Parties* (London: Zed Books).

Selcuk, F. (1998) 'A Brief Account of the Turkish Economy, 1987–1996', in Rittenberg, L. (ed.) *The Political Economy of Turkey in the Post-Soviet Era: Going West and Looking East?* (Santa Barbara: Praeger Publishers), pp. 17–33.

Shannon, T. R. (1989) *An Introduction to the World-System Perspective* (Boulder, San Francisco and London: Westview Press).

Shannon, T. R. (1990) *An Introduction to World System Perspective* (Boulder, CO: Westview).

Sharma, A. (2006) 'Flexibility, Employment and Labour Market Reforms in India', *Economic and Political Weekly*, 26 May, pp. 2078–2085.

Sharman, J. C. (2005) 'South Pacific Tax Havens: From Leaders in the Race to the Bottom to Laggards in the Race to the Top?', *Accounting Forum*, 29 (3), pp. 311–323.

Sharman, J. C. (2007) 'The Bark *is* the Bite: International Organisations and Blacklisting', unpublished manuscript.

Shaw, T., Cooper, A. F. and Antkiewicz, A. (2007) 'Global and/or Regional Development at the Start of the 21st Century? China, India and (South) Africa', *Third World Quarterly*, 28 (7), pp. 1255–1270.

Shields, S. (2003) 'The Charge of the "Right Brigade": Transnational Social Forces and the Neoliberal Configuration of Poland's Transition', *New Political Economy*, 8 (2), pp. 225–244.

Shields, S. (2004) 'Global Restructuring and the Polish State: Transition, Transformation, or Transnationalization?', *Review of International Political Economy*, 11 (1), pp. 132–154.

Shields, S. (2006) 'Historicizing Transition: The Polish Political Economy in a Period of Global Structural Change – Eastern Central Europe's Passive Revolution?', *International Politics*, 43 (4), pp. 474–499.

Shiva, V. (1997) *Biopiracy: The Plunder of Nature and Knowledge* (Boston, MA: South End Press).

Shiva, V. (2006) *Earth Democracy: Justice, Sustainability and Peace* (London: Zed Books).

Silver, B. (1995) 'World-Scale Patterns of Labor-Capital Conflict: Labor Unrest Long Waves & Cycles of Hegemony', *Review*, 18, pp. 1–53.

Silver, B. J. (2003) *Forces of Labor: Workers' Movements and Globalization since 1870* (Cambridge: Cambridge University Press).

Silver, B. J. and Arrighi, G. (2001) 'Workers North and South', *Socialist Register* (London: The Merlin Press), pp. 53–76.

Silver, B. and Slater, E. (1999) 'The Social Origins of World Hegemonies', in Arrighi, G. et al. (eds) *Chaos and Governance in the Modern World-System* (Minneapolis: University of Minnesota Press), pp. 151–216.

Singh, B. N. P (1997) 'Three Years' Achievement of the New Economic Policy in India', in Gupta, K. R. (ed.) *Liberalisation and Globalisation of the Indian Economy* (New Delhi: Atlanti), pp. 1–16.

Simmons, D. (2002) 'Some Legal Issues Arising out of the OECD Reports on Harmful Tax Competition', in Biswas, R. (ed.) *International Tax Competition: Globalisation and Fiscal Sovereignty* (London: Commonwealth Secretariat).

Simon, R. (2010) 'Perestroika, Passive Revolution and the Contemporary Russian State', *Capital & Class*, 102 (forthcoming).

Simpson, G. R. (2005) 'In Europe, Finance Lobby Sways Terror-Funding Law', *The Wall Street Journal Europe* (24 May).

Skocpol, T. (1977) 'Wallerstein's World Capitalist System: A Theoretical and Historical Critique', *American Journal of Sociology*, 82 (5), pp. 1075–1090.

Sklair, L. (1997) 'Social Movements for Global Capitalism: The Transnational Capitalist Class in Action', *Review of International Political Economy*, 4 (3), pp. 514–537.

Sklair, L. (2001) *The Transnational Capitalist Class* (Malden, MA: Blackwell Publishers).

Slay, B. (1994) *The Polish Economy: Crisis, Reform, and Transition* (Princeton, NJ, London: Princeton University Press).

Smil, V. (2008) *Energy in Nature and Society: General Energetics of Complex Systems* (Cambridge, MA: MIT Press).

Smith, D. A. and Lee, S. H. (1990) 'Limits on a Semiperipheral Success Story? State Dependent Development and the Prospects for South Korean Democratization', in Martin, W. (ed.) *Semiperipheral States in the World-Economy* (New York: Greenwood).

Smith, J. (2008) *Social Movements for Global Democracy* (Baltimore: Johns Hopkins University Press).

Smith, S., Booth, K. and Zalewski, M. (eds) (1996) *International Theory: Positivism & Beyond* (Cambridge: Cambridge University Press).

Soederberg, S. (2004) *The Politics of the New International Financial Architecture: Reimposing Neoliberal Domination in the Global South* (London and New York: Zed Books).

Solinger, D. (2003) 'China's Urban Workers and the WTO', *The China Journal*, January, pp. 61–87.

Spencer, H. (1882) *First Principles of a New System of Philosophy*, 4th edn (New York: D. Appleton and Co).

Srinivasan T. N. and Tendulkar, S. D. (2003) *Reintegrating India with the World Economy* (Washington, DC: Peterson Institute).

Stevis, D. and Boswell, T. (2008) *Globalization and Labor: Democratizing Global Governance* (Lanham, MD: Rowman and Littlefield).

Stopford, J. and Strange, S. (1991) *Rival States, Rival Firms: Competition for World Marker Share* (Cambridge: Cambridge University Press).

Strange, G. (2002) 'Globalization, Regionalism and Labour Interests in the New International Political Economy', *New Political Economy*, 7 (3), pp. 343–365.

Strange, G. (2006) 'The Left Against Europe? A Citical Engagement with New Constitutionalism and Structural Dependence Theory', *Government and Opposition*, 41 (2), pp. 197–229.

Strange, S. (1987) 'The Persistent Myth of Lost Hegemony', *International Organisation*, 41 (4), pp. 551–574.

Strange, S. (1988) *States and Markets* (London: Frances Pinter).

Strange, S. (1995) 'The Defective State', *Daedalus*, 124 (2), pp. 55–74.

Strange, S. (1996) *The Retreat of the State: The Diffusion of Power in the World Economy* (Cambridge: Cambridge University Press).

Strong, Pauline Turner. (1999) *Captive Selves, Captivating Others: The Politics and Poetics of Colonial American Captivity; Narratives* (Westview Press/Perseus Books).

Sunkel, O. (1972) 'Big Business and "Depencia" ', *Foreign Affairs*, 50, pp. 517–531.

Suter, C. (1992) *Debt Cycles in the World Economy: Foreign Loans, Financial Crises and Debt Settlements, 1820–1987* (Boulder, CO: Westview).

Szacki, J. (1995) *Liberalism After Communism* (Budapest: Central European University Press).

Szelenyi, I. and Kostello, E. (1996) 'The Market Transition Debate: Toward a Synthesis?', *American Journal of Sociology*, 101 (4), pp. 1082–1096.

Tainter, J. (1988) *The Collapse of Complex Societies* (New York: Cambridge University Press).

Taussig, M. (1993) *Mimesis and Alterity* (London: Routledge).

Taylor, P. (1996) *The Way the Modern World Works: World Hegemony to World Impasse* (New York: Wiley).

Teoh, S. W., Sathirathai, S., Lam, D., Lai, C. and Cahreaonwongsak, K. (2007) *Microeconomics and Competitiveness Paper*, available at http://www.isc.hbs.edu/pdf/Student_Projects/Thailand_AutomotiveCluster_2007.pdf.

Thai Farmers Bank Survey (1986), (Bankok: Thai Farmers Bank).

The Economist (1989) 'Country Report on Poland', December.

Thun, E. (2008) *Changing Lanes in China: Direct Foreign Interest, Local Governments and Auto Sector Development* (Cambridge: Cambridge University Press).

Tilly, C. (2007) *Democracy* (New York: Cambridge University Press).

Todorova, Maria. (1997) *Imagining the Balkans.* (New York and Oxford: Oxford University Press).

Tomasic, D. (1953) *The Impact of Russian Culture on Soviet Communism* (Glencoe: Free Press).

Treisman, D. (2007) 'Putin's *Silovarchs*', *Orbis*, Winter, pp. 141–153.

Trotsky, L. (1977) *The History of the Russian Revolution* (London: Pluto Press).

United Kingdom Public Record Office (1967–1969) *Tax Havens* (London, Archive Folder: IR 40/16743).

United Kingdom Public Record Office (1973) *Tax Havens in Cayman Islands* (London, Archive Folder: FCO 44/861).

UNDP (2005) *Human Development Report.*

UNICO (1995) *The Study on Industrial Sector Development Supporting Industries in the Kingdom of Thailand*, Japan International Cooperation Agency (JICA) and Department of Industrial Promotion, Ministry of Industry.

van Apeldoorn, B. (2000) 'Transnational Class Agency and European Governance: The Case of the European Round Table of Industrialists', *New Political Economy*, 5 (2), pp. 157–181.

van Apeldoorn, B. (2004) 'Theorizing the Transnational: A Historical Materialist Approach', *Journal of International Relations & Development*, 7 (2), pp. 142–176.

van de Mieroop, M. (2007) *A History of the Ancient Near East, ca. 3000–323 BC*, 2nd edn (Malden, MA: Blackwell).

van der Pijl, K. (1984) *The Making of an Atlantic Ruling Class* (London: Verso).

van der Pijl, K. (1995) 'The Second Glorious Revolution: Globalizing Elites and Historical Change', in Hettne, B. (ed.) *International Political Economy: Understanding Global Disorder* (London: Zed Books), pp. 100–128.

van der Pijl, K. (1998) *Transnational Classes and International Relations* (London: Routledge).

van der Pijl, K. (2004) 'Two Faces of the Transnational Cadre Under Neo-Liberalism', *Journal of International Relations & Development*, 7 (2), pp. 177–207.

van der Pijl, K. (2006) *Global Rivalries: From the Cold War to Iraq* (London: Pluto Press).

Vlcek, W. (2004) 'The OECD and Offshore Financial Centres: Rearguard Action Against Globalisation?' *Global Change, Peace and Security*, 16 (3), pp. 227–242.

Vlcek, W. (2007) 'Why Worry? The Impact of the OECD Harmful Tax Competition Initiative for Caribbean Offshore Financial Centres', *The Round Table: The Commonwealth Journal of International Affairs*, 96 (390), pp. 331–346.

Vlcek, W. (2008a) *Offshore Finance and Small States: Sovereignty, Size and Money* (Basingstoke: Palgrave Macmillan).

Vlcek, W. (2008b) 'Competitive or Coercive? The Experience of Caribbean Offshore Financial Centres with Global Governance', *The Round Table*, 97 (396), pp. 439–452.

Vlcek, W. (2009) 'The Caribbean Confronts the OECD: Tax Competition and Diplomacy', in Cooper, A. F. and Shaw, T. M. (eds) *The Diplomacy of Small States* (Basingstoke: Palgrave Macmillan), pp. 164–179.

Von Wehrlof, C. (2000) ' "Globalization" and the "permanent" Process of "primitive accumulation": The Example of the MAI, the Multilateral Agreement on Investment', *Journal of World-Systems Research*, 6 (3), pp. 728–747.

Wade, R. (1990) *Governing the Market* (Princeton, NJ: Princeton University Press).

Wagar, W. (1996) 'Toward a Praxis of World Integration', *Journal of World-Systems Research*, 2 (2) http://jwsr.ucr.edu/index.php.

Wagar, W. (1999) *A Short History of the Future*, 3rd edn (Chicago, IL: University of Chicago Press).

Walicki, A. (1988) 'Liberalism in Poland', *Critical Review*, 2 (1), pp. 8–38.

Walker, J. W. (2007) 'Learning Strategic Depth: Implications of Turkey's New Foreign Policy Doctrine', *Insight Turkey*, 9 (3), pp. 32–47.

Wallerstein, I. (1974) *The Modern World-System Volume I: Capitalist Agriculture and the Origins of the European World-Economy in the Sixteenth Century* (New York: Academic Press).

Wallerstein, I. (1976) 'Semi-Peripheral Countries and the Contemporary World Crisis', *Theory and Society*, 3 (4), pp. 461–483.

Wallerstein, I. (1979) *The Capitalist World Economy* (Cambridge: Polity).

Wallerstein, I. (1980) *The Modern World System, Volume II: Mercantilism and the Consolidation of the European World Economy 1600–1750* (New York: Academic Press).

Wallerstein, I. (1985) 'The Relevance of the Concept of Semi-Periphery to Southern Europe', in Arrighi, G. (ed.) *Semiperipheral Development* (London: Sage), pp. 31–39.

Wallerstein, I. (1989) *The Modern World System III: The Second Era of Great Expansion of the Capitalist World-Economy, 1730–1840s* (New York: Academic Press).

Wallerstein, I. (1992) 'The West, Capitalism, and the Modern World-System', *Review*, XV (4) Fall, pp. 561–619.

Wallerstein, I. (1995) 'Three Paths of Upward Mobility Within the Capitalist World-System', in Sanderson, S. (ed.) *Sociological Works: Comparative and Historical Readings on Society* (Oxford: Oxford University Press).

Wallerstein, I. (1998) *Utopistics, or, Historical Choices of the Twenty-First Century* (New York: The New Press).

Wallerstein, I. (2000) [1974] 'The Rise and Future Demise of the World Capitalist System: Concepts for Comparative Analysis', in Wallerstein, I. (ed.) *The Essential Wallerstein* (New York: The New Press).

Wallerstein, I. (2004a) *World-Systems Analysis* (Durham: Duke University Press).

Wallerstein, I. (ed.) (2004b) *The Modern World-System in the Longue-Duree* (Boulder CO: Paradigm).

Wallerstein, I. (2005) 'After Developmentalism and Globalization, What?', *Social Forces*, 83 (3), pp. 1263–1278.

Wallerstein, I. (2006) *World Systems Analysis: An Introduction* (Durham: Duke University Press).

Wallerstein, I. and Kasaba, R. (1987) 'The Incorporation of the Ottoman Empire into the World-Economy', in Huri Islamoglu-Inan (ed.) *The Ottoman Empire and the World-Economy* (Cambridge: Cambridge University Press), pp. 88–97.

Wallis, V. (2008) 'Capitalist and Socialist Responses to the Ecological Crisis', *Monthly Review*, November, pp. 25–40.

Walton, J. and Seddon, M. (1994) *Free Markets and Food Riots: The Politics of Global Adjustment* (Cambridge, MA: Blackwell).

Wattanuruk, P. (1994) 'Thailand's Automotive and Auto Parts Industry: Gearing up for Growth', *Market Intelligence Report* (Bangkok: Office of the Board of Investment).

Weaver, F. (2000) *Latin America in the World Economy: Mercantile Colonialism to Global Capitalism* (Colorado: Westview).

Wechsler, W. F. (2001) 'Follow the Money', *Foreign Affairs*, 80 (4), pp. 40–57.

Weil, R. (1994) 'China at the Brink: Class Contradictions of Market Socialism', *Monthly Review*, 46 (7), pp. 10–36.

White, L. (1943) 'Energy and the Evolution of Culture', *American Anthropologist*, 45 (3), pp. 335–356.

Wierzbicki, P. (1985) *Mysli staroswieckiego Polaka* (London: Aneks).

Wilkin, P. (2008) 'Global Communication and Political Culture in the Semiperiphery: The Rise of the Globo Corporation', *Review of International Studies*, 34, Special Issue, pp. 93–113.

Wilkinson, D. (1987) 'Central Civilization', *Comparative Civilizations Review*, 17, pp. 31–59.

Wittfogel, K. (1957) *Oriental Despotism* (Yale: Yale University Press).

Wolf, M. (2008) 'Global Impact: A Waking Giant Tugging Hard at Its Chains', in FT.com. http://us.ft.com/ftgateway/superpage.ft?news_id=fto0124200807353919111

Womack, J. R., Jones, D. T. and Roos, D. (1990) *The Machine That Changed the World* (New York: Rawson Associates).

Woodward, R. (2004) 'Global Monitor – The Organisation for Economic Cooperation and Development', *New Political Economy*, 9 (1), pp. 113–127.

World Bank (1996) *World Development Report: From Plan to Market* (New York: Oxford University Press).

World Bank (2005) *Global Monitoring Report: Millennium Development Goals: From Consensus to Momentum* (Washington DC: World Bank Publications).

World Bank and International Monetary Fund (2003) *Financial Sector Assessment Program Review, Lessons, and Issues Going Forward* (Washington, DC: World Bank International Monetary Fund).

World Bank (2008) *World Development Indicators* (Washington, DC: The World Bank Group) World Party, http://csf.colorado.edu/wsystems/archive/praxis/wp/index.htm

Worth, O. (2005) *Hegemony, International Political Economy and Post-Communist Russia* (Aldershot: Ashgate).

Yoshihara, M. (1988) *The Rise of Ersatz Capitalism in South-east Asia* (Singapore: Oxford University Press).

York, R. and Rosa, E. (2003) 'Key Challenges to Ecological Modernization Theory: Institutional Efficacy, Case Study Evidence, Units of Analysis, and the Pace of Eco-Efficiency', *Organization & Environment*, 16 (3), pp. 273–288.

Zloch-Christy, I. (ed.) (1995) *Privatization and Foreign Investment in Eastern Europe* (Westport: Praeger Publishers).

Zhibin Gu, G. (2006) *China and the New World Order: How Entrepreneurship, Globalization, and Borderless Business are Reshaping China and the World* (Palo Alto, CA: Fultus Corporation).

Zubek, V. (1997) 'The End of Liberalism? Economic Liberalization and the Transformation of Post-Communist Poland', *Communist and Post-Communist Studies*, 30 (2), pp. 181–203.

Index